Contents

THE
NORTH AMERICAN FREE TRADE AGREEMENT

THE
NORTH AMERICAN FREE TRADE AGREEMENT

Labor, Industry, and Government Perspectives

Edited by MARIO F. BOGNANNO
and KATHRYN J. READY

PRAEGER

Westport, Connecticut
London

DEC 0 4 1995   ABD 7154

Library of Congress Cataloging-in-Publication Data

The North American Free Trade Agreement : labor, industry, and
  government perspectives / edited by Mario F. Bognanno and Kathryn J.
  Ready.
       p.   cm.
    Includes bibliographical references and index.
    ISBN 0–275–94675–4 (alk. paper : pbk.)
    1. Free trade—North America—Congresses.   2. Industrial
relations—North America—Congresses.   3. Collective Bargaining—
North America—Congresses.   4. Canada.   Treaties, etc.   1992, Oct.
7—Congresses.   I. Bognanno, Mario Frank.   II. Ready, Kathryn J.
HF1746.N67   1993
382′.911812—dc20   93–19094

British Library Cataloguing in Publication Data is available.

A hardcover edition of *The North American Free Trade Agreement* is available from the
Quroum Books imprint of Greenwood Publishing Group, Inc. (ISBN: 0–89930–849–X).

Library of Congress Catalog Card Number: 93–19094
ISBN: 0–275–94675–4

First published in 1993

Praeger Publishers, 88 Post Road West, Westport, CT 06881
An imprint of Greenwood Publishing Group, Inc.

Printed in the United States of America

The paper used in this book complies with the
Permanent Paper Standard issued by the National
Information Standards Organization (Z39.48–1984).

10 9 8 7 6 5 4 3 2

to my son Dayton
who entered and enriched my life during this debate

kjr

to my wife
for her loving support during still another project

mfb

Preface

For more than two years former U.S. President George Bush, former Canadian Prime Minister Brian Mulroney, and Mexican President Carlos Salinas pressed hard for a North American Free Trade Agreement (NAFTA), reaching an accord in August 1992 and signing it in December 1992. During the months leading up to its fruition, labor, industry, environmental, and religious groups from the three participating countries actively debated and lobbied their respective trade negotiators to gain support for their unique concerns. Lobbying by these groups continues, particularly in the United States, as policy deliberations shift from treaty negotiations, to the submission of enabling legislation, and ultimately to congressional authorization.

In view of the debate that was building among the interest groups commenting on NAFTA, a decision was made to bring together, in common forum, the relevant "actors"—labor, industry, and government—for a more formal discussion about the issues dividing them. Thus, on November 19–20, 1991, a conference was held at the Minneapolis Convention Center, bringing together leading representatives from labor, industry, and government from the three NAFTA countries.

This book both presents and discusses the principal ideas exchanged at this conference, and more. Part I of the book is a short monograph containing economic comparisons among the three NAFTA countries, their reasons for supporting NAFTA, and the major controversies surrounding NAFTA as perceived by labor and environmental groups. This discussion is supplemented by an analysis of several papers and recorded remarks that were presented at the conference. A summary of the proposed NAFTA agreement with possible inclusions that have been put forth by various groups provides impetus for additional debate as NAFTA enters the legislative circuit of the three countries involved. Part II presents several of the papers and recorded remarks that were delivered at the conference.

The book is intended for policymakers, business managers, labor organizations, environmentalists, academics, students, and others who have an interest in understanding and exploring the issues surrounding the NAFTA debate, particularly viewed from the perspective of labor and the environment. It provides the reader with the positions the "actors" have taken on NAFTA and it documents the support for these positions.

We would like to recognize three organizations that made this conference, and ultimately this book, possible. First, the Twin City Area Labor Management Council (TCALMC) and its board of directors should be recognized for exercising the courage and leadership needed to bring under one roof leaders from North America's labor, industry, and government organizations to debate NAFTA—a matter of great importance and about which the invited speakers and their organizations were clearly divided. Second, the Industrial Relations Center, University of Minnesota, provided the academic leadership and conference support that a project like this needed to be the success that it was. Finally, we must thank the Canadian Embassy in Washington, who generously underwrote a significant share of the expenses associated with bringing together the large field of leaders that was required for this undertaking.

We would like to thank Jeff Bangsberg, TCALMC director, for the many hours he spent organizing the conference's sessions, arranging for speakers, and managing conference logistics. TCALMC's assistant director, Robert Patterson, and its secretary, Carol Thomalla, made sure that the conference ran smoothly. To them, and to Joyce Hegstrom and Donna D'Andrea, Industrial Relations Center, who aided with conference preparations, we extend our deep appreciation. Research and assistance were provided by the University of Wisconsin–Eau Claire, and the Industrial Relations Center, University of Minnesota. In particular, we want to recognize the Industrial Relations Center's Cynthia Mutz, Stacie Jo Walker, and Marjorie Whitehill for clerical support, and Binod Thapa, graduate student in Industrial Relations, for research assistance.

Mario F. Bognanno
Kathryn J. Ready

Introduction: NAFTA and Its Actors

Kathryn J. Ready and Mario F. Bognanno

Debate surrounding the North American Free Trade Agreement (NAFTA) has escalated among the three countries involved—the United States, Canada, and Mexico. The 1992 presidential election campaign in the United States provided impetus for ongoing discussions. Over the months ahead this debate will no doubt center on dissimilarities in NAFTA policy that exist between the Clinton White House and Congress and the need for supplemental "side" agreements to remedy these differences. In Canada and Mexico the debate tempo increased as trade negotiations were approaching finality. Moreover, debate in these countries is expected to accelerate in advance of Canada's forthcoming 1993 and Mexico's forthcoming 1994 national elections.

NAFTA discussions initially seemed to feature intergovernment and industry-based trade and tariff tug-of-wars. However, during 1991 and 1992 the debate's center of gravity changed to concerns about the impact NAFTA will have on workers and the environment. Proponents of NAFTA claim that the accord will increase trade throughout the Americas, moderate product prices, and create new jobs in all three countries. Critics claim just as adamantly that the proposed accord will degrade blue-collar employment, wages, and environmental standards throughout North America. Moreover, they claim that jobs will move to Mexico due in part to the wide disparity in labor market regulations and wages existing between the United States/Canada and Mexico. While many claim that Canada has already lost several thousand jobs as a result of the U.S.-Canada Free Trade Agreement, some U.S. and Canadian groups fear that both countries will experience significant job losses to Mexico, a low-wage developing country that is ripe with opportunities for investment and poised for economic growth. Much of the labor debate has focused on predicting whether NAFTA will cause permanent job loss and unprecedented unemployment rates. Workers fear job displacement during economic times that have already caused significant job losses in well-paying industrial sectors, particularly manufacturing, and continued pressure to hold down real wage gains.

According to the Bureau of Labor Statistics, factory jobs in the United States during August 1992 were at their lowest level since April 1983. Over 17 million workers were either unemployed or underemployed, amounting to 13 percent of the workforce. The largest sectoral losers were industrial machinery, electronic equipment, aircraft and transportation equipment, and instruments. Compounding the unemployment problem is the realization that less than half of the jobless workers—4.5 million—qualified for unemployment benefits in the United States. Canada echoes the unemployment plight of the United States, with a record 10.3 percent unemployment rate in 1991. Understandably, labor organizations and allied progressive groups in the United States and Canada fear additional job losses as a result of a free trade agreement. They contend that adequate job safeguards should be incorporated into NAFTA—safeguards that allow for a smooth restructuring of employment opportunities by industries. Moreover, they see NAFTA as being helpful to Mexican conglomerates and U.S. and Canadian multinational corporations, but skirting labor, health, safety, and environmental standards.

In addition to worker displacement, the prospect of environmental problems stemming from Mexico's lax enforcement of environmental standards has tilted the debate toward a concern that with NAFTA the environment of the northern hemisphere will suffer. Labor and a broad-based coalition of consumer, farmer, religious, and environmental groups argue that environmental safeguards must necessarily be part of any free trade agreement. Some firms moving into Mexico have been accused of favoring raw economic exploitation of Mexican labor at the expense of environmental protection.

The building debate was the catalyst leading to the organization of a conference entitled "The North American Free Trade: Labor, Industry, and Government Policy Perspectives," which was held on November 19–20, 1991, in Minneapolis. The conference was jointly sponsored by the Industrial Relations Center, University of Minnesota, and the Twin City Area Labor Management Council with financial support from the Embassy of Canada in Washington, D.C. The conference was the first of its kind; representatives from labor, industry, and government from the three member countries— the United States, Canada, and Mexico—were invited to attend to share and discuss their different perspectives about the North American Free Trade Agreement (NAFTA). In addition to this distinguishing character, the conference emphasized NAFTA and its labor market and environmental implications, rather than exclusively emphasizing NAFTA and its product market effects: greater trade through tariff reductions.

The central question addressed by this conference was: What are or what should be the social, economic, and industrial relations opportunities and consequences of enhanced international commerce in North America? Consequently, the conference participants examined significant trade and industrial relations issues arising out of the formation of a North American free trade region. In particular, they discussed the social, employment, wage, regulatory, and collective bargaining issues surrounding the regional trade dialogue.

Lessons learned from the U.S.-Canada Free Trade Agreement were highlighted as the starting point for the development of NAFTA. Other topics that were examined included international unionism and transnational collective bargaining; regional trade and labor-management cooperation; impact of easing trade barriers on unions and industry and mutual concerns raised by this innovation; trade's impact on collective bargaining at the firm-bargaining unit level; and social issues raised by the regionalization of trade relationships.

This book is divided into two distinct parts. Part I is a short monograph presenting information on the events leading up to the proposed NAFTA agreement, including differences in trade policies, the impact of maquiladoras, the controversies surrounding the agreement's negotiations, and a brief summary of how select industries may be affected by the agreement. We also examine the parties' views about trade, jobs, and the environment by summarizing many of the arguments presented by leading government, labor, and industry participants at the conference. Finally, we summarize the proposed agreement and present possible supplements to the agreement that will continue to be debated as NAFTA enters the mainstream of congressional debate in 1993.

Part II contains a collection of several of the papers and recorded remarks that were presented at the conference. By and large these papers and remarks are relatively brief, containing a wealth of data. Mainly, however, they serve to delineate the nature of the political, social, and economic problems facing the three countries, but particularly the United States, which must be solved if President Clinton and his counterparts from Mexico and Canada hope to build broad-based support for NAFTA.

Part I

BACKGROUND

NAFTA: Labor, Industry, and Government Perspectives

Kathryn J. Ready

BACKGROUND TO AGREEMENT

The United States and Mexico first indicated their intent to enter into a comprehensive free trade agreement during 1990. Canada's involvement with U.S. trade as outlined in the U.S.-Canada Free Trade Agreement of 1988 resulted in Canada becoming the third party to the NAFTA negotiations in 1991. A U.S./Mexican/Canadian agreement or a North American bloc agreement would result in the world's largest free market with 364 million consumers and a combined economic output of $6 trillion. NAFTA would encompass an economic alliance between two developed countries and low-income, newly industrializing country.

The discussion about a free trade agreement has generated a great deal of publicity and controversy on both sides of the border and across many different groups. Both proponents and critics believe the agreement will have a significant impact on the economies of the countries involved given the volume of trade, differences in the rates of return on capital and wage rates, and opportunities due to differences in employment, living, and environmental standards.

During the early part of 1991 a formal announcement to seek NAFTA was accompanied by the Bush administration's request for fast-track negotiating status. In granting fast-track authority to the president, Congress expedites the negotiation of trade agreements by permitting the president to negotiate international trade treaties and submit them to Congress for approval without amendments.[1] Congress then has ninety days to approve or reject the proposal. During May 1991 Congress granted fast track for NAFTA and in June 1991 allowed for a two-year extension of fast-track procedures.[2]

NAFTA negotiations were concluded on August 12, 1992, and implementing legislation was sent to Congress. Congress will discuss the proposed NAFTA during the 1993 session.

The NAFTA agenda is divided into six areas: market access (tariffs and nontariff barriers, rules of origin, government procurement, automobiles, and other industrial sectors); regulations (safeguards, subsidies, trade remedies, and standards); services (principles of services, financial services, insurance, land transportation, telecommunications, and other services); investment; intellectual property; and dispute settlement.

The agreement indicated strict rules of origin, safeguard clauses, and up to fifteen-year phase-in periods for the elimination of tariffs governing import-sensitive industries such as agriculture and textiles and apparels. The Bush administration pledged to work with Congress to ensure an adequately funded worker adjustment program either through an expansion of existing programs, or through the creation of a new program. The plan called for joint projects to be undertaken to address problems posed by occupational health and safety and child labor. This plan was denounced by many groups as inadequate.

The Bush administration and many in the U.S. business community claimed that NAFTA would allow U.S. manufacturers to take advantage of market specialization and lower Mexican wages to establish production-sharing arrangements and exploit economies of scale within North America. NAFTA is likely to make Mexico a more attractive prospect for foreign investment because it will guarantee firms secure and permanent access to "tariff-free" U.S. and Canadian markets. Even though most of the tariffs between the United States and Mexico have been removed or reduced since Mexico joined GATT in 1986, some tariff and many nontariff barriers remain.

NAFTA was a political issue heavily debated by U.S. presidential candidates George Bush, Bill Clinton, and Ross Perot. Subsequent to the November 1992 election, the political scene has shifted from the White House to Congress, where the agreement's implementing legislation will be debated. Already NAFTA provisions are stimulating major differences in the approach that should be taken for a free trade agreement. Several proposals have been put forward in Congress, including one by Congressman William Gephardt who has proposed incorporating an exchange transaction tax that would be used to fund relocations and retraining of workers displaced by NAFTA. This is merely the onset of continued debate as the NAFTA agreement is just beginning to be analyzed by political parties in the United States, Canada, and Mexico.

The major issue addressed in NAFTA negotiations is not whether the United States should trade with Mexico and Canada or whether capital should be allowed to move among the countries. The question focuses on how and under what conditions such increased trade and investment should take place. Canada and Mexico are already among the United States' most

Table 1.1
U.S. Trade with Canada and Mexico (in Billions of Dollars)

	1986	1987	1988	1989	1990	1991	1992
U.S. Trade with Canada	124	131	153	167	175	182	189
U.S. Trade with Mexico	30	35	44	52	59	64	75

Source: Department of Commerce, International Monetary Fund, International Financial Statistics, 1992

Table 1.2
Trade Balances of Participating NAFTA Countries (in Billions of Dollars)

	1988	1989	1990	1991	1992
United States with Canada	-$11.7	-$11.3	-$10.8	-$8.6	-$7.9
United States with Mexico	-3.1	-2.6	-2.4	1.4	5.4
Canada with Mexico	-668.0*	-909.0*	-995.0*	-1.7	-1.6

*in millions of dollars
Source: U.S. Department of Commerce, 1993

important trading partners. U.S. trade with Canada and Mexico is growing. Table 1.1 shows the increased trade generated from 1986 to 1992 between the United States and Mexico and the United States and Canada.

The resulting trade balances show an increase in U.S. imports and exports to Mexico and significant increases in Canadian imports from Mexico. Table 1.2 shows the resulting trade balance relationships among the three member countries. NAFTA trade comparisons by country are shown in Table 1.3. The U.S. trade deficit with Canada has been falling since 1988 and by 1992 reached $7.9 billion. Canadians are experiencing a growing trade deficit with Mexico, totaling almost $2 billion in 1992. The United States experienced a positive trade balance with Mexico in 1992 when $5.4 billion more goods were exported to Mexico than had been imported.

Former President Bush indicated that the implementation of a free trade agreement with Mexico is only the first step toward developing similar agreements with other Latin American countries. These discussions are already taking place under the Enterprise for the Americas Initiative, which would promote trade and investment, eventually culminating in a hemispheric free-trade zone. Bush envisioned NAFTA as a means of securing a solid export market in Mexico, strengthening Mexican President Salinas de Gortari's bold economic reforms, and enhancing U.S. competitiveness worldwide. Promoting worldwide competitiveness is a primary concern as the

Table 1.3
NAFTA by Country Trade Comparisons, 1992 (in Billions of Dollars)

U.S. exports to Canada	$90.6
U.S. imports from Canada	<u>98.5</u>
Total U.S./Canadian Trade	$189.1
U.S. exports to Mexico	$40.6
U.S. imports from Mexico	<u>35.2</u>
Total U.S./Mexican Trade	$75.8
Canadian exports to Mexico	$771*
Canadian imports to Mexico	<u>2751*</u>
Total Canadian/Mexican Trade	$3522*

*in millions of dollars
Source: U.S. Department of Commerce, 1992.

European Economic Community and the Pacific Rim are moving toward the formation of regional trading blocs.

Why Did the United States Become Interested in Securing NAFTA?

Robert Lawrence, professor of international trade and investment at Harvard University, attributes the move toward NAFTA as a response to the decline in U.S. productivity growth (see Chapter 14, this volume). Since 1973 output per worker in the United States has risen at only a 0.8% annual rate, compared with a 2.5% rate over the previous twenty-five years.[3]

Lawrence claims that during the 1970s the United States dealt with productivity declines by increasing the number of women and baby boomers in the labor force. During the 1980s the United States modified this strategy by spending more than was produced and borrowing the rest in order to continue fueling the economy. This practice resulted in the service sector of the economy growing due to its dependence on domestic spending. As a consequence, interest rates increased and the manufacturing sector declined.

Lawrence predicts that during the 1990s the United States can expect only 2% real GNP growth per year.[4] The slowing of labor force growth, continued slow productivity performance of the 1980s, and the move to reduce both the budget deficit and the trade deficit all contribute to this forecast. Ultimately this means that the United States cannot rely on growth to occur in the service sector of the economy as in the past, but must depend on international trade to stimulate demand. Designing policy initiatives that will result in spurring improvements in productivity and in performance becomes the goal in stimulating economic growth.[5]

GATT versus Regional Trade Agreements

Current U.S. trade policy calls for freer trade, improved market access abroad, fewer obstacles to exports, and fewer restrictions on imports. The United States has advocated freer trade since 1947 through the General Agreement on Tariffs and Trade (GATT). GATT encompasses a multilateral approach to trade intended to lower tariff barriers among its members. It also provides for regional trading arrangements in which members within a region receive preferential treatment from the other members of that region (e.g., the European Community), which was essentially a violation of the "most favored nation" treatment intent of GATT.[6] As the number of countries belonging to GATT grew to over 135 by the early 1990s and the enforcement against violating member-nations waned, individual member countries sought their own means for securing reduced trade barriers.

GATT was not equipped to handle institutional developments within economies in which nontariff barriers remained. Lawrence attributes the U.S. movement away from multilateral trade to GATT's shortcomings. The United States, recognizing GATT's shortcomings, entered into a "multitrack" approach, broadening its scope during the late 1980s.

During the recent Uruguay Round of GATT negotiations, the United States sought to address issues such as intellectual property rights, trade-related investment measures to improve the dispute settlements of GATT, the introduction of services into GATT, and reforms to agriculture. At the same time, the United States sought to impose unilateral trade measures such as antidumping and safeguard provisions and voluntary restraint arrangements. In order to succeed, the United States recognized that bilateral agreements between willing parties, rather than enforcement of unilateral demands, was the trade strategy to pursue. It was in this vein that the United States embraced the Canadian initiative during the 1980s, culminating in the U.S.-Canada Free Trade Agreement. In part, based on the success of the U.S.-Canada FTA, the United States has moved to secure NAFTA.

How Did Mexico's Trade Policies Differ from the United States'?

Mexico, by contrast, embarked on a policy of substantial import protection in the post–World War II period. Mexico's trade policies historically have been characterized by high import tariffs, import licensing requirements, official import reference prices, domestic content requirements, and subsidies in order to discourage imports and encourage domestic industrialization. Mexico protected its own markets by nationalizing several industries, including oil, power generation, and telephone. Mexico's policymakers believed that opening their underdeveloped domestic markets would lead to exploitation by wealthier, predatory countries.[7]

During the world debt crisis of 1982 and the softening of the oil market, Mexico faced severe economic problems as a result of its dependence on petroleum, which accounted for almost 80% of its total export earnings. Account deficits could no longer be financed by borrowing from abroad, and imports were severely curtailed. Mexico realized that foreign competition was needed to help restructure Mexican industries to leverage comparative advantages in order to become more competitive.

In 1986 Mexico joined GATT, permitting regional free trade agreements and, in 1987, announced its Pact for Economic Growth and Stability—a dramatic plan to freeze wages and prices and to restructure the economy. These actions led to privatization of state-owned industries[8] and deregulation in order to increase domestic competitiveness and productivity and to curb inflation.[9]

Mexico embarked on a policy of gradual trade liberalization (by lowering tariffs and removing import quotas) throughout the 1980s. Average tariffs were lowered from 100 to only 10 percent. The highest tariffs were on manufactured and consumer goods, automobile, processed agricultural, and petrochemical products. By 1990 import licenses were reduced to a weighted average rate of just over 6 percent and applied to less than 3 percent of Mexican tariff categories. Official reference prices for imports were eliminated.[10] These policy changes led to significant devaluing of the peso and unprecedented inflationary rates. Presently Mexico continues to struggle with inflation rates of 15 to 20 percent. Mexico's underdeveloped infrastructure in the areas of highways, railroads, bridges, utilities, ports, storage facilities, and trucking services also has inhibited trade.

Despite Mexico's shortcomings, policy changes have resulted in an improved general economic climate according to William Cavitt, director of the Office of Canada, U.S. Department of Commerce. He notes that during the past several years real economic growth in Mexico has increased, exceeding population growth. Inflation has been reduced, external debt as a percentage of gross domestic product has been reduced, foreign direct investment is up,[11] and U.S. merchandise exports to Mexico have doubled from 1987 to 1990 (see Chapter 4, this volume).

Cavitt observes that Mexico would benefit from NAFTA because it would provide access to U.S. and Canadian finance and technology, and to their huge product markets. It would help Mexico finance its economic growth, service its foreign debt, and lower its current account deficit. Moreover, investment would generate jobs for Mexico's rapidly expanding workforce.

Jeff Faux and Thea Lee of the Economic Policy Institute report that Mexico's labor force is currently growing at a rate of one million per year, while only about 300,000 to 400,000 jobs per year are being created by the formal economy. Even at extremely high future growth rates of 5 or 6 percent, the Mexican economy would not be able to generate enough jobs to reduce unemployment significantly from its current rate of about 20 percent. Between 1985 and March 1990 net new employment creation amounted to only 33,513 jobs in Mexican manufacturing and 242,441 in the maquiladoras (assembly plants located along the border).[12] While investment is increasing in the export-processing maquiladoras, firms producing primarily for the Mexican market have gone out of business.[13]

Mexican economists foresee three phases of restructuring for Mexico's industry.[14] During an initial period as many as half of the remaining jobs in Mexican industry will be lost due to inability to compete with imports. A second phase will result in more Mexican industries closing as has happened in the former East Germany. Only a few sectors such as cement, glass, and ceramic tiles will be able to compete successfully.

During a third period there will be a net inflow of foreign direct investment as more U.S. and Canadian companies move production to Mexico. Mexican university economists predict that direct foreign investment in Mexico could double to $60 billion by the year 2000. However, Alejandro Alvarez of the Economics Faculty of the National Autonomous University (UNAM) concludes that investment in export industries will create only 12% of the jobs that will be needed in Mexico by the year 2000 due to Mexico's growing population.

Cavitt summarizes the benefits of a free trade agreement with Mexico in Chapter 5 (this volume). First, NAFTA would contribute to long-term economic prosperity, stability, and growth in Mexico. It would help the United States by controlling such bilateral problems as illegal immigration, drugs, and pollution. Second, NAFTA would advance the cause of economic reform in Latin America. Mexico, as a leader among the Latin American countries, could serve as a model for market-oriented policies and reforms elsewhere in the hemisphere, including Bush's Enterprise for the Americas Initiative. Third, U.S. business would benefit by major trade and investment opportunities in Mexico with guaranteed access to that market. Mexico is the fastest growing U.S. export market and has a high capacity to consume U.S. goods.

Comparing the United States and Mexico

Mexico is the third largest U.S. trading partner behind Canada and Japan. Although the Mexican market is currently only one-tenth the size of the U.S. market in GDP terms, it is expanding rapidly. With a population of 90 million, 47 percent of whom are under the age of fifteen, Mexico holds

Table 1.4
North American Economic Overview, Selected Statistics

	United States	Canada	Mexico
Population (in millions, 1991)	252.5	26.8	90.0
Labor Force (in millions, 1989)	123.8	13.5	31.8
Labor Force (% of pop.)	50.3	52.0	38.4
Birth Rate (per 1,000 pop.)	15.0	14.0	29.0
Population Growth Rate (%, 1991)	0.8	1.1	2.2
Women Laborers (% of labor force)	44.5	43.9	27.8
Unemployment Rate (%, 1991)	6.7	10.3	20.0

Source: World Economic Forum International Monetary Fund International Labor Organization, 1992.

great potential as a marketplace for U.S. exports. Table 1.4 presents a breakdown of selected labor market statistics among the three NAFTA countries.

The United States exports and imports largely manufactured goods with Mexico. In 1991 manufactured goods accounted for over three-fourths of U.S. exports to Mexico and over two-thirds of U.S. imports from Mexico. One estimate indicates that the elimination of trade barriers between the United States and Mexico would result in a $1.6 billion increase in Mexican exports to the United States, largely from the manufacturing sector.[15] Almost 60 percent of Mexican manufactured exports are between related parties such as multinational corporations doing business in both countries.[16]

Proponents of NAFTA argue that Mexico presents significant opportunities for U.S. export market development because once the tariffs are removed, the net result should be increased demand for U.S. products. Tariff reductions have contributed to increased U.S. exports to Mexico from $14 billion in 1987 to $40.6 billion in 1992. In 1991 Mexico accounted for 9.2 percent of overall U.S. exports and 6 percent of its imports, compared with Mexico's dependence on the United States for 70 percent of both imports and exports. According to the U.S. Department of Commerce, for every $1 billion increase in U.S. exports to Mexico, approximately 20,000 U.S. jobs would be created. Table 1.5 presents United States-Mexican merchandise trade.

According to Cavitt, 44 percent of Mexican exports enter the United States duty-free. While the United States has agreed to further reduce tariffs on goods, the United States is holding back on further liberalization in such import-sensitive industries as steel and textiles. Strict rules of origin are needed in NAFTA, especially in the automotive sector, so that third-party countries cannot use Mexico or Canada as a "packaging station" to enter the U.S. market through a North American back door.[17]

U.S. tariffs on Mexican goods vary considerably, although the average

Table 1.5

United States-Mexico Merchandise Trade (in U.S. $ billions)

	1989	1990	1991	1992
Principal U.S. Exports to Mexico				
Electrical Machinery, Apparatus	3.6	3.8	4.4	5.3
Auto/Motor Vehicle Parts	2.0	2.9	3.2	3.9
Chemicals	2.2	2.3	2.7	3.2
Telecommunications Equipment	1.0	1.2	1.3	1.5
Office Machinery & Computers	.8	.8	1.1	1.3
Principal U.S. Imports from Mexico				
Electrical Machinery, Apparatus	4.2	4.6	4.8	5.5
Crude Oil	4.0	4.8	4.3	4.4
Autos/Motor Vehicles	1.2	2.2	2.6	2.6
TV's and Radios	1.6	1.5	1.6	1.9
Auto/Motor Vehicle Parts	1.1	1.2	1.4	2.0

Sources: U.S. Department of Commerce, American Embassy, Mexico City, Bank of Mexico, 1993.

U.S. tariff on Mexican goods is only 3.8 percent compared with the average Mexican tariff of 10 percent. In 1989 products with a tariff of 10 percent or less accounted for almost 80 percent of Mexican exports to the United States, while goods subject to a tariff of 30 percent or more made up .5 percent of total exports. Almost 10 percent of Mexican imports to the United States enter duty-free under the Generalized System of Preferences for less developed countries. Mexico is classified as a "beneficiary developing country," meaning the United States had voluntarily agreed to grant preferential tariff treatment until July 4, 1993.[18]

U.S. quotas and high tariffs on some Mexican goods are perceived by many Mexicans as proof that the U.S. market is relatively more closed than Mexico's. Mexicans argue that U.S. protectionist policies result in effectively blocking a comparative trade advantage with the United States. For example, Mexican agricultural products (e.g., cotton, dairy products, sugar, sugar-containing products, and peanuts) exported to the United States are subject to significant quotas. Outside of the agricultural sector, certain steel mill products and textiles are also subject to steep quotas.

Major economic differences exist between the United States and Mexico. Table 1.6 presents a comparison of trade statistics for the three member NAFTA countries. The U.S. gross domestic product is approximately $5.4 trillion, compared with Mexico's $180 billion, or 3 percent of the United States'. Mexico's GDP growth rate is over three times the rate of growth

Table 1.6
NAFTA Participants, Trade Comparisons

	United States	Canada	Mexico
GDP (billions constant 1985 dollars)	5951	552	334
GDP Growth (%, 1991)	-0.7	-2.0	3.6
GNP ($ billion, 1989)	5237.7	500.3	170.1
GNP per Capita ($, 1989)	21,110.0	19,020.0	1990.0
GNP Growth Rate (%, 1990)	0.9	1.1	3.5*
Government Budget Deficit (billions)	280.6	16.5	5.0**
Consumer Price Inflation (%, 1991)	4.3	5.6	22.7*
Exports ($ billion, 1990)	394.0	123.0	24.6*
Imports ($ billion, 1990)	495.0	116.1	25.7*
Merchandise Trade Balance (millions, 1991)	-73.6	5.9	-11.1

*Estimate
**Surplus
Sources: World Bank, *Economic Report of the President*, U.S. Department of Commerce,
International Monetary Fund, International Labor Organization, World Economic Forum,
1992.

Table 1.7
Comparison of North American Wages, 1990

United States	Canada	Mexico
$14.83	$15.94	$1.85

Hourly compensation costs in U.S. dollars for production workers in manufacturing.

Source: U.S. Department of Labor, Bureau of Labor Statistics, "International Comparisons of
Hourly Compensation Costs for Production Workers in Manufacturing, 1990," Report 803,
May 1991.

for the United States and Canada. Per capita income in the United States
is over $21,000 per year compared with $1,990 in Mexico—only about 9
percent as large. Mexico's imports and exports are only about 20 percent as
large as Canada's and only 5 to 6 percent as large as the United States'.

Mexican hourly wages average about 10 percent of those in the United
States,[19] although wages are considerably lower in the maquiladoras than in
other areas of Mexico. See Table 1.7 for a comparison of U.S., Canadian,
and Mexican manufacturing wages. Measured in U.S. dollars, real wages of

Mexican workers have plunged 64 percent since 1982. In that year, workers received nearly 40 percent of Mexico's GDP; however, their share had fallen to 24 percent by 1991.[20]

What Impact Have Maquiladoras Had on U.S.-Mexican Trade?

Many have pointed to the maquiladora industry as an example of the kind of polluting, low-wage industry that should not serve as a model for further U.S.-Mexican economic cooperation. They claim that the industry has unfairly taken jobs away from U.S. workers by taking advantage of both lower wages and the lax enforcement of labor and environmental regulations in Mexico.

Under the maquiladora system, U.S. manufactured parts are shipped to Mexico for assembly, then shipped back for distribution. Imported component parts are placed "in-bond" to avoid taxes, because the parts will be used to manufacture items for export. When these finished products are exported from Mexico, no export fee or value-added tax is charged by the Mexican government, and the U.S. government imposes only a value-added tariff. Machinery and components to be used in the in-bond production of a maquiladora plant may also be imported in-bond, duty-free from any country. Maquila plants may sell up to 20 percent of their output in Mexico, provided they do not compete with Mexican products. Over 90 percent of maquila output is exported and 90 percent of that goes to the United States.[21]

Forty-five percent of U.S. imports from Mexico are products from the maquiladora industries in which duty is added only on the value added in Mexico due to the Generalized System of Preferences (GSP). GSP permits the importation of many maquiladora products without payment of U.S. duties, provided that a minimum of 35 percent of the product content is a product of Mexico. The Mexican government treats the maquiladora program as a vehicle to transfer technology to Mexican industry, to upgrade workers' skills, to improve employment and income in the border area, and to increase demand for Mexican manufactured goods.

Statistics on foreign ownership of maquiladora plants vary. U.S.-owned maquiladora plants account for between 65 and 95 percent of all maquiladoras in Mexico. In 1990 over two thousand maquiladoras operated along U.S.-Mexican border and brought in $3.2 billion to the Mexican economy.[22] See Table 1.8 for an examination of maquiladora plants. Maquiladoras employ five hundred thousand people in Mexico at an average wage approximately half that prevailing in the rest of Mexico's manufacturing sector or approximately one-fourteenth of the U.S. manufacturing wages. The General Accounting Office estimates that by 1995 the maquila industry will employ approximately one million workers.[23]

Female employees comprise about 60 percent of all maquila workers.[24]

Table 1.8
Maquiladora Statistics

Year	Plant	Aggregate Value	Workers		Total Employees
			% Men	% Women	
1985	789	325,249.7	25.72	56.11	217,544
1986	987	792,017.9	26.76	54.67	268,388
1987	1,259	2,235,149.6	28.13	53.03	322,743
1988	1,490	5,263,925.0	30.84	50.53	389,245
1989	1,795	7,499,322.0	31.23	49.48	437,064
1990	2,078	N/A	39.08	60.91	500,000

Note: 1990 data use December 1990 estimate.
*As of August 1990
Source: Business Mexico, Mar. 1991.

The high percentage of women employed in maquiladoras has been viewed as a means to exploit politically inexperienced women, destroy the opportunities for males as breadwinners (75 percent of men sharing households with women maquiladora workers are either unemployed or underemployed),[25] promote single parent households, exacerbate unemployment among men, and prevent technology transfer because of prevailing stereotypes about women. On the other hand, some favor the employment of women because it represents the first step in emancipating women from low wages.[26]

The U.S. International Trade Commission has studied the maquiladora program four times since 1970.[27] In each instance, they found that the likely economic effects of the elimination of production sharing would be that most of the products of the maquiladoras would continue to be imported, and of wholly foreign origin, most likely from the Far East. If this occurred, U.S. and Mexican exports would lose out to the benefit of Far Eastern exporters. There would be no U.S. jobs producing the components and no Mexican jobs assembling those components. In a worst case scenario, the United States would lose the estimated 154,000 jobs currently producing components for assembly in Mexico and Mexico would lose 438,000 assembly jobs.

Mexican Labor

Concern on the part of U.S. and Canadian labor unions has arisen over the lax enforcement of Mexican labor laws. The Mexican government in its attempt to increase trade has ignored many restrictive regulations in order to encourage foreign investors. For example, despite regulations that guarantee collective bargaining rights to Mexican employees and compensation for layoffs, plant closing, and work-related injuries, these regulations are often not enforced in the maquila district.

Mexico does have laws that dictate employment relations. Mexican law requires certain minimum fringe benefits for all permanent employees, including six days' paid vacation annually, in addition to a 25 percent vacation pay premium. Seven paid federal holidays, a profit-sharing plan, and an employer-paid payroll tax that funds employee daycare centers. Employees are paid fifteen days' salary as a Christmas bonus each year. After one year of employment, a Mexican worker is considered tenured and can be dismissed only for causes specifically enumerated in the Mexican Federal Labor Law. However, these protective labor requirements are often overlooked in the low-wage maquila areas, partly as an incentive to bring in foreign investment.[28]

The official PRI government labor union is the Confederation of Mexican Workers (CTM).[29] On February 24, 1992, CTM once again "reelected" ninety-two-year-old Fidel Velazquez as secretary general for another six-year term. Through elite negotiations and alliances with PRI governments, Velazquez has manipulated CTM since the 1940s. For fifty years Velazquez and his labor bosses have effectively constrained the wage and benefit demands of rank-and-file CTM members in exchange for CTM elites' guaranteed access to public offices and government-sponsored patronage.[30] The Mexican labor hierarchy has a history of corrupt practices. They commonly receive higher wages or kickbacks, while union rank-and-file workers are forced to accept wages set by government and business development strategies.

CTM claims to represent over 75 percent of all organized workers in Mexico. Reliable Mexican data on union membership do not exist although one estimate claims that 35 percent of workers are organized. The U.S. Commerce Department estimates that in the industrialized sector more than 90 percent of all production workers in establishments employing over twenty-five workers are organized.[31] Except for the Matamoros maquila area, which is highly unionized, most maquilas are not organized and U.S. firms often conduct antiunion campaigns in order to remain so.

Mexican labor supports President Salinas and his NAFTA initiative. Erfani (1992) suggests that this support may be because a NAFTA-inspired maquiladora expansion on the border would involve CTM unionization of new plants rather than independent union formation of a more militant strain. Erfani also points out that if the PRI were to lose control of the presidency in 1994,[32] the privileged patronage positions of CTM bosses would be undermined as CTM ties to national government dissolved.

Manfred Fiedler, vice president of Honeywell, explains major differences existing between U.S. and Mexican labor agreements (see Chapter 9, this volume). Fiedler claims that labor relations and labor agreements in Mexico lack the flexibility needed to adjust to Mexico's changing economic situation. Labor contracts have tended to emphasize the protection of employees at the expense of the employer by using severance pay and longevity pay. He argues that the relations between employees and the unions are less stringent in Mexico than they are in the United States and are governed by mutual respect; therefore, a cooperative negotiating method will continue. The potential foreign trade agreement between the United States and Mexico will strongly favor a gradual homologation between the labor laws of both countries.

While the AFL-CIO would like to see joint efforts across the border among the various unions, the difference in the structures of the unions between the United States and Mexico makes this dialogue somewhat more difficult to plan at a national level. In order for this dialogue to occur, Pharris Harvey, executive director of the International Labor Rights Education and Research Fund, argues that the three national union centers should begin to develop joint research centers where collective bargaining agreements, labor statistics, company data, and other relevant information can be gathered, analyzed, and shared (see Chapter 12, this volume).

Harvey claims that while building solidarity and membership is important for labor unions' survival they are not the only groups facing this problem. Environmentalists, community development organizations, alternative political groups, religious groups, and consumer advocates also have related interests. Groups are forming such as the Mobilization on Development, Trade, Labor and Environment (MODTLE). This group is critical of and challenges NAFTA. MODTLE organized over issues such as wages and social protection, health care, education, cultural respect, and integrity of communities. Likewise, the Coalition for Justice in the Maquiladoras, a multisectoral group supported by organized labor, religious, community, and development groups in the United States and Mexico is working to develop a code of conduct for American firms working in the border region of Mexico. Harvey points out that common action across all three countries is difficult due to wage competition and the vast shortage of jobs experienced by all three countries.

Joe Mangone, director of the UAW National Community Action Program, and M. E. Nichols, executive vice president of the International Communication Workers of America, claim that cooperation and international solidarity among the unions in the three countries are imperative (see Chapters 16 and 18, this volume). The most common forms of multinational support and cooperation have consisted of information exchanges related to organizing or bargaining; industry-wide and company-wide meetings of unionists to discuss relevant developments; regional meetings for workers in particular companies or industries to exchange information and discuss strategies; and educational conferences to address the problems of women workers, white-collar workers, skilled workers, and others.

 ## WHAT IS THE DEBATE OVER NAFTA ABOUT?

Studies about NAFTA

The public debate about NAFTA has been dominated by econometric models calculating gains in income and employment over current trends for all three countries. For the most part, these models have indicated projected gains in exports, output, and employment for the United States. William C. Gruben, senior economics and policy advisor to the Federal Reserve Bank of Dallas, analyzes the effects of NAFTA on the U.S. labor market in Chapter 10 of this volume. Gruben suggests that while studies of the impacts of NAFTA vary in their conclusions, they generally imply that the impact on U.S. employment will be small overall, but that the U.S. gainers will either offset or more than offset the losers.[33] He concludes that negative employment effects will be concentrated in relatively few industries and that these impacts will be stretched out over time. Skilled workers will benefit and unskilled workers will be at a disadvantage. The effects will be positive for those who work in heavily capitalized industries that already face a good deal of international competition and negative for those who work in industries that use relatively small amounts of physical capital per worker or that have been protected from international competition.

Gruben bases his conclusions in part on two often cited studies—the International Trade Commission study (1990) and the Peat Marwick study (1991)—which evaluate the impact of NAFTA on U.S. labor. Jeff Faux and Thea Lee of the Economic Policy Institute claim that these models have assumed away many of the questions they purport to answer (see Chapter 8, this volume). They argue that the models assume that a free trade agreement will not facilitate a shift in productive investment from the United States to Mexico. They clam that this assumption about capital mobility is pivotal to the ongoing debate.[34]

Specifically, Faux and Lee claim that the International Trade Commission study acknowledges the possibility of capital flow from the United States to Mexico following the signing of an agreement, but does not factor this possibility into its predictions about employment and thus leads to conclusions that are highly suspect. Faux and Lee refute the authors' conclusion in the Peat Marwick study that an additional $25 billion investment in the Mexican economy would not replace any physical plant and equipment that otherwise would have been located in the United States. Faux and Lee point out that the United States is the major foreign investor in Mexico, and a massive shift in investment from the United States to Mexico has occurred during the past ten years.

Table 1.9
Unemployment Rates of NAFTA Participants

	1987	1988	1989	1990	1991
United States	6.2	5.5	5.3	5.4	6.7
Canada	8.8	7.8	7.5	8.1	10.3
Mexico	19.0	19.0	20.0	18.0	20.0

Source: U.S. Department of Commerce, 1992.

Labor Claims NAFTA Will Result in Job Loss

U.S. labor spokespersons vary in their degree of opposition to NAFTA and its enduring negotiation process. U.S. House of Representatives Majority Leader Richard A. Gephardt advised the White House to withdraw the proposal when he spoke at the opening session of the Trade for the 21st Century Conference on September 7, 1992, after Bush released the text of the agreement. AFL-CIO Vice President Jack Sheinkman and AFL-CIO chief economist Rudy Oswald have warned that NAFTA as drafted will result in a substantial net movement of jobs out of the United States, and even more damaging, lead to a dramatic lowering of wage levels and living standards in the United States.[35] The loss of jobs is particularly crucial considering the increased unemployment rates in both the United States and Canada as shown in Table 1.9.

Some labor spokespersons early on (e.g., Faux and Oswald) focused on actively fighting the fast-track procedure, which would permit a negotiated NAFTA to become law without the input of various labor and environmental groups, and subsequently opposed NAFTA. Other labor spokespersons (e.g., Scholssberg) have resigned themselves to the inevitability of some form of NAFTA and have chosen to focus on how such increased trade and investment should take place.[36]

Labor's central economic objection to NAFTA is that it provides an incentive for U.S. producers to respond to market competition with a low-wage strategy, which will lower incomes and productivity over the long run, rather than the more difficult approach of producing high value-added, high-quality, high-wage products more efficiently. As a result, manufacturing potential in the United States will be further eroded. Mark Anderson of the AFL-CIO points to the tens of thousands of workers across the United States working for companies like Electrolux, Tyco, Zenith, Westinghouse, Farah, GE, AT&T, GM, Ford, and Chrysler who have seen their jobs lost to Mexico (see Chapter 2, this volume).[37] Moreover, U.S. labor groups fear not only job losses, but also lower wages and less stringent health, safety, and environmental regulations in Mexico.

Table 1.10
U.S., Canada and Mexico Wages: Four Major Industries (in U.S. dollars)

	Textile	Chemical	Electronic	Automotive
USA	9.74	18.19	14.31	21.51
Canada	11.23	15.51	13.99	17.74
Mexico	1.27	1.30	1.04	2.15

Source: The American Chamber—Mexico, 1990.

Labor claims that corporations seeking to maximize profits will locate production where overall costs—including wages, corporate taxes, and the costs incurred in complying with environmental or workplace safety regulations—are lowest. Faux and Lee point to the loss of jobs experienced by many Canadians after the Canada-U.S. Free Trade Agreement in 1989 and the growth of the maquiladora area in Mexico as examples. Workers in U.S. manufacturing industries are particularly concerned that the dramatic difference in manufacturing wages in Mexico—$2.35 per hour in 1992 or 15 percent of the $16.17 per hour earned by U.S. production workers—will entice companies to move across the border. For U.S., Canadian, and Mexican wage comparisons see Table 1.10. For average manufacturing wages worldwide see Table 1.11.

Faux and Lee estimate that the loss of U.S. jobs during the 1980s caused real earnings to decline about 20 percent for those workers with high school educations.[38]

Increased competition may drive down real wages in the United States as a result of an increase in the number of imports from Mexico. Labor-intensive industries, such as wearing apparel, shoes, and hand-picked agricultural products may be hardest hit because wages in these industries make up a significant portion of unit costs of goods. Also, these are goods the United States already substantially protects through import restrictions.[39] Labor claims that given the current projections, job losses during the next ten years will cause further deterioration of living standards in the United States.[40]

James Cypher estimates that about 220,000 U.S. jobs will move to Mexico over the next five years as a result of investment shifts brought about by NAFTA (see Chapter 7, this volume). A second estimate of job displacement has been made by economists Sam Bowles, Gerald Epstein, Timothy Koechlin, and Mehrene Larudee.[41] They find that 290,000 to 490,000 U.S. jobs will be lost over the next ten years, as U.S. and foreign investors build new capacity in Mexico rather than in the United States, attracted by improved access to the U.S. market and a more stable investment climate in Mexico. They base their estimates on historical examples of the increases in U.S.

Table 1.11
Average Manufacturing Wages, Worldwide (in U.S. dollars)

	1986	1987	1988	1989
EEC	13.21	13.40	13.85	14.31
Denmark	11.08	14.54	15.86	15.16
Belgium	12.31	15.04	15.54	15.18
Germany	13.29	16.91	18.11	17.58
Luxemburg	10.63	13.03	13.88	N/A
Ireland	7.81	9.08	9.74	9.42
England	7.54	9.97	10.46	10.44
France	10.27	12.42	12.96	12.72
Spain	6.43	7.86	8.61	9.10
Greece	4.07	4.61	5.22	5.48
Holand	12.57	15.60	16.22	15.54
Italy	9.91	12.14	12.87	13.23
Portugal	2.08	2.51	2.67	2.77
Eastern Europe				
Yugoslavia	1.32	1.40	N/A	N/A
Hungary	0.78	0.83	N/A	N/A
Asia				
Japan	9.31	10.83	12.80	12.63
Hong Kong	1.88	2.09	2.40	2.79
Korea	1.45	1.76	2.50	3.57
Singapore	2.23	2.31	2.67	3.09
Taiwan	1.73	2.26	2.82	3.53
Others				
Canada	11.00	11.95	13.53	14.72
Costa Rica	N/A	1.32	N/A	N/A
Mexico	1.50	1.57	1.99	2.32

Source: The American Chamber—Mexico, 1990.

foreign direct investment that took place when Ireland and Spain joined the European Community.

Faux and Lee argue that U.S. workers displaced by trade end up moving down the job ladder, to lower-paying jobs, or off the ladder to permanent unemployment, not up to better jobs than they started with. On the other hand, Rudiger Dornbusch among others has argued that the bad (low-wage) jobs will move to Mexico while U.S. workers will move up the ladder to the high-paying, high-tech jobs that the agreement will create.[42]

Cheap labor will be a major attraction for corporations relocating their production in Mexico while retaining free access to the U.S. market. Mexico has a growing supply of labor. Mexico had 48 million people between the ages of 15 and 64 as of 1988, compared with 162 million in the United States and 18 million in Canada. By 2025 Mexico is projected to more than double its population aged 15 to 64 to 97 million, while the population in that age bracket will only rise to 188 million in the United States and 19 million in Canada.

Faux and Lee voice labor's concerns by claiming the economic losses of the administration's proposed Free Trade Agreement will far outweigh the potential gains. They claim NAFTA will result in a net loss of jobs and incomes for U.S. workers. U.S. workers who lose their jobs to import competition are reemployed at much lower wages—if they are reemployed at all. Complicating this loss is the reduction in trade adjustment assistance available for these displaced workers. The Reagan and Bush administrations cut trade adjustment assistance from $1.6 billion in 1980 to $270 million (budget authority) in 1991 and consistently tried to eliminate it.

Faux and Lee claim that U.S. financial institutions are vulnerable to a future economic crisis in Mexico that could result in demands for a U.S. bailout of the Mexican economy. They argue that NAFTA cannot be compared to the European Community's acceptance of Spain and Portugal. U.S.-Mexican wage gaps are much greater; Mexico has a larger population; and the European Community has retraining, safety net, and subsidy programs unknown in the United States. They argue that Mexico's promises to strengthen environmental and worker protection are unreliable. The institutions that promote and guarantee these protections—the judiciary, environmental, and labor groups—are not autonomous and independent of the government in Mexico.

Faux and Lee, referencing congressional testimony presented earlier, note that Mexico's primary economic problem is not trade, but debt. They claim that the administration's proposal is an effort to have U.S. workers pay with their jobs and incomes for the bad loans made to Mexico by first world banks and international lenders. The long-term impact on the U.S. economy will be to encourage U.S. producers to seek low-wage solutions to the problems of international competition,[43] rather than to invest in productivity improvement and technological innovation. Faux and Lee conclude that short of debt relief, strict standards written into NAFTA should entail harmonization of labor and environmental protection practices, political liberalization in Mexico, and policies to assure the successful adjustment of U.S. workers, industries, and communities.

In April 1992 labor urged Congress to pass the Save American Jobs Act. The legislation is sponsored by Senator Howard M. Metzenbaum (D-Ohio), who chairs the labor subcommittee of the Senate Labor and Human Resources Committee, which held the hearings. Similar legislation has been introduced in the House by Representative William D. Ford (D-Mich.). The Senate bill requires companies that run away to low-wage countries to provide severance pay, continue health care coverage for a year, and render retraining and relocation expenses up to $10,000 for each displaced employee. In addition, federal grants and loans would be cut off for a five-year period for the runaway firms, while companies that do not move out would be rewarded with a preference for federal contracts.[44]

Countering Labor's Job Loss Claims

Proponents of NAFTA argue that trade integration with Mexico is essential to building a more cost-competitive U.S. manufacturing sector. Parts production and assembly can take place where each is most advantageous. This will result in the United States becoming export-competitive even in third world markets.[45] The lack of investment and the depressed living standards of the 1980s will give way to a major upward adjustment in Mexican spending. Mexican wages will rise, the internal market will expand, and a good part of the extra demand will spill over to the United States in orders for export industries.

NAFTA will not necessarily result in permanent job loss according to Lawrence (see Chapter 14, this volume). He argues that Mexico's low-wage advantage will not result in Mexico overtaking American firms. He claims that while there are some areas where cheap labor may be exploited, this is clearly not the case for all industries. Some industries are much more dependent on skill, high-level technology, and quality, and will not be adversely affected.

Lawrence argues that jobs will be created not only by Mexican consumers purchasing U.S. products, but also by producer and investment goods (e.g., machinery) that will fuel the economy. He claims that the result will be Mexico specializing in labor-intensive activities and the United States specializing in technology-intensive industries. He argues that this change should result in the upgrading of the U.S. labor force by ultimately providing higher wages and better employment opportunities.

Lawrence does not feel that increased investments in Mexico will result in larger trade deficits. He claims that although these gains will be relatively small when considering the size of the U.S. economy and the fact that only

Table 1.12
NAFTA Countries' Government Budget Deficit (in U.S. Billions)

	1987	1988	1989	1990	1991
United States (year ended Sept. 30)	147.5	155.5	143.8	218.1	280.6
Canada (year ended Mar. 31)	15.8	11.7	11.7	15.7	16.5
Mexico (year ended Dec. 31)	11.9	17.7	10.0	9.1	5.0*

*Surplus
Source: International Monetary Fund, 1992.

6 percent of U.S. international trade occurs with Mexico, the net result in the short and medium terms will be positive because 70 percent of Mexico's imports come from the United States. An additional gain will be to stem the tide of immigration as living standards improve in Mexico.

Lawrence claims that all countries benefit when the country they are conducting trade with relaxes its barriers. This is particularly important for the United States and Canada; their deficits continue to grow, totaling $280.6 billion and $16.5 billion, respectively, in 1991, while Mexico experienced a budget surplus of $5.0 billion as shown in Table 1.12.

Lawrence points to the benefits experienced among European Community countries in their moves to increase trade among members. Another example is Bush's Enterprise for the America's Initiative, which has been useful in increasing trade between Latin American countries and the United States.

Cavitt cites six reasons why NAFTA will not result in a massive shift of U.S. jobs and plants to Mexico. First, any plant that could benefit from virtually free trade with Mexico could have moved there any time in the past twenty-five years under the maquiladora plan. Second, total production and marketing costs are what matter, not wages alone. Third, Mexican wages reflect Mexican productivity. Output per worker in the United States is five to six times that of Mexico. Since 1980 output per person employed in U.S. manufacturing has grown 2.5 times faster than in Mexican manufacturing. Fourth, most exports from Mexico are already duty-free or virtually duty-free. The average U.S. tariff on goods from Mexico is only 4 percent. Therefore, the elimination of those tariffs will be insignificant. Fifth, there is a shortage of skilled labor in Mexico. There are few technical schools and graduates. One study shows that Mexican engineers, technicians, supervisors, and managers in Sedad Juarez earn salaries of 60 to 90 percent of their American counterparts in El Paso. Finally, the Mexican social infrastructure is inadequate to meet current basic needs. Inadequacies include roads, bridges, border crossings, municipal transit, housing, health care, child care facilities, and even basic sewage disposal.

U.S. corporate interests that sought an extension of the fast-track agreement is represented by the Coalition for Trade Expansion, a lobbying umbrella that includes more than five hundred corporations and lobbyists from five key business trade associations: The Business Roundtable, U.S. Chamber of Commerce, Emergency Committee for American Trade, the National Association of Manufacturers, and National Foreign Trade Council. Many members of these associations have been reluctant to make the massive long-term investment in plant and equipment needed to take full advantage of cheaper costs in Mexico because of concern over the unstable political climate. Specifically, they fear a return of hostility toward foreign investment and the threat of nationalization. They are working to promote liberal trade and investment policies that cannot easily be reversed by a future Mexican government.[46]

Calman Cohen, vice president of the Emergency Committee for American Trade (ECAT), an organization of over sixty U.S. firms with extensive overseas business activities, indicates strong support among its members for NAFTA. In Chapter 6 of this volume Cohen argues that NAFTA will encourage U.S. firms manufacturing in Mexico and the United States to find ways to rationalize production and become more competitive. He argues that NAFTA will not lead to increased maquiladoras but to their obsolescence because they are a result of an inefficient Mexican economy. He concludes that NAFTA presents an opportunity for the three member countries to redefine their home markets, thereby improving the economic welfare of the population of all three countries.

How Does Canada View NAFTA?

The arguments for and against NAFTA must be considered in conjunction with the effect that NAFTA will have on the previously negotiated Canadian-U.S. Free Trade Agreement. The U.S./Canadian/Mexican Free Trade Zone would be the world's largest free market with a total output of $6 trillion and a total trade of $225 billion. While Mexico is Canada's largest trading partner in Latin America, bilateral merchandise trade between the two countries in 1992 was $2.9 billion annually.[47] Canada is the largest trading partner of the United States. Total bilateral trade in goods and services was $212.7 billion in 1990, up from $169 billion in 1988 or a $47 billion increase in four years.[48]

During the 1980s Canadians were confronted with escalating prices due to the lack of competition occurring within its borders. Considerable benefits could be realized through specialization by allowing Canadian firms to enjoy scale economies and by enhancing competition in Canada. The United States stood to gain as Canadian tariffs against American products were higher in virtually every product category than American tariffs were against Canadians. Free trade meant the eventual elimination of these barriers.

In 1988 the United States and Canada agreed to a FTA that took effect January 1, 1989. The U.S. Department of Commerce has summarized the major provisions of the U.S.-Canada Free Trade Agreement as follows:[49]

1. Tariffs: The major focus of the agreement is to eliminate all tariffs on the other country's products within ten years. Almost three-fourths of U.S. goods entering Canada are already duty-free. The U.S.-Canadian free trade agreement placed the remaining types of goods on three lists depending on whether duties are to be eliminated in 1989, 1993, or 1998. It provides a mechanism for accelerating the timetable of tariff reductions if both sides agree.[50]

2. Rules of Origin: While tariffs will be eliminated on products originating in Canada and the United States, they are retained for products originating in third countries. The rules of origin established a percentage of Canadian or U.S. content for the products to qualify for duty-free treatment.

3. Government Procurement: The agreement incorporates the GATT requirement that purchases by specified government agencies valued at more than $171,000 are to be open to free competition, and lowered the dollar threshold to $425,000 in some cases.

4. Restraints: The agreement forbids government to place new restrictions on business services and secured access to the telecommunications network. It applies the principle of "national treatment"—requiring both governments to treat the other nation's service providers the same as their own.

5. Investment: The agreement eliminates certain trade-related "performance requirements" that the Canadian regulatory agency, Investment Canada, has imposed on U.S. firms. It narrows the range of conditions under which Investment Canada may review acquisitions by U.S. firms. Only acquisitions valued at more than $150 million (1992) Canadian dollars will be eligible for review.

6. Border-Crossing Procedures: The procedures are simplified for four categories of visitors to Canada: business visitors, traders and investors, intracompany transferees, and professional service providers.

7. Energy: The agreement eliminates all remaining tariffs on energy products and forbids introduction of new trade regulations with respect to those products that would put the other party at a disadvantage.

8. Dispute Settlement: The agreement establishes a "Canadian-U.S. Trade Commission" to supervise the agreement's implementation and to handle disputes except in the areas of financial services, antidumping, and countervailing duties.

The FTA between the United States and Canada is comprehensively addressed in Chapter 17 of this volume by Keith Martin. Martin, director of policy for the Canadian Chamber of Commerce, supports NAFTA and all avenues available to liberalize trade including GATT, the Canadian-U.S. FTA, and NAFTA. Martin discusses Canadian objectives in NAFTA as they relate to technical and legal issues, government procurement, agriculture, energy, safeguards, subsidies and countervailing duties, dumping and antidumping duties, services transportation, telecommunications, intellectual property, and general dispute settlement.

Martin concludes that by participating in the process Canadians protect their own interests within the FTA while exploring the possibility of gaining preferred access to the potentially dynamic Mexican market. Their involvement also permits them to reevaluate issues that were not fully negotiated in the U.S.-Canada FTA and permits them to diversify their trade relations, positioning them for global competitiveness.

Sunder Magun, of the Economic Council of Canada, also recognizes Canadian gains via NAFTA (see Chapter 15, this volume). He claims that each country has a unique pattern of international specialization and will build upon its strengths. Canada will benefit from direct export gains in Mexican markets, trade diversion gains in Mexico, and productivity gains resulting from industry rationalization across the three economies. Gains will accrue to Canada when real incomes of Mexicans rise, generating increased demand as a result of NAFTA.

According to Cavitt, the gains from the U.S.-Canada agreement included greater market access, more secure market access, and freedom for market forces to work (see Chapter 4). The United States attained elimination of Canadian tariffs, which averaged 9.9 percent and were among the highest in the industrialized world. The United States also attained a 10 percent growth in the size of its domestic market, increasing from $250 million to $276 million. Canada also achieved greater market access; however, U.S. tariffs averaged only a 3.3 percent on dutiable imports from Canada.

Despite the glowing reports, the U.S.-Canada FTA has met with harsh criticism in Canada. Sentiment is running 2 to 1 against the broader NAFTA agreement.[51] While the business community was almost unanimous in its support for the Canada-U.S. deal, opponents built a broad-based coalition among trade unions, political parties, nationalists, the artistic community, and intellectuals.[52] Both the Liberal party and the other main opposition party, the New Democratic party, are against the treaty as it now stands. Many of these critics are using NAFTA as a vehicle for attacking the existing U.S.-Canada Free Trade Agreement.

According to Bruce Campbell, research fellow at the Canadian Center for Policy Alternatives, the Canadian labor movement's position on NAFTA is that an economically integrated North American economy based on the model already in place, the Canada-U.S. Free Trade Agreement, is undesirable (see Chapter 3, this volume). Canadian workers envision NAFTA—with low-wage maquiladora factories with their lack of effective unions, workplace health and safety regulations, and other labor and environmental standards—as an unfair economic playing field that can only have a negative effect on jobs and living standards. They see it exacerbating a process, entrenched in the FTA, of lowest common denominator competition or competitive poverty among workers and communities.

Campbell claims that the Canadian labor movement opposition to NAFTA is based on the following expectations: (1) that the essential terms and conditions of the FTA will remain in place in a trilateral accord; (2) that the U.S. government will extract further adverse concessions from Canada; (3) that the free trade-driven restructuring of the Canadian economy, most visibly in manufacturing, and the resulting job losses will be exacerbated; (4) that the harmonization effect of free trade or downward pull on Canadian wages, labor, social, and environmental standards will quicken; and (5) that NAFTA will reinforce the process of economic and political disintegration currently underway in Canada.

The Canadian labor movement points out that tight monetary policy imposed by the conservatives in an attempt to bring down inflation has resulted in soaring interest rates and depreciation of the Canadian dollar. As a result Canadians have found themselves priced out of the American market and facing rising unemployment levels. Industry has fled Canada and Canadians have recognized gains from shopping in U.S. border cities.

Many Canadians claim that jobs have been lost as a result of the U.S.-Canada FTA. Estimates of job losses vary, ranging from 267,000 manufacturing jobs to as many as 425,000 jobs. The Conservative government blamed the loss of jobs on the overvalued Canadian dollar and the recession. Opponents claim that Canada's well-developed social insurance, safety net, and public investment policies are already being eroded by the trade agreement with the United States. Under conditions of free trade, competition has increased between political jurisdictions to attract investment. This competition invariably puts downward pressure on wages, social benefits, and workplace health and safety standards.

The sectors with the highest job losses are those that employ more women and immigrants (textiles and clothing and food processing). Eighty percent of the jobs lost occur in manufacturing. The new employment opportunities that are being created in Canada are mostly lower-paying, nonunion jobs in the service sector.[53]

The Action Canada Network, which is comprised of nearly forty major Canadian groups, has reported that the United States has two main objectives in its trade talks with Canada and Mexico. The first is "to secure access to Mexico's petroleum" much as the United States gained access to Canadian petroleum in the FTA. The second major U.S. objective is "to establish permanent investment and services codes favorable to transnational corporations."[54]

Even if Canada rejects NAFTA, it is likely that the United States and Mexico would go ahead with the agreement. This would result in the United States having a huge edge over Canada in attracting foreign transplants because only the United States would then be able to ship duty-free products to both Canada and Mexico. An attempt by Canada to roll back free trade with the United States would threaten $175 billion in cross-border business.

By contrast Canada's trade with Mexico is only $2.5 billion per year. The Conservative government had the votes to push NAFTA through Parliament, however, to have done so might have harmed its chances of prevailing in the upcoming 1993 general election. The New Democrat Liberal coalition is having some success with the electorate in campaigning against NAFTA. The New Democrats want to rip up the U.S.-Canada deal, and the more moderate Liberals want to see it renegotiated.[55]

Jeremy Wright, global economist from Itchenhouse, Ottawa, in Chapter 23, outlines the major labor differences among the three NAFTA countries. Significant differences occur in industrial relations, employment standards, and occupational safety and health standards. Wright argues that NAFTA must establish *ex ante* enforceable provisions for the highest possible international environmental, health and safety, and labor standards. These could take the form of "snap-back," (tariff reductions snapping back if the labor and environmental rules are not implemented). Firm-specific or product-specific duties could also be imposed in the same way as "countervail" now operates. Failure to meet the highest environmental and social and labor standards would be deemed to be a "trade-distorting" subsidy.

The Impact of Free Trade on the Collective Bargaining Agreement: United States and Canada

Morley Gunderson and Anil Verma conclude that little systematic analyses of the impact of free trade on the broader area of labor relations in general or on the collective bargaining agreement in particular has been conducted (see Chapter 11, this volume).[56] They maintain that the legislative and regulatory mechanisms for dealing with the adjustment consequences of free trade will be affected in an indeterminate fashion. On the one hand, the adjustment consequences will increase the need for legislation and programs in such areas as advance notice, severance pay, seniority for layoffs and recalls, subcontracting, successor rights, wage claims under bankruptcy, retraining and relocation, and income support programs like unemployment insurance. As well, there will be pressure to downsize through such mechanisms as early retirement, attrition, worksharing, and leaves of absence. There will be continued pressure for wage concessions and breaks in traditional pattern bargains to gear settlements to the affected organization's ability to pay in a particular situation. The upside adjustment consequences will put pressure on adaptability and flexibility to meet the rapidly changing needs and skill shortages. This could imply fewer and broader job categories, multiskilling for a variety of tasks, retraining provisions, and a deemphasis on seniority as the main criterion for promotion.

On the other hand, free trade can also make it more difficult to institute or expand programs like these because it is more difficult to pass their cost on to employers who can more easily relocate to areas where there are minimal regulations, and export to areas where there is more costly regulation. This is part of the idea that competitive pressures on the product market side lead to a "forced harmonization" of laws and regulations in the labor market. This occurs because under free trade, businesses can more easily invest and locate in areas of minimal regulatory cost and export to the areas of more costly regulation. Jurisdictions will increasingly compete to attract and retain business by offering a regulatory climate that is conducive to business. In the policy debate over these issues, the relative power of employers increases because of the enhanced "threat effect" that greater investment and location decisions carry.

While the pressures toward harmonization may be toward the lowest common denominator (i.e., the least regulatory environment) this need not always be the case. Some jurisdictions may seek to compete for business on the basis of providing a safety net or publicly supported training, despite the costs. As well, political agreements across countries can lead to upward harmonization if that is the collective will. This is perhaps best illustrated by the European Economic Community, where there is considerable political pressure (e.g., through the Social Charter) to harmonize upwards to the *higher* standards of countries like Germany, to avoid social dumping of countries with low wages and labor standards. In the European Community, however, the regulatory costs are protected somewhat by the common tariff.

According to Gunderson and Verma, a common market involves the free trade of goods and services, but it also includes the free mobility of labor and a common external tariff. Neither of the latter two characteristics is incorporated in NAFTA. This means that NAFTA does not have to deal with labor compensation even though huge discrepancies exist between Mexico and the United States and Canada, and the absence of a common external tariff means that the free trade countries could not agree to an "upward harmonization" of their labor legislative initiatives, with the cost consequences of those initiatives being protected by the common external tariff, as is the case with the European Economic Community.

PROPOSED NAFTA

The proposed NAFTA involves an ambitious effort to eliminate barriers to agricultural, manufacturing, and services trade, to remove investment restrictions, and to protect intellectual property rights. Highlights of NAFTA according to the White House, Office of the Press Secretary, in a memorandum released August 12, 1992:

Tariff Elimination. Approximately 65 percent of U.S. industrial and agricultural exports to Mexico will be eligible for duty-free treatment either immediately or within five years. Mexico's tariffs currently average 10 percent, which is two-and-a-half times the average U.S. tariff.

Increased Investment. Mexican "domestic content" rules will be eliminated, permitting additional sourcing of U.S. inputs and, for the first time, U.S. firms operating in Mexico will receive the same treatment as Mexican-owned firms. Mexico has agreed to drop export performance requirements, which presently force companies to export as a condition of being allowed to invest.

Protection of Intellectual Property Rights. NAFTA will provide a higher level of protection for intellectual property rights than any other bilateral or multilateral agreement. These rights are crucial for U.S. high technology, pharmaceuticals, biotechnology, sound recordings, motion pictures, and computer software. Producers that rely heavily on protection for their patents, copyrights, and trademarks will realize substantial gains under NAFTA. The agreement will also limit compulsory licensing, resolving an important concern with Canada.

How Will Industries Be Affected by NAFTA?

Automotive Trade

Automobiles and automobile parts are key economic sectors in Canada, with a high percentage of Canadian manufacturing jobs linked directly or indirectly. The auto industry in Canada constitutes a significant volume of trade with the United States ($40.4 billion in 1988, or 31.4 percent of bilateral trade in manufactures).[57] U.S. automotive exports to Canada and Mexico totaled $28.5 billion in 1991. Similarly, automobiles and automotive parts are the largest component of manufactured trade between the United States and Mexico. The United States exported $5.7 billion in autos and parts to Mexico in 1991 out of a total $33 billion in exports.

NAFTA will lower Mexican tariffs on autos from 20 percent to 10 percent immediately, and then to zero over ten years. Tariffs on most auto parts will be lowered to zero within five years.

NAFTA mandates tough rules of origin, specifying that vehicles must contain 62.5 percent North American content to qualify for NAFTA tariff preferences. This increased percentage should aid in preventing "screwdriver" assembly plants using insufficient North American content from benefiting from NAFTA tariff cuts. The 62.5 percent North American content requirement is considerably more than the 50 percent required by the U.S.-Canada Free Trade Agreement.

NAFTA contains tracing requirements so that individual parts can be identified to determine the North American content of major components and subassemblies (e.g., engines). This strict rule of origin is important in ensuring that the benefits of NAFTA flow to firms that produce in North America.

NAFTA will eliminate over ten years requirements that automakers supplying the Mexican market produce the cars in Mexico and buy Mexican parts. It eliminates mandatory export quotas and other performance requirements previously imposed on foreign-owned automotive manufacturing facilities in Mexico and eliminates Mexican import restrictions on buses and trucks within five years. These provisions should result in increased demand in Mexico for U.S. autos and auto parts.

Textiles and Apparel

Mexico's textile and apparel market is a $6.4 billion market. U.S. textile exports to Mexico reached $1.1 billion in 1991.

NAFTA will immediately eliminate barriers to trade between Mexico and the United States on over 20 percent, or some $250 million, of textile and apparel exports. This includes key U.S. exports, such as denim, underwear, thread, and many household furnishings. NAFTA will eliminate, over six years, barriers to another $700 million worth of U.S. textile exports, including yarns, most household furnishings, most fabrics, and certain other apparel.

NAFTA will provide strong rules of origin, requiring that garments must be manufactured in North America generally from the yarn-spinning stage forward to qualify for duty-free status, thus preventing Mexico from serving as an export platform for "free riders" outside North America. The proposed NAFTA provides safeguards that may be invoked such as tariffs and quotas if imports cause damage to the U.S. industry.

Agriculture

Mexico imported $3 billion worth of U.S. agricultural goods in 1991, making it the third largest U.S. market. The NAFTA will immediately eliminate Mexican import licenses, which covered 25 percent of U.S. agricultural exports in 1991, and will phase out remaining Mexican tariffs within ten to fifteen years. One-half of U.S. farm exports to Mexico will enter Mexico duty-free on the day NAFTA enters into force. All remaining tariffs on agricultural goods will be eliminated within fifteen years. Mexican tariffs now generally range from 10 to 20 percent. NAFTA's tariff reductions and elimination of Mexican import licenses should spur increased U.S. agricultural exports.

Grains

NAFTA will eliminate immediately Mexico's licensing requirements for wheat and corn and will allow unrestricted access for those commodities, as well as other grains, rice, oilseeds, and oilseed products within ten to fifteen years.

Dairy and Poultry

NAFTA will immediately eliminate Mexico's licensing requirements for poultry, eggs, cheeses, and nonfat dry milk and remove all further trade barriers within ten to fifteen years.

Livestock

NAFTA will lock in the U.S. current duty-free access to the Mexican market for cattle and beef, and will eliminate within ten years all remaining Mexican tariffs on U.S. livestock and poultry exports. NAFTA contains safeguard measures that automatically increase duties for certain sensitive products to protect U.S. farmers if import volumes rise too rapidly during the transition.

Electronics

U.S. exports of electronics products to Canada and Mexico totaled $4.5 billion in 1991, and have been growing 20 percent annually.

Most Mexican tariffs on telecommunications equipment, computers and parts, and electronic components will be eliminated immediately, with others eliminated within five years.

Pharmaceuticals

In 1991 the United States exported $645 million in pharmaceuticals to Mexico and $121 million to Canada.

Mexico will immediately eliminate its import licenses on pharmaceuticals, which now range between 10 and 20 percent. In addition, NAFTA will virtually eliminate compulsory licensing for pharmaceuticals and extend the term of patent protection to at least twenty years, versus the current ten years in Canada. Mexico also will substantially open its government procurement market for pharmaceuticals.

Entertainment

NAFTA will open Mexico's cable television market to U.S. and Canadian investment, given U.S. broadcasters the right to broadcast across the Mexican border, and remove Mexican import restrictions on U.S. motion pictures.

Energy and Petrochemicals

NAFTA provides access for U.S. firms to Mexico's electricity, petrochemical, gas, and energy services and equipment markets.

NAFTA increases government procurement opportunities. NAFTA provides significant opportunities to sell to state-owned PEMEX and CFE (the State Electricity Commission) under open and competitive bidding rules. NAFTA allows private foreign ownership and operation of electric generating plants for self-generation, co-generation, and independent power plants. NAFTA immediately lifts trade and investment restrictions on most petrochemicals, the lifting investment restrictions on fourteen of the nineteen previously restricted basic petrochemicals and on sixty-six secondary petrochemicals.

NAFTA provides for performance incentives in services contracts such as drilling activities. NAFTA permits U.S. firms to negotiate directly with Mexican buyers of natural gas and electricity and to conclude contracts with the buyers together with PEMEX or CFE.

Benefits of NAFTA in Key Service Sectors

Expanded Trade in Financial Services

Mexico's closed financial services markets will be opened and U.S. banks and securities firms will be allowed to establish wholly owned subsidiaries and engage in the same range of operations as similar Mexican firms. Transitional restrictions will be phased out by January 1, 2000, and Mexico's ability to place future constraints on foreign-owned firms will be limited. Other types of financial firms, including leasing and consumer finance, will also be able to establish operations in Mexico when the agreement goes into effect and will not be subject to any limitations after a short transitional period. Mexicans and Canadians will be guaranteed the right to purchase financial services from firms in the United States.

New Opportunities in Insurance

NAFTA eliminates restrictions on U.S. ownership and provision of services in the $3.5 billion Mexican insurance market.

U.S. and Canadian firms with existing joint ventures will be permitted to obtain 100 percent ownership by 1996; new entrants to the market can obtain a majority stake in Mexican firms by 1998 and 100 percent ownership by the year 2000. New entrants may start their own wholly owned firms in Mexico immediately, subject to certain size limitations in effect until January 1, 2000. U.S. insurance companies may sell cargo insurance, and reinsurance on a cross-border basis in Mexico. They may also sell life, health, and travel insurance to Mexican residents who come to the United States.

Land Transportation

NAFTA opens Mexico's market for international truck, bus, and rail transport, and locks in U.S. access to Canada's already open transportation market. Over 90 percent of U.S. trade with Mexico is shipped by land.

NAFTA will permit U.S. trucking companies to carry international cargo to the Mexican states contiguous to the United States by the end of 1995, and to have cross-border access to all of Mexico by the end of 1999. Currently, U.S. and Canadian truckers are denied the right to carry cargo or to set up subsidiaries in Mexico, forcing them to "hand off" trailers to Mexican drivers and return home empty.

NAFTA will provide U.S. and Canadian charter and tour bus operators full and immediate access to the cross-border market. Regular bus route companies will gain full cross-border access by the end of 1996. U.S. and Canadian trucking and bus companies gained the right to set up international cargo subsidiaries or new companies in Mexico, and to acquire minority ownership by the end of 1995, majority ownership by 2000, and 100 percent ownership by 2003.

NAFTA opens the Mexican market permanently for U.S. and Canadian railroads, locking in the market-oriented reforms undertaken by the Mexican National Railroad, by permitting U.S. and Canadian railroads to market their services directly to customers, use their own locomotives, construct and own terminals in Mexico, and provide infrastructure financing. NAFTA also opens investment and operating access for port facilities in Mexico, increasing options for U.S. intermodal companies.

Telecommunications Trade

U.S. exports of equipment to Mexico totaled $1.274 billion in 1991 and had already reached $1.1 billion by September of 1992.

NAFTA eliminates discriminatory restrictions on U.S. and Canadian sales to and investments in the $6 billion Mexican market for telecommunications equipment and services. It improves opportunities for U.S. and Canadian exports of enhanced services to Mexico, a market expected to grown from $22 million in 1991 to over $100 million by 1995. NAFTA also improves prospects for exports of cross-border enhanced services, which totaled $27 million in 1990. NAFTA eliminates investment restrictions in most enhanced services immediately, and eliminates all investment and other restrictions on packet-switched services in 1995. NAFTA should enable U.S. and Canadian firms to operate state-of-the-art, private intracorporate communications systems throughout North America with guaranteed access to public communications facilities while doing business in and with Mexico.

NAFTA eliminates product standards as a barrier to telecommunications trade by providing for mutual recognition of test data from all competent test facilities in NAFTA countries.

Early Responses to the Proposed NAFTA

As Steven Schlossberg, director of the Washington branch of the International Labor Office, pointed out in round-table discussions relevant to the concerns he develops in Chapter 21, we have to take care of the automobile industry, the electronics industry, certain agricultural industries. We have to take care of textiles and garments. We might have to take care of them for twenty-five years. We have to retrain people, see that people do not starve.

Agriculture

Some opponents to NAFTA fear that U.S. standards may be "harmonized down" in order to adjust for substandard Mexican imports. The reduction in import controls engendered by NAFTA could allow the introduction of pesticides, toxins, or other harmful products into the United States. This concern cannot be trivialized because in 1991 agricultural products accounted for over $5.5 billion of U.S.-Mexican trade.[58] In 1989 the United States purchased 90 percent of Mexico's agricultural exports, and supplied 75 percent of Mexico's agricultural imports.

At the Trade for the 21st Century Conference held in Washington on September 7, 1992, Leland Swenson, president of the National Farmers Union, warned of the exposure consumers could receive to pesticides and chemicals long banned in the United States. He produced a list of fifty-eight pesticides not under U.S. bans that are used on fruits and vegetables by Mexican producers.

On the other hand, the U.S. International Trade Commission claims that NAFTA will significantly affect the level of U.S. trade with Mexico in agricultural products. It could increase U.S. citrus fruit and winter vegetable imports from Mexico considerably, and increase U.S. exports of corn, sorghum, and soybeans. The United States could also experience a moderate increase in beef, sorghum, and oilseed imports from Mexico. U.S. fruit and vegetable growers fear competition—especially since imports of these commodities from Mexico doubled during the 1980s.

Automobiles

The auto industry has been a major investor in Mexican maquiladoras. Organized labor in the United States has expressed concern that the U.S.-based automobile industry would relocate to Mexico, resulting in significant numbers of U.S. jobs lost. Owen Bieber, United Auto Workers president, in a recent Senate hearing testified that maquiladora plants involved in the production of cars and transportation equipment expanded from 12,000 jobs in 1982 to 90,000 to 1989.[59] General Motors Corp., with 55,000 workers in Mexico, is the nation's largest private employer.[60]

Mexico imposes many restrictions on its automotive sector, such as local content regulations, rules of origin, and prorated import and export ceilings. The Big Three U.S. auto manufacturers—Ford, Chrysler, and GM—lobbied for the creation of a two-tier system within NAFTA. Their proposal would give preferential treatment to automobile firms already established in Mexico by requiring different phase-in periods and separate local content requirements for those seeking to enter the market. The Big Three argue that this mechanism is necessary in order to level the playing field; they need time to adjust their present operations, which were designed under the restrictive Mexican laws governing this sector. This proposal did not become part of the current NAFTA.

The Big Three were not united in their preferred policy regarding rules of origin. While GM of Canada favored retaining the 50 percent rule of origin, Ford and Chrysler of Canada were in favor of increasing the content requirement to 60 percent and the U.S. auto industry was seeking 65 percent.

Energy and Petrochemicals

The energy sector was another problematic area of negotiations. The United States wanted energy on the negotiating table, but Mexico declined. The Mexican constitution prohibits foreign investment in large parts of the oil industry. However, given the Mexican oil industry's need for both funds and technology, many analysts speculate that certain arrangements such as subcontracting or the refining of secondary petrochemicals will allow Mexico to access both the technology and the financing that it needs, without compromising its constitution.

How Will Investors Be Helped?

NAFTA provides for nondiscrimination against U.S. companies establishing, acquiring, or operating businesses in Canada or Mexico and vice versa. The repatriation of capital to the United States including profits and royalties cannot be blocked. It eliminates the approval needed for new investments in most sectors. NAFTA prohibited the parties from requiring companies to export as a condition for investing and from offering incentives that discriminate against imports. Performance requirements dictating that exports balance imports and local content be used are no longer in effect. Investors maintain the right and direct access to international arbitration for disputes with host governments. Investors may seek binding awards of money damages for violators of the NAFTA investment provision.

Private commercial disputes will be resolved. Each country must have legal mechanisms in place to enforce arbitration contracts and awards and will take steps to promote other forms of dispute settlement. In addition, a special committee under the NAFTA Trade Commission will examine and report on dispute settlement issues in the three countries.

RECOMMENDATIONS FOR AN IMPROVED NAFTA

Environmental Standards

Several major environmental groups have split over the agreement. Some fear that Mexico will become a "pollution haven" for U.S. companies seeking to escape tough U.S. environmental laws; others think that Mexico will become more environmentally conscious if it becomes wealthier through liberalized trade. The National Wildlife Federation and the World Wildlife Fund expressed support for its environmental provisions, while three other major groups—the Sierra Club, Friends of the Earth, and Public Citizen—called for the pact's rejection.[61]

Some environmentalists fear that in a zone free of tariffs, Mexico would have a competitive advantage due to its alleged low environmental standards and weak enforcement of existing rules. Proponents of NAFTA argue that trade liberalization, by generating wealth, would provide Mexico with the resources to improve its environmental record. NAFTA could aid environmental problems by easing the transfer of more efficient technology and stimulating economic growth so that more resources would be available. On the other hand, opponents argue that to date the rules have not been enforced and that NAFTA should address environmental considerations.

Critics of NAFTA question the paltry monetary amounts available for environmental safeguards, pollution controls, and development of infrastructure. Mexico's entire budget for environmental matters is about $38 million a year for SEDUE (Secretariat of Urban Development and Ecology), the agency in Mexico responsible for the environment, compared to $5.5 billion for the Environmental Protection Agency (EPA) in the United States. Critics claim significant resource gaps exist. According to data provided by the Congressional Research Service, based on information obtained from EPA, the U.S. per capita spending on environmental protection totaled $24.40 in 1991 compared with the SEDUE budget per person of $0.48 in Mexico.

Complicating the low revenue available for environmental concerns, public input into the process of environmental standard setting and enforcement is virtually nonexistent in Mexico. As previously mentioned, General Motors is one of Mexico's largest private employers and also one of the major polluters in the maquila area. The National Toxics Campaign recently conducted the largest environmental testing program ever undertaken among maquiladora industries. Preliminary results showed that conditions "are even worse than imagined." The highest level of toxic contamination was 2.8 million parts per billion of the toxic solvent xylene taken from a sample discharge from the GM facility in Matamoros. Xylene can cause respiratory irritation, amnesia, brain hemorrhage, internal bleeding, and damage to the lungs, liver, and kidneys. Ignorant of the results, GM issued a statement that its facilities are "operated in compliance with all applicable environmental, health, and safety laws, including the proper handling and disposal of hazardous waste materials at plants on both sides of the border."[62]

Environmentalists claim that the agreement must address environmental issues. They claim that Mexico will need money to train personnel, to develop the technical capacity to deal with the complex environmental problems that will accompany the agreement, and to create sufficient infrastructure to absorb new development. In order to guarantee sustainable development, natural resources must be conserved, waste and pollution minimized, standards harmonized, and money made available for enforcement of environmental laws.

Two proposals have been advanced for subsidizing the enforcement, environmental monitoring, and infrastructure development from the industries benefiting from free trade. These proposals are currently not part of the proposed NAFTA. One approach would be to assess a user fee. The Mexican government has debated charging the maquiladoras a fee to finance the creation of a regulatory infrastructure. This financing would go directly for communities where the businesses would be located, so that those communities could set up police forces, fire departments, and so forth. A second proposal involves the creation of a bonding system or up-front trust fund that would monitor environmental problems.

The Coalition for Justice in the Maquiladoras, a coalition of more than sixty organizations including the AFL-CIO, American Agriculture Movement, Child Labor Coalition, Consumer Federation of America, Environmental Action, Greenpeace, and Public Citizen have been actively opposing NAFTA. The coalition is "trying to educate the public about the conditions in the maquiladora plants and to correct those conditions." They have proposed a Maquiladora Standards of Conduct, which would establish ethical practices for corporations. The coalition also released preliminary studies showing the major U.S. corporations are responsible for widespread illegal dumping of toxic chemicals in sewers and waterways in Mexico. The coalition continues to pressure U.S. legislators to incorporate the standards of conduct in any trade negotiations with the Mexican government.

Although comprehensive data concerning the full extent of health and safety dangers for Mexican workers in the maquiladoras are lacking, there is ample evidence that health and safety rules are not enforced and that workers suffer a high rate of industrial injuries and illnesses. Mexico currently has the standards but no money to enforce them. The incidence of fatal workplace accidents in Mexico is reported to be twenty times higher than in the United States and six times higher than in Canada.[63]

Enforcement of workplace health and safety standards has been an issue. The proposed NAFTA does contain a provision for dispute settlement. Panels of scientific experts will be established in trade disputes for environmental and health science issues. The complaining party maintains the burden of proving that an environmental or health measure is inconsistent with the agreement. The proposed mechanism for enforcement includes endorsement of relevant International Labor Organization (ILO) conventions and passage of necessary legislation for compliance by all three countries as a basis for bringing standards up to an internationally accepted norm. Increased budgets for enforcement, trade sanctions against companies that cut costs by producing for export in areas of lax enforcement or loose laws, and access to the courts of any of the countries involved in cross-border transactions affected by the practice at issue are also sought.

On February 25, 1992, a Border Environmental Plan was introduced by the U.S. and Mexican administrations to address the problems of air and water pollution, hazardous waste, chemical spills, pesticides, and enforcement. Funding for the first stages (1992–94) of the integrated environmental plan for the border area will come from the Mexican and U.S. governments, state and local governments, and the private sector. Mexico has committed $460 million over three years for border environmental initiatives while Bush's FY1993 budget includes $241 million, including $75 million for the *colonias* (unincorporated communities on the U.S. side of the border that often lack effective sanitation services and running water) and over $120 million for border wastewater treatment plants.

Curbing Child Labor Law Violations

Curbing the rampant violators of child labor laws in Mexico has been a main concern. Half of Mexico's population is under the age of eighteen. It is illegal in Mexico to hire children under fourteen, but the Mexico City Assembly recently estimated that anywhere from 5 to 10 million children are employed illegally, often in hazardous jobs despite the fact that children are required by law to stay in school until sixth grade.[64] Due to the lack of enforcement many children may easily enter the workforce. The national labor code (which legislates child labor codes) gives the federal government jurisdiction over only a limited number of industries that make up only 3 percent of businesses in the state.

The AFL-CIO's "Policy Recommendations for 1992"[65] claim that in order to prevent countries from seeking to attract industry through the exploitation of workers, international agreements are needed to improve labor standards. In pursuit of this goal, they argue that the United States should fully utilize the workers rights provision in Section 301 of the 1988 Trade Act, to penalize those countries where basic rights and standards are denied. Provisions of the Generalized System of Preferences concerning labor rights must be enforced, and countries that abuse worker rights should be immediately removed from the program. The persistent use of child labor should be addressed through the enactment of legislation that would prohibit imports of products produced by children, with stiff criminal penalties for violators of that ban.

Trade Adjustment Assistance

Labor strongly supports investments for increased worker assistance. Some groups have argued that this could most easily be obtained through the inclusion of a "social charter" in NAFTA, something like the European Social Charter. Schlossberg supports the incorporation of a social dimension in NAFTA similar to that embodied in the European Community's progress toward integration. A Social Dimension has two aspects: (1) a Social Charter, which establishes the principle that trade should not be based on "social dumping," where poorer countries follow low-wage, low-regulation strategies in order to increase exports; and (2) the Structural Funds, which help redistribute resources to poorer countries, regions, and disadvantaged groups.

The European Economic Community contains a Social Charter guaranteeing rights to social assistance, collective bargaining, vocational training, and health and safety protections.[66] The Europeans have also created a $68 billion Regional Development Fund[67] to narrow the gap in per capita income between rich and poor countries within the market—a gap that is only one-fifth as wide as the one between the United States and Mexico.[68]

Critics of NAFTA have argued that the administration and Congress must develop a credible and comprehensive strategy for worker training and job creation because funding has traditionally not been made available for dislocated workers. The Trade Adjustment Assistance (TAA) program and the Job Training Partnership Act have been underfunded and the Bush administration further cut their budgets. In Bush's proposed budget for the fiscal year 1993, the administration reduced funding for worker retraining programs by 6.6 percent (nominal terms). The training component of TAA was eliminated and TAA benefits were cut in half. The TAA is the only U.S. program that comes close to meeting international standards in terms of duration of assistance and provision of training for dislocated workers; it requires major improvements in benefits, eligibility rules, and funding in order to provide meaningful help for workers who will be injured as a result of NAFTA.[69]

The current losers in trade adjustment assistance include firms, workers, and communities where policies have not been adequately developed to deal with dislocation. Lawrence advocates skill acquisition and training and a wage compensation program for displaced workers. While he claims the concept of trade adjustment assistance is good, the mechanisms for implementation are not in place. Lawrence also advocates the adoption of an insurance program that would permit communities to insure their tax base, thereby offsetting some of the downward spiral that individual communities experience in the face of plant closure.

Gary Sorensen, assistant commissioner for job service and unemployment insurance in the Minnesota Department of Jobs and Training, advocates education and economic development issues as top priorities (see Chapter 22, this volume). Improvements in vocational and technical education are needed. He advocates the evaluation of training in the workplace so that training does not continue for jobs that are going to be low-wage, low-skill, or obsolete in a few years. Improved methods of moving dislocated workers into new employment or with a minimum of training are needed. He claims the assumption that all displaced workers need retraining is both costly and irrational. Increased training will make it easier to make the transition into a new job if displacement does occur and it will be significantly less costly to taxpayers.

Sorensen highlights problems with trade assistance implementation on the state level. The job service offices administer trade assistance programs. Dislocated worker programs are serviced by private industry councils, job services, and other vendors. Due to vendor independence, information on openings and qualified individuals is not shared. On-the-job training contracts need to be encouraged and early intervention must be improved.

Improved training provisions in the state's unemployment compensation law are also needed. For example, current Minnesota law prohibits training for anyone with marketable skills, including basic entry skills. Under existing law, if a new job does not work out—and it is not due to illness or something directly attributable to the employer—individuals are disqualified when they come back to reopen an unemployment claim.

Democrats and Republicans in the United States differ on their approaches to job training. President Clinton favors active government involvement in comprehensive training and apprenticeship programs. To help pay for it, he wants companies to spend 1.5 percent of their payrolls on training. Clinton wants to set up a national network of community centers to give dropouts remedial education and skills training. He has proposed a national apprenticeship program for the 56 percent of students who do not go to college. Clinton also promises to create a national training policy by coordinating current schemes.[70]

Former president Bush suggested adding $2 billion a year to what the government spends on programs for young people and disadvantaged and dislocated workers. Funding for dislocated workers would rise from $750 million a year to $2 billion by 1994 and eligibility would be increased. Bush also proposed a Youth Training Corps, modeled after Job Corps, which would reopen closed military bases as training centers for 43,000 youths. He wanted the government to spend $100 million a year to start youth apprenticeship programs. These initiatives would cost $1 billion a year, of which $600 million would be new money.

WILL THE PROPOSED NAFTA BE THE FINAL NAFTA?

Due to the many different viewpoints expressed from labor, industry, environmentalists, and government officials, there have been many possibilities suggested for an enhanced NAFTA. Possible provisions yet to be addressed in NAFTA include guarantees that the trade agreement will not result in a mass exodus of jobs across the border; economic development assistance, much like the European Economic Community's efforts to help Portugal and Spain; provisions made for displaced workers to be compensated with adjustment assistance programs that focus on retraining; a Social Charter akin to the European model with minimum standards on wages, benefits, safety, environment, and worker protection; significant debt relief and/or increased U.S. aid for Mexico; improvements in the infrastructure of the border areas, including sewers, water, adequate housing, and schools; the elimination of unfair labor practices such as the use of child labor and the denial of effective representation for workers; necessary increases in compensation for Mexican workers with U.S. companies; enforceable environmental, safety, and health regulations; and Maquiladora Standards of Conduct that would establish ethical practices for business (proposed by the Coalition for Justice in the Maquiladoras).[71]

Specific suggestions for an improved NAFTA have been made by various groups. The Mobilization on Development, Trade, Labor and the Environment (MODTLE) has recommended that the following provisions be incorporated into NAFTA:

1. Preservation of strong standards. Harmonization language in NAFTA should spell out strong environmental and consumer protection standards that all countries should respect. Violations would constitute unfair trade practices. No ceiling or trade penalties should be imposed for countries enacting more restrictive standards.

2. Compensatory investment program. A mechanism should be established within NAFTA to ensure that those who benefit from NAFTA help pay the added burden for environmental protection created by the agreement.

3. Prevention of environmental dumping. A mechanism should be included in NAFTA that would allow countervailing duties to be imposed upon industries that do not meet applicable pollution control standards.

4. Recognition of the legitimacy of environmental protection language. Provisions of NAFTA must recognize the legitimacy of bona fide environmental measures even where they affect the flow of international commerce.

5. Informed public participation. Formal mechanisms for public participation must be established in the negotiation, implementation, and enforcement of NAFTA.

6. Elimination of trade in hazardous waste and the restriction of environmental runaway production. Hazardous wastes must be disposed of in the country of origin.

MODTLE also recommended labor rights and standards for NAFTA:

1. Enforcement of the rights of free association, collective bargaining, nondiscrimination, and equal remuneration for work of equal value. The right to strike and nondiscriminatory wages and conditions of employment must be assured in order to ensure that workers are not discriminated against or inhibited in accruing and maintaining effective union representation.

2. Trade-linked fair labor practices enforcement mechanism. Mechanism whereby infractions of labor rights or workplace standards in production for export can be challenged by trade unions or individuals in each country and, after reasonably swift adjudication, trade concessions or benefits can be removed from violators or punitive actions taken.

3. Workplace health and safety standards. Workplace health and safety standards for export production in all three countries must be in conformity with regionally

set standards that are not lower than the standards required by any of the three countries.

4. Living wage provision.

5. Social infrastructure investment. A provision whereby companies that invest in other countries contribute their fair share to support social infrastructure in the communities in which they operate, including such areas as medical care, community development, and education.

6. Program to eradicate child labor. This includes improved inspection and legal enforcement.

7. Reexamination of migrant program.

Separately, labor has voiced similar concerns. The AFL-CIO has recently listed issues that must be addressed if a new trade agreement is to be successful.[72]

1. Provisions must be included in any trade agreement whereby infractions of labor rights or workplace standards in production for export can be addressed by trade actions by any of the three countries. Areas that should be dealt with by these provisions include the right to organize and bargain collectively, strong workplace health and safety standards, an appropriate minimum wage structure, and the elimination of child labor.

2. The huge wage differential among the three countries should be addressed by encouraging an increase in compensation for Mexican workers. This is particularly important for those who are employed by U.S. companies exporting to this market. The AFL-CIO claims that current levels of compensation for these workers have no relationship to their productivity.

3. Provisions to address the existing environmental degradation of the border area, and provision of funds for increased enforcement of environmental laws and regulations in all three countries must be provided. Violations of environmental standards should be addressed.

4. There must be no change in current U.S. trade remedy law, including safeguards, subsidies, dumping, Section 301, and Section 337.

5. Legislation should be enacted that would deny trade benefits to companies that transfer production to Mexico.

6. Funds must be provided to improve the infrastructure of the border area, including sewers, water, electricity, housing, and schools.

7. Additional debt relief for Mexico should be provided so that it can begin investing at home to improve the standard of living of its people.

8. Protection must be provided for import-sensitive industries in the United States.

9. Tough rules of origin—with content requirements of at least 80 percent—must prevent other countries from taking advantage of the agreement and transhipping goods through Mexico or Canada into the U.S. market. For textile and apparel products, a 100 percent rule of origin should be negotiated.

10. An adequately funded trade adjustment assistance program with reasonable el-

igibility standards to provide assistance to those who are displaced, including income maintenance, special health care protection, and worker retraining must be established. Funding should be provided through the allocation of existing tariff revenues or the imposition of an import surcharge.

11. Requirements that all internationally traded goods are marked with their country of origin.

12. Safeguards to protect U.S. workers against import surges.

13. Strict limitations on "temporary entry" of persons to provide services, including transportation, and banning entry to affect labor disputes. Any temporary entrant must be paid and work under conditions prevailing in the host country.

14. Preservation of federal, state and local "Buy American" laws and regulations.

15. Equal market access for cultural industries.

16. Safeguards for U.S. automotive production, equivalent to existing provisions in Mexico and Canada.

17. Provisions addressing the needs of import-sensitive industries, such as textiles, apparel, electrical, electronic, glass, meat, tuna, sugar and light-duty trucks.

18. A cross-border transaction tax to help fund programs to improve food safety inspections and customs services; the infrastructure in the border area covering water treatment, electricity, housing and schools; Trade Adjustment Assistance for those hurt by trade.

President Clinton has indicated that he will ask Congress to take several unilateral actions to supplement the trade deal. He argues for significant retraining, health benefits, and income supplements to workers displaced by the agreement as well as assistance to communities to create jobs; enhanced environmental protections; and special assistance to farmers, including retraining, aid in shifting to alternate corps, and bans on products that do not meet U.S. pesticide standards. He advocates legislation to give American citizens the right to challenge objectionable environmental practices by the Mexicans or the Canadians, and the right to defend challenges to U.S. laws. Enforcement of cross-border provisions prohibiting the import of strikebreakers, as well as tough inspections to assure that Mexican truckers meet U.S. safety and training standards are also proposed.

Clinton has also said he will negotiate supplemental agreements with Canada and Mexico to establish an Environmental Protection Commission with substantial powers and resources to prevent and clean up water pollution and a commission for worker standards and safety[73] with extensive powers to educate, train, and develop minimum standards, as well as authority for dispute resolution and remedies. He also will work toward legislative authority to negotiate another agreement to deal with unexpected import surges. In general, Clinton argues that the key to improving U.S. performance in the global marketplace is to invest more in education, worker training, and infrastructure to improve productivity.

Trade officials said administration support is behind a plan advanced by Senator Max Baucus, Chairman of the Finance Committee's International Trade Subcommittee.[74] This plan would permit the boards to investigate complaints that companies doing business in Mexico were in violation of labor or environmental standards. If a company was found guilty and Mexico ignored the Commission's findings, the U.S. government could impose punitive tariffs on the company's exports to the United States. In cases of "systematic and persistent" violations by a company in one country, the other two countries would be able to levy trade sanctions.

The United States, Canada and Mexico differ on enforcement power within NAFTA. The United States is promoting a plan in which the boards could use trade sanctions as an enforcement vehicle, but the Canadians are opposed. The United States is pushing an additional agreement to limit unexpected surges in imports, but Canada and Mexico believe that provisions in NAFTA already cover those concerns. Under the free trade pact, when imports from Mexico or Canada threaten "serious injury" to U.S. companies, the United States can reimpose, for as long as four years, tariffs that existed before the agreement took effect. In addition, the United States retains its rights under international trade law to impose quotas on goods if U.S. companies are especially threatened.

Given the many provisions that have been proposed specifically by environmental and labor groups, the NAFTA debate promises to be a lengthy process where the parties will continue to support their agendas. NAFTA was delayed in June 1993 when a federal district court ruled that the Clinton administration must file an environmental impact study.

CONCLUSIONS

While the debate concerning NAFTA has been waged during the past three years, the critical debate is only just beginning. During the early stages, the debate focused on if negotiations should take place and if so was fast tracking the preferred mode. The debate has moved much further with the realization that increased trade among the three countries is a reality. Today the debate focuses on the rules that the three countries want to play by. Strict proponents would have NAFTA address only trade issues, whereas other groups (environmentalists and labor groups) want to see the inclusion of more regulatory mechanisms for the parties and environment to be affected.

According to a joint communication issued by the participating countries, the goal of the proposed NAFTA is to eliminate obstacles to the flow of goods, services, and investment, provide for intellectual property rights protection, and establish a fair and expeditious dispute settlement mechanism. While the proposed NAFTA addresses these three major areas, much of the debate centers on workers and environment, which constitute the "fallout" of the trade sanctions. Critics claim that U.S., Mexican, and Canadian workers will be thrown into competition with each other to attract investment by offering the lowest wages and the least restrictive regulations. Overall standards will decline as competitive pressures induce companies to move to lower-wage, lower-standard areas, driving down wages and funding available for higher-standard areas. In this scenario, the United States and Canada would have to lower standards, taking two steps back.

Comparative advantages do exist among the three member countries to NAFTA. Mexico's comparative advantage lies in its growing population and ability to provide a low-wage, low-skilled workforce particularly in assembly operations. Mexico does have weaker enforcement capabilities in the areas of environment, child labor protections, collective bargaining freedoms, and worker protection. Canada has vast natural resources, a highly trained workforce, developed infrastructure, and safety nets for workers although they are losing ground to the United States, where much of their industry is relocating. The United States is fearful of losing to the Mexican economy despite their skilled workforce and high productivity levels. The United States has the technological know-how, a skilled workforce, and environmental protections, but is losing ground as industries that previously employed low-skilled workers at premium wages relocate. These workers do not have the safety net provisions available to Canadian workers and will require retraining as low-skilled jobs disappear and real wages fall. NAFTA will force Canada and the United States to review their labor market adjustment policies such as retraining and worker adjustment programs.

Mexico stands to benefit the most from NAFTA. NAFTA will raise wages and standards of living in Mexico and should ultimately decrease pressure for unauthorized immigration to the United States. Mexican infrastructure including highways and communication systems will improve. Mexico will become more of a market economy characterized by competition, increased jobs, and increased investment flow resulting in a more stable economy.

Proponents of NAFTA claim that Mexico's environment will be positively affected; studies have shown that as countries become more industrialized, resources are generated to improve the environment and pollution decreases. Proponents further point to the efforts that Mexico has made to move its standards up to international levels. Critics point to the disastrous effects that NAFTA will have on the Mexican environment. Regardless of the position taken, the debate yet to be waged will be over the measurement and achievement of properly enforced minimum standard provisions.

The NAFTA agreement affirms the goal of all three nations to promote sustainable development and strengthen the development and enforcement of environmental laws and regulations. Historically investment liberalization has resulted in increased investments and increased exports. Integrated production will resulted in U.S. and Canadian firms being more competitive against European and Japanese producers. Proponents conclude that NAFTA will both increase exports and expand the number of jobs in the United States and Canada as Mexico becomes increasingly reliant on exports. The United States and Canada would be the natural benefactors as trade liberalization favors these countries over possible outsiders. If this scenario develops, then the United States, Canada, and Mexico are taking "three steps forward" in establishing a trading bloc that will be economically competitive in a global society.

The creation of a North American free trade zone touched off predictable protests throughout the world, notably in Asia. Asian government and industry leaders professed concern that industrial investment could shift from them to Mexico. Asian companies will begin studying how they can benefit from combining their strengths with Mexico and the United States. As NAFTA unfolds, firms outside the United States may consider consolidating U.S., Canadian, and Mexican subsidiaries in order to develop an integrated approach to doing business in North America.

NOTES

1. The fast-track rule covers all trade pacts, including the pending multilateral Uruguay Round of the General Agreement on Tariffs and Trade (GATT). GATT explicitly allows regional free trade agreements even if there is intended political integration. Both the European Common Market and the European Free Trade Association took advantage of this exception to the general GATT rule of most favored nation treatment (Dornbusch, 1990).

2. Fast tracking is highly controversial and first passed during the Reagan administration. In the past fifteen years, the United States has completed more than eighty-nine multilateral agreements that did not go through a fast-track process. There have only been three trade agreements that went through this procedure, including the Canadian-U.S. Free Trade Agreement.

3. Had productivity kept up with its earlier pace, today's median family income would be $47,000 instead of the current $35,000. Christopher Farrell and Michael J. Mandel, "Industrial Policy Call It What You Will, The Nation Needs a Plan to Nurture Growth." *Business Week*, Apr. 6, 1992, pp. 70–75.

4. According to Murray (1993) during 1982, productivity growth surged reaching 2.9%. According to Robert Gordon, a Northwestern economist, this growth has been attributed to a temporary response to the recession where companies failed to get rid of redundant workers when the economy slowed between 1987 and 1991 and then belatedly shed workers in 1992. George Perry of the Brookings Institution claims that this productivity increase is due to the use of computers in the workplace. Laura D'Andrea Tyson, chair of President's Council of Economic Advisors, and Secretary of Labor Robert Reich are less optimistic about the move toward long-term productivity growth. Reich points to the fact that there has not been an increase in jobs, nor real wages.

5. There are many ways of approaching this productivity problem including increasing research spending across a wide range of technologies, financial support to high-tech areas, and promoting tax laws that make it cheaper for the private sector to invest in research, development, and new equipment. Smaller companies could get technical assistance to learn the latest manufacturing techniques. Building up the infrastructure, especially by encouraging the development of high-speed com-

munications networks, could also be utilized. Trade policy could focus on opening up foreign markets while resisting protectionism at home.

6. All countries that are party to GATT must be treated at least as well as the most favored country.

7. Sidney Weintraub, *A Marriage of Convenience: Relations Between Mexico and the U.S.*, Twentieth Century Fund Report (New York: Oxford University Press, 1990), p. 70.

8. Since 1982 three-quarters of the nearly 1,155 state-owned companies have been privatized, most recently Mexico's giant telephone monopoly (Kootnikoff, 1991).

9. In many Mexican markets prices were administered through either monopoly-management policy or government controls. Prices were normally insulated from market forces.

10. U.S. International Trade Commission, *Review of Trade and Investment Liberalization Measures by Mexico and Prospects for Future U.S.-Mexican Relations*, Investigation No. 332–282, Phase II: Summary of Views on Prospects for Future U.S.-Mexican Relations, Oct. 1990, Washington, D.C.

11. U.S. investors account for 65 percent of direct foreign investment in Mexico.

12. *La Jornada*, Mexico City, Oct. 8, 1990, p. 44.

13. *Economic Justice Report*, vol. 2, no. 3, Oct. 1991, p. 4.

14. Edur Velasco Arregui, "El Desafio Sindical al TLC: productividad, empleo y salarios," *El Cotidiano*, no. 41, mayo–junion de 1991, Universidad Autonoma Metropolitana Unidad Azacapotzalco, Mexico, pp. 23–24.

15. Alexander Yeats and Refik Erzan, "U.S.-Latin American Trade Areas: Some Empirical Evidence," in Sylvia Saboria, *Premise and the Promise: Free Trade in the Americas. U.S.-Third World Policy Perspectives*, no. 18, July 1992.

16. Sidney Weintraub, "The Canadian Stake in U.S.-Mexico Free Trade Negotiations," *Business in the Contemporary World*, vol. 3, no. 1, Autumn 1990, pp. 127–30.

17. Carla Hills, testimony before the Senate Finance Committee, May 7, 1991; and text of Bush Action Plan submitted to Congress on May 1, 1991.

18. Walter E. Greene, "The Maquiladora—Japan's New Competitive Weapon," *Business*, vol. 39, no. 4, Oct.–Dec. 1989, pp. 52–56.

19. Sidney Weintrub, "The Canadian Stake in U.S.-Mexico Free Trade Negotiations," *Business in the Contemporary World*, vol. 3, no. 1, Autumn 1990, pp. 127–30.

20. "Mexico's Road to Nowhere," *Dollars & Sense*, Apr. 1992, p. 14.

21. Susanna Peters, "Labor Law for the Maquiladoras: Choosing Between Workers' Rights and Foreign Investment," *Comparative Labor Law Journal*, vol. 11, no. 2, Winter 1990, pp. 226–48.

22. Lawrence Kootnikoff, "Coming Together," *Business Mexico*, vol. 1, no. 1, Mar. 1991, pp. 4–38.

23. U.S. International Trade Commission, Publication No. 2053, *The Use and Economic Impact of TSUS Items 806.30 and 807.00*, Aug. 16, 1988, report to the Subcommittee on Trade, Committee on Ways and Means, U.S. House of Representatives.

24. Some estimates indicate that as high as 80 percent of all maquila workers are female.

25. M. Patricia Fernandez Kelly, "Technology and Employment along the U.S.-

Mexican Border," in *The U.S. and Mexico: Face to Face with New Technology*, U.S.-Third World Policy Perspectives, no. 8, Overseas Development Council 151 (C. Thorup ed. 1987).

26. Susanna Peters, "Labor Law for the Maquiladoras: Choosing Between Workers' Rights and Foreign Investment," *Comparative Labor Law Journal*, vol. 11, no. 2, Winter 1990, pp. 226–48.

27. See William Cavitt, Chapter 5, this volume, for further discussion of the maquiladoras.

28. In Mexico the normal wage negotiation process involves the labor union notifying the employer that the labor contract's term is coming to an end (usually a thirty-day advance notice is given). Large industries, like oil (Pemex Monopoly), power generation (CFE Monopoly), sugar refining, and steel conduct national bargaining, which includes a mix of wage increases and other compensation usually every year. Benefits obtained by these groups are generally higher than those obtained by individual companies.

29. The PRI government-leaning unions include the Federation of Syndicates of Workers in Service of the State (FSTSE), the Revolutionary Mexican Workers' Confederation (CROM), the Regional Confederation of Workers and Peasants (CROC), the National Syndicate of Railroad Workers of the Mexican Republic, and the National Syndicate of Mining and Metallurigical Workers of the Mexican Republic. Besides these government-leaning unions, there are many independent unions with a variety of political/ideological tendencies. See Julie A. Erfani, "NAFTA's Ties to Political Authoritarianism in Mexico," *Industrial Relations Research Association*, Proceedings of the 1992 spring meeting, May 6–9, 1992, Denver, Colo., pp. 530–34.

30. See Kevin J. Middlebrook, "The Sounds of Silence: Organized Labour's Response to Economic Crisis in Mexico," *Journal of Latin American Studies* 21 (May 1989), pp. 195–220.

31. U.S. Department of Commerce, *Investing in Mexico*, Overseas Business Reports 5 (Dec. 1985).

32. As per authoritarian PRI custom, the outgoing PRI president characteristically selects his successor in the year preceding the national "election." For the coming 1994 succession, this selection process, known as the *dedazo*, will occur in 1993 when Salinas will reveal his choice for PRI presidential candidate. The Mexican Revolution that founded the current Mexican regime began with a call for "effective suffragate and no reelection" to rid themselves of the former dictatorial powers.

33. Robert Lawrence concurs with Gruben's conclusions regarding NAFTA studies that have been conducted.

34. Mark Anderson of the AFL-CIO concurs with Jeff Faux and Thea Lee's supposition that capital investments may shift from the United States to Mexico.

35. John Oravec, "Trade Conference Zeroes in on NAFTA Defects." *AFL-CIO News*, Sept. 14, 1992, p. 4.

36. Steve Schlossberg, in Chapter 21, claims that since NAFTA undoubtedly will occur, labor should focus on "conditions" under which it will happen. These conditions should be considered as "social charter" provisions akin to the provisions set forth within the European Economic Community.

37. For a partial list of plants and jobs that have relocated to Mexico, see "Jobs Exported to Mexico," *AFL-CIO News*, Apr. 29, 1991.

38. Faux's estimate of a reduction in real earnings of blue-collar workers during

the 1980s is consistent with Lawrence's view that the manufacturing sector decline is due in part to higher interest rates while the service sector grew due to its dependence on domestic spending.

39. Sidney Weintraub, "Jobs on the Line," *Business Mexico*, vol. 1, no. 1, Mar. 1991, pp. 10–11.

40. Real wages in Mexico may be similarly affected. Cavitt indicates that between 1981 and 1989, real wages in Mexico fell 40 percent.

41. Timothy Koechlin, et al., "Effect of the North American Free Trade Agreement on Investment, Employment and Wages in Mexico and the U.S.," mimeo, Feb. 1992.

42. Rudiger Dornbusch, "U.S.-Mexico Free Trade: Good Jobs at Good Wages," testimony before the Subcommittee on Labor-Management Relations and Employment Opportunities, Committee on Education and Labor, U.S. House of Representatives, Apr. 30, 1991.

43. A report issued by the Office of Technology Assessment indicated that a trade accord could lead to downward pressure on U.S. wages and labor standards, with less-educated U.S. workers likely to lose 1 percent of their inflation-adjusted wages annually. The report also concludes that wages in Mexico would probably remain low in the short run, held down by unemployment and underemployment, which could increase emigration to the United States; however, the report did not attempt to estimate job losses or gains.

44. John R. Oravec, "Workers Ask Congress to Save U.S. Jobs," *AFL-CIO News*, vol. 37, no. 8, Apr. 13, 1992, p. 1.

45. Rudiger Dornbusch, "Its Time to Open Up Trade with Mexico," *Challenge*, vol. 33, no. 6, Nov.–Dec. 1990, pp. 52–55.

46. U.S. International Trade Commission, *Review of Trade and Investment Liberalization Measures by Mexico and Prospects for Future U.S.-Mexico Relations*, Investigation No. 332–282, USITC Publication 2275, Washington, Apr. 1990, p. xi.

47. *Survey of Current Business*, U.S. Department of Commerce; *U.S. Foreign Travel Update*, U.S. Department of Commerce; *Exports/Imports by Country*, Statistics Canada, 1993.

48. Statistics obtained from Chapter 5.

49. U.S. Department of Commerce, *United States Trade Performance in 1988* (Sept. 1989), appendix A, Ann H. Hughes, "U.S.-Canada Free Trade Agreement," pp. 57–60.

50. NAFTA may require longer phase-in periods than provided for in the Canadian-U.S. FTA. Mexico may demand that a longer transitional period be invoked for its tariff reductions, to reflect its status as a developing country.

51. William C. Symonds and Paul Magnusson, "In Canada, The Free-Trade Deal Is Hardly Home Free," *Business Week*, Sept. 7, 1992, p. 53.

52. Lawrence Kootnikoff, "Coming Together," *Business Mexico*, vol. 1, no. 1, Mar. 1991, pp. 4–38.

53. Economic Justice Report, vol. 2, no. 3, Oct. 1991, p. 2.

54. John Dillon, "Trade Talks Are the Key to the 'New World Order,'" *Pro-Canada Dossier* (Mar.–Apr. 1991), pp. 17–18.

55. William C. Symonds and Paul Magnusson, "In Canada, The Free-Trade Deal Is Hardly Home Free," *Business Week*, Sept. 7, 1992, p. 53.

56. The paper, "Provisions of Collective Agreements: A Comparison of Selected

Portions of Labor Agreements Negotiated in Canada and the U.S.," by Marcus Hart Sandver examines specific contractual provisions between U.S. and Canadian firms. He concludes that Canadian agreements contain more detailed management right clauses and stronger union security provisions resulting in more explicit stated rights for both labor and management than is commonly found in collective bargaining agreements negotiated in the United States.

57. Jeffrey Schott and Gary Hufbauer, "The Realities of a NA Economic Alliance" (Washington, D.C.: Institute for International Economics, 1990).

58. Foreign Agricultural Trade of the U.S.: Jan./Feb. 1992 Washington, D.C.: Dept. of Agriculture, Economic Research Service, 1992.

59. John R. Oravec, "Workers Ask Congress to Save U.S. Jobs," AFL-CIO News, vol. 37, no. 8, Apr. 13, 1992, pp. 1, 3.

60. Paul Magusson, et al., "The Mexico Pact: Worth the Price?" Business Week, May 27, 1991, pp. 32–35.

61. Rose Gutfeld, "Free Trade Accord May Hurt Workers in U.S., Study Says," Wall Street Journal, Oct. 1, 1992, p. A3.

62. Bureau of National Affairs, "Operating Standards for Maquiladoras Sought in U.S.-Mexico FTA Legislation," International Trade Reporter, Feb. 20, 1991, vol. 8, no. 8, p. 279.

63. Edur Velasco Arregui, "El Desafío Sindical al TLC: productividad, empleo y salarios," El Cotidiano, no. 41, may–junio de 1991, Universidad Autonoma Metropolitana Unidad Azacapotzalco, Mexico, p. 12 of prepublication draft.

64. Matt Moffett, "Working Children Underage Laborers Fill Mexican Factories, Stir U.S. Trade Debate," Wall Street Journal, Apr. 8, 1991, pp. A1, A14.

65. "The Pocketbook Issues AFL-CIO Policy Recommendations for 1992," p. 23, pamphlet reprinted from the National Economy section of the Report of the Executive of the AFL-CIO to the Nineteenth Convention, Detroit, Nov. 1991.

66. The Social Charter actually contains twelve provisions that are currently being negotiated among the twelve European Community members. These provisions are freedom of movement, freedom of choice in employment and remuneration, improvement of living and working conditions, social protection, freedom of association and collective bargaining, vocational training, equal treatment for men and women, information/consultation and participation for workers, health and safety, protection of children and adolescents, rights of elderly persons and rights of disabled persons.

67. This fund was developed out of the fear that "social dumping" would occur whereby capital and labor would relocate to the poorest/cheapest countries, namely, Spain and Portugal.

68. Lane Kirkland, "U.S.-Mexico Trade Pact: A Disaster Worthy of Stalin's Worst," Wall Street Journal, Apr. 18, 1991, p. A15.

69. Sheldon Friedman, "Trade Adjustment Assistance Time for Action, Not False Promises," AFL-CIO Reviews the Issues, Report No. 53, Sept. 1991.

70. Aaron Bernstein and Susan Garland, "There's More Than One Way to Say 'Job Training,'" Business Week, Sept. 7, 1992, p. 30.

71. Joe Mangone, director of the UAW National Community Action Program, claims that the UAW has been a part of, and worked with, the Coalition and the AFL-CIO in promoting the coalition.

72. "The Pocketbook Issues AFL-CIO Policy Recommendations for 1992," p. 26, pamphlet reprinted from the National Economy section of the Report of the Executive

Council of the AFL-CIO to the Nineteenth Convention on the Economic Situation, Detroit, Nov. 1991. See also John R. Oravec, "AFL-CIO Lists Problems with Mexican Trade Pact," *AFL-CIO News*, Vol. 38, No. 5, Mar. 1, 1993, p. 5.

73. Gerald Seib, "Clinton Backs the North American Trade Pact, But Candidates' Stances on Issue Aren't Clear," *Wall Street Journal*, Oct. 5, 1992, p. A14.

74. Bob Davis, "U.S., Canada, Mexico Find Differences on How to Give Teeth to Free Trade Pact," *Wall Street Journal*, Mar. 19, 1993, p. A2.

Part II

PROCEEDINGS

2

North American Free Trade Agreement's Impact on Labor

Mark Anderson

A new trade agreement with Mexico, unless carefully structured, will only encourage greater capital outflows from the United States, bring about an increase in imports from Mexico, and reduce domestic employment as the United States remains mired in a recession. At the same time, it will do little to promote equitable economic development in Mexico, or to improve the standard of living for the vast majority of Mexican citizens unless there are explicit provisions within the agreement to do so.

What is at stake is not more or less trade with Mexico, but the nature and quality of that trade. The United States will stand to lose in the competition for world markets if the economic relationship emerging with Mexico contributes to the further deindustrialization of the American economy, and to the erosion of the skill base of this country. By the same token, a trade accord that ignores the social dimension of economic integration, that is, the problems of ordinary people, may actually serve to increase tensions and frictions between the two countries, sharpening differences and blocking the development of a more harmonious relationship.

This second point is vital for both the interests of the United States and Mexico. A bad trade agreement for the United States would result in less job creation, less productivity increases, and regression in environmental and other social standards. For Mexico, it could well reduce that country's comparative advantage to simply cheap labor, turning Mexico's economy into one large export platform and sacrificing balanced and equitable economic development.

We have a vivid illustration of what will result from an ill-conceived trade agreement in the operation of the so-called maquiladora program. During the 1980s U.S. companies invested hundreds of millions of dollars in Mexico

to produce goods for export to the United States. The exodus of manufacturing facilities from the United States to Mexico has left hundreds of thousands of American workers jobless and their communities in economic
disarray. Meanwhile, some five hundred thousand Mexicans work for substandard wages and under substandard working conditions, producing products destined almost entirely for the U.S. market.

This transfer of production to Mexico turns the traditional concept of
international trade on its head. Here, an industry's competitiveness or a
nation's comparative advantage is not determined on the basis of the cost
or quality of the completed product. Rather, comparisons can now be made
for each stage of the production process in deciding on foreign or domestic
sourcing. It permits U.S. corporations to sidestep the problems of productivity and fair competition and get by in the short term with the easiest
solution: cheap labor.

The historic strength of the U.S. economy has been based on a variety of
factors, including a highly educated, productive, and well-paid workforce;
ample capital and natural resources; innovative production techniques;
strong managerial skills; and continued technological advances. Together,
these elements have led to the high standard of living enjoyed by many
Americans. This wealth and its continued growth also require the buying
power of the U.S. worker-consumer.

Now, a company can separate decent and justifiable wage levels from all
other aspects of production. Mexico's single comparative advantage is the
poverty that forces its citizens to work for subsistence wages. The skill,
productivity, and contributions of U.S. workers become irrelevant in this
context, and the growth of this activity threatens one of the essential pillars
of the American economy. No matter how productive, U.S. workers cannot
compete with labor costs of less than one dollar an hour.

The debate on the likely employment impact of a free trade agreement
has been clouded by supposedly sophisticated economic studies and models
that tend to downplay negative employment effects. This type of analysis
merely serves to camouflage the obvious.

The one thing we do know is the some five hundred thousand Mexican
workers produce goods destined almost solely for the U.S. market. If this
market was being serviced by domestic production, even taking productivity differences into account, U.S. employment would clearly be hundreds
of thousands higher. Tens of thousands of workers across America in
companies like Electrolux, Tyco, Zenith, Westinghouse, Farah, GE, AT&T,
GM, Ford, and Chrysler—to name only a few—have seen their jobs
disappear to Mexico.

One of the stated reasons of the Bush administration for establishing a
free trade area with Mexico was that it would help Mexico develop more
rapidly by encouraging additional investment from the United States. Yet
common to most of the economic studies cited by the administration to
support its contention that there would be no U.S. employment losses, was

the assumption that shifts in investment from the United States to Mexico would be negligible if not nonexistent. Clearly, such an assumption has no relationship to reality. More recent studies that factor in modest shifts in investment conclude that as many as 550,000 jobs would be lost over ten years as a result of the proposed agreement.

This should come as no surprise. Why should firms invest in the United States if they can move a hundred yards across the Rio Grande and dramatically reduce their social and labor costs? Common sense—even without the experience of the maquiladora program and newer economic studies—tells us that a free trade agreement with a country where wages are less than one-tenth of the United States', and costs associated with decent labor standards or environmental protection need not be paid, will harm U.S. employment, income, and productivity.

Nevertheless, negotiations, if properly oriented, do provide an opportunity to begin to make some progress on problems that are present for ordinary people in both countries. If they remain narrow in scope—relying solely on so-called free market mechanisms, to simply expand existing patterns of trade and investment—these problems will only grow.

The following elements are among those that must be addressed, if a new trade arrangement is to be successful.

Labor Rights and Standards. Provisions must be included in any trade agreement whereby infractions of labor rights or workplace standards in production for export can be addressed by trade actions by any of the three countries. Areas that should be dealt with by these provisions include the right to organize and bargain collectively, strong workplace health and safety standards, an appropriate minimum wage structure, and the elimination of child labor. For example, concerning workplace health and safety standards, an agreement should include, in addition to the concept noted above, a program for improving such standards in all three countries to levels that reflect the best practice in any of the three countries. Such an effort would require increased levels of enforcement and increased funding to insure compliance.

In addition, this negotiation would provide the opportunity to creatively address the huge differential in wage levels among the three countries by encouraging an increase in compensation for Mexican workers. This is particularly important for those who are employed by U.S. companies exporting to this market. It is clear that current levels of compensation for these workers have no relationship to their productivity.

The Environment. An agreement must contain provisions to address the existing environmental degradation of the border area, and provide funds for increased enforcement of environmental laws and regulations in all three countries. It is essential that an agreement specifically permit trade actions to address violations of environmental standards. The recent GATT panel decision, objecting to U.S. controls on tuna imports from Mexico that do not meet U.S. standards for protecting dolphins, underscores the importance of this objective. It is incumbent upon the United State to insure that an agreement prevents the relocation of production or the existence of investment incentives based on inadequate environmental protection or lax enforcement. In this regard, it is important to include provisions in an agreement that would insure that companies fully disclose the nature of their production process, methods used to comply with environmental standards, and the manner used to dispose of toxic materials.

Beyond the issue of addressing the responsibilities of corporations for environmental pollution, an agreement must contain provisions, with appropriate funding, directed at improving the infrastructure of the border area, with particular emphasis on sewers, water, electricity, and housing. These problems are directly related to the poverty caused by low wage levels, and must be dealt with a variety of ways if an agreement is to provide benefits to people on either side of the border.

It should be emphasized that it is essential that both labor and environmental issues be addressed within any trade agreement. Current activities on labor and the environment, running parallel to the trade negotiations, are inadequate to the task of meaningfully addressing the complexities present in the evolving relationship between the United States and Mexico.

Rules of Origin. Rules of origin negotiated in the U.S.-Canadian trade agreement are inadequate to the goal of creating a preferential trade area between the two countries, and therefore, are particularly inadequate for an expanded North American trade area. It is essential, therefore, for any agreement to contain a rule of origin, that at a minimum, requires that 80 percent of the direct cost of manufacturing be of North American origin in order to qualify for preferential treatment. For textile and apparel products a 100 percent rule of origin would be appropriate. Such rules should be made applicable at the time an agreement enters into force. Reliance on a "substantial transformation" system, or changes in tariff classification to confer preferential treatment, should be rejected.

Government Procurement. Government procurement poses serious problems in any trade agreement with Mexico. The economic structure of Mexico depends heavily on parastatal firms and is dominated by a variety of monopolies and duopolies. Under these circumstances it makes little sense for the United States to open up federal government procurement to Mexican bids since there can be no assurance that reciprocal treatment would be forthcoming. Similarly, trade negotiated procurement policies should not be extended to the state and local level.

Agriculture. Any agreement should exempt trade in fruits and vegetables from coverage, extend the current exemption of dairy products in the U.S.-Canadian agreement to Mexico, and permit the continued enforcement of both Section 22 of the Farm Bill and provisions of the Meat Import Act. It is also essential to insure that U.S. pesticide residue and other food safety standards are applied in an effective and nondiscriminatory way to both domestic and foreign-produced items.

Services and Investment. Efforts by the administration to liberalize trade in services may be paid for by concessions in trade in goods, and may unnecessarily restrict the ability of government to regulate commerce and protect the public welfare. Maritime, aviation, and land transportation services should be excluded from discussions.

An agreement must not restrict the rights of U.S. states to regulate financial insurance services. The ability of states, for example, to maintain exclusive state funds for worker compensation insurance must be maintained, and any agreement must allow other states to develop such a program should they wish.

Concerning investment, the United States should concentrate on the immediate elimination of those measures explicitly designed to promote exports. U.S. acquiescence to the use of such measures has been harmful to U.S. workers, and their elimination should be a major goal of the negotiations. The regulation of investment flows per se should not be viewed negatively, and any agreement should not limit the right of countries to monitor, review, and, if appropriate, restrict foreign investment. Suggestions by some, to extend Overseas Private Investment Corporation (OPIC) insurance programs to U.S. investors in Mexico, should be rejected.

Trade Rules. No changes should be negotiated in current U.S. trade remedy law, including safeguards, subsidies, dumping, Section 301, and Section 337. It is particularly important for an agreement to address problems concerning two-tier energy-pricing structures and third-country dumping. In addition, the United States must address, in a meaningful fashion, the fact that a considerable part of Mexico's productive capacity involves a clear and direct government role, and is therefore at odds with the concept of free trade.

Tariff and and Nontariff Barriers. As a general rule, tariff negotiations should first achieve a binding of tariff rates, with further negotiations proceeding from that basis. The structure should not be based on a so-called balance of concessions, but should first seek the equalization of tariff rates, followed by mutual, staged reductions. We believe that it would be unwise to perpetuate, over time, the tariff inequities currently present in the trading relationship of the United States, Mexico, and Canada. Concerning textiles and apparel, any increases in imports from Mexico must be balanced by decreases in quota allocations to other exporting countries.

Beyond these issues, the AFL-CIO believes that it is incumbent upon the administration to establish a meaningful, well-financed trade adjustment assistance program, including income maintenance and worker retraining programs to provide real help to those workers who are displaced both directly and indirectly by trade. Workers have been promised such a program many times in the past, only to find that the reality of assistance has fallen short of the rhetoric.

It is also appropriate for an agreement to contain provisions providing additional debt relief for Mexico, so that it can begin investing at home to improve the standard of living of its people. If the United States is truly interested in helping its neighbor, such relief should have a central place in that effort.

The North American trade negotiations provide the opportunity to begin to examine the complexities present in economic relations among the three nations. Regrettably, the priorities of the Bush administration did not address issues that were of direct importance to the vast majority of people in the two countries. While commerce today is indeed global, social protection and regulation—factors necessary to humanize the market and help promote a more equitable distribution of wealth—remain the responsibility of national governments and national institutions. How this conflict is resolved will be of major importance in the establishment of a North American trade area.

3

A Canadian Labor Perspective on a North American Free Trade Agreement

Bruce Campbell

The Canadian labor movement's position on a North American Free Trade Agreement is that an economically integrated North American economy based on the model already in place, the Canada-U.S. Free Trade Agreement (FTA), is undesirable. Canadian workers see NAFTA, with its high productivity low-wage maquiladora factories, lack of effective unions, and labor standards, as an unfair economic playing field that can only have negative effects on their jobs and their living standards. They see it as exacerbating a process, entrenched in the FTA, of lowest common denominator competition or competitive poverty among workers and communities.

It is important to understand that the debate over NAFTA in Canada is less about what might happen in an uncertain future than it is a debate about three years of experience with the Canada-U.S. trade deal and the likely consequences of extending it to Mexico. It is not therefore an abstract debate but rather one that centers on the effects free trade has already had.

The Canadian labor movement opposition to NAFTA is based on the following expectations: (1) that the essential terms and conditions of the FTA will remain in place in a trilateral accord; (2) that the U.S. government will extract further concessions negative to Canada; (3) that the free trade-driven restructuring of the Canadian economy, most visibly in manufacturing, and the resulting job loss will be exacerbated; (4) that the harmonization effect of free trade or downward pull on Canadian wages and labor, social, and environmental standards will quicken; and (5) that NAFTA will reinforce the process of economic and political disintegration currently underway in Canada.

Let us examine these concerns one at a time. The main accomplishment of the FTA is that it secures the rights and freedoms of corporations and thereby circumscribes the power of governments, present and future, to intervene in their economies. It formalizes in treaty a specific paradigm of economic development, a neoconservative paradigm, foreclosing other national development options. For example, key provisions in the FTA prevent Canadian governments from bringing in policies that favor nationally owned companies over U.S.-owned companies, policies without which many of leading Canadian companies would not have come into existence. Other provisions prevent governments from requiring U.S. corporations operating in Canada to meet certain performance requirements, that is, requirements that they locate a certain amount of production and maintain certain minimal employment levels in Canada if they want to sell freely on the Canadian market (this was the essential idea behind the content requirements of the auto pact that were severely weakened by the FTA); that they export a certain portion of what they produce; that they employ Canadians in the management and on the boards of their Canadian subsidiaries.

Many years of experience in an economy that has by far the highest level of foreign ownership in the industrialized world have demonstrated that such regulation is needed to ensure that transnationals bring benefits to Canada. More than 50 percent of manufacturing sales in Canada are by foreign (mainly U.S.-controlled) corporations. Two-thirds of U.S. exports to Canada are intrafirm, that is, from parent companies to their Canadian subsidiaries, not transactions on an open market. A recent study found that thirty-two of the fifty largest importers to Canada were foreign-owned. These thirty-two corporations accounted for 70 percent of imports into Canada. There is no historical example of a country that has achieved a strong, technologically sophisticated, internationally competitive manufacturing base without intervention by government, whether through discrimination in favor of national firms, restrictions on foreign takeovers, intervention in capital markets, protection, performance requirements, or other means. Germany, Japan, Korea, Sweden, and the United States in an earlier period are all such examples.

Still other FTA provisions limit the ability of governments to reserve certain economic activity for the public domain (besides existing activities, which are grandfathered). Over a year ago, for example, Canada's largest province, Ontario, elected a social democratic government. One of its central election promises was to replace private auto insurance with a publicly administered system similar to ones already in existence in three other provinces. The FTA allows governments to do this in theory, but in practice makes implementation virtually impossible. Article 2010 requires prior consultation with the U.S. government and is subject to the nullification and impairment clause (Article 2011), which says that even if an action is compatible with the agreement, if it reduces benefits otherwise expected the United States is entitled to compensation. Moreover, Article 1605 requires "fair market compensation" for U.S. firms for measures "tantamount to expropriation." Canadian law does not give this right to Canadian companies. Thus, U.S. auto insurance companies currently active in Ontario have conducted studies claiming that they would be entitled under the FTA to billions of dollars in compensation if Ontario brought in its public auto insurance scheme. No such legal compensation obligation would be required vis-à-vis Canadian companies, but in practice not extending compensation would be politically unacceptable. At a trade ministers meeting in Seattle Carla Hills, the U.S. trade representative, told Canadian trade minister Michael Wilson that Ontario's proposed policy violated the FTA and implied that the United States would exact a very high price if Ontario were to proceed.

Consequently, a beleaguered Ontario government, weakened by a free trade-driven restructuring process that has seen the large-scale exodus of production facilities, the loss of hundreds of thousands of manufacturing jobs, the erosion of its tax base, and the growth of its deficit, admitted defeat and announced that it was reneging on its promise to the Ontario voters to bring in public auto insurance. This is clear evidence that the FTA is working as its proponents intended. (It is important to note as well that if the FTA had been in place in the 1960s, these same provisions and the same corporate pressure would have prevented Canada from brining in its publicly funded and administered medicare system, which is far superior, to the American medical care system.)

These examples demonstrate how the FTA greatly reduces the policy tools available to foster national economic development. Its fundamental provisions will also be included in NAFTA. To expect otherwise is naive to say the least. The FTA limits choices and reduces the power of governments. But it does not transfer power, like the European Community does, to supranational institutions. The FTA transfers power to the corporations and establishes the United States as the enforcer of the new order. Canada has surrendered sovereignty without having gained any voice in a supranational institution. One has to ask: To what extent is democracy compromised when a government relinquishes so much sovereignty? Government is the only, at least potentially, democratic forum for the expression of the values and priorities of a society. Corporations are not democratic nor do they claim to be. They are not accountable to the communities in which they operate and do not claim such responsibility. Capital desires mobility, a borderless world free from constraints. Most workers are not able, nor do they want to, move beyond their national borders. They want to stay and build their communities, to rear their children and put down roots.

"Money has no heart, no soul, no conscience, no homeland." That is the way Frank Stronach, chairman of the large Canadian auto parts manufacturer, Magna, put it as he announced his company's plans to set up a joint venture in the maquiladora to make bumpers for Volkswagen. Ironically,

Stronach was one of the few corporate executives who opposed the FTA, not on the grounds that it would threaten the viability of his company, but that it would threaten the viability of Canada.

The current NAFTA negotiations have become a vehicle for reopening the bilateral FTA, enabling the United States to extract concessions that it did not achieve in the original round of negotiations. High on the U.S. hit list are restrictions on Canadian farm marketing boards such as the Canadian Wheat Board, which gives Canadian farmers some protection against price gouging by the giant private conglomerates that dominate the international grain trade; further concessions from the already beleaguered film, recording, publishing, and broadcast industries; and perhaps most important, inclusion in NAFTA of an intellectual property code to entrench the monopoly protection for corporate property such as patents and copyrights. If knowledge-based production is the key to competitiveness and this knowledge can be privately appropriated and monopolized for long periods of time, this is an important advantage for U.S. corporations that now hold the vast majority of patents in North America. Moreover, a NAFTA code could serve as the model for the intellectual property regime that the United States wants to have inserted in GATT. In the first round Canada made a number of concessions in this area but balked at the last moment at going all the way with U.S. demands for a code that completely prohibited the compulsory licensing of patents.

Canadian labor critics see NAFTA as prolonging a very destructive and painful economic restructuring process that has accelerated dramatically over the past three years. Throughout the 1980s employment in Canadian manufacturing remained constant. There was drop of 270,000 jobs during the 1981–82 recession but those jobs eventually came back.

Beginning in 1989 the Canadian manufacturing sector shrank by 435,000 jobs net (see Table 3.1), or 22 percent of the total workforce. Manufacturing employment has dropped to just 15 percent of total Canadian employment, the lowest level of any industrialized country. To compare this hollowing out of Canadian manufacturing with what has been happening in the United States, the U.S. manufacturing workforce fell by only 4.6 percent during the same period. Those who say that this is only a cyclical downturn should examine the figures on plant closings in Ontario, the manufacturing heartland of Canada. In 1981–82 22 percent of workers who lost their jobs did so as a result of permanent plant closings. In the free trade era 65 percent of the lost jobs have been due to permanent plant closings.

Thousands of Canadian manufacturing jobs have been lost as corporations have relocated plants in the U.S. Sun Belt states and the maquiladora to take advantage of low wages, weak labor and inadequate environmental laws. James Stanford, in a study published in January 1992 by the Canadian Centre for Policy Alternatives entitled *Going South, Cheap Labour as an UnFair Subsidy in North American Free Trade*, shows that the right-to-work laws

Table 3.1
Canada: The Manufacturing Crisis

	EMPLOYMENT AS % MANUFACT. (TOTAL JUNE 1989)	% CHANGE REAL OUTPUT (MAY 1989-MAR. 1991)	% CHANGE IN EMPLOYMENT (JUNE 1989-MAR. 1991)	
TOTAL MANUFACTURING	100% 2M	-12.4	-21.7	(-435,000)
FOOD AND BEVERAGES	12.8	-1.5	-22.6	(-58,000
RUBBER	1.3	-21.9	-16.6	(-4,200)
PLASTIC	3.0	-14.5	17.7	(-10,600)
LEATHER	0.9	-23.6	-37.2	(-6,700)
TEXTILES	3.3	-16.5	-27.1	(-17,800)
CLOTHING	4.6	-14.8	-22.9	(-21,100)
WOOD	6.2	-25.4	-33.3	(-41,000)
FURNITURE AND FIXTURES	3.3	-26.0	-29.4	(-19,500)
PAPER AND ALLIED	6.5	-2.5	-13.0	(-17,100)
PRINTING AND PUBLISHING	7.4	-13.8	-19.3	(-28,400)
PRIMARY METAL	5.3	-12.2	-21.5	(-22,500)
FABRICATED METAL PRODUCTS	8.2	-13.9	-27.5	(-44,900)
MACHINERY	5.3	-17.5	-23.2	(-24,700)
TRANSPORTATION EQUIPMENT	11.5	-19.8	-15.0	(-33,200)
• AIRCRAFT		-2.8	+1.6	(+700)
• AUTO/TRUCK		-20.4	-16.6	(-12,500)
• AUTO PARTS		-26.3	-21.0	(-15,600)
ELECTRICAL	6.5	-7.7	-22.5	(-29,200)
NON METALLIC MINERAL PRODUCTS	2.9	-30.6	-30.6	(-17,800)
REFINED PETROLEUM AND COAL PRODUCTS	1.0	-5.2	-12.2	(-2,500)
CHEMICALS	5.2	-6.7	13.2	(-13,700)

Source: Statistics Canada Cat. 72–002 Employment, Earnings and Hours: Cat. 15–001 G.O.P.
   by Industry. Only the latter (output) series is seasonally adjusted.

in the Deep South are deliberate government restrictions on labor practices that have had the effect of suppressing or subsidizing the wage costs of manufacturers there (involuntarily paid for by the workers) by 15 percent of their total wage costs. Stanford concludes that this constitutes an unfair subsidy and that the Canadian government should retaliate by imposing a countervailing duty on all manufactured imports from states with right-to-work laws.

The question of jobs is important because during the free trade debate the Conservative government and proponents claimed that hundreds of thousands of jobs would be created under the FTA. Econometric models predicted increases in employment and income with great certainty and precision. They greatly oversimplified a complex economic reality, narrowly defined the FTA as being essentially about tariffs, and made unrealistic assumptions about what would happen to such variables as productivity and exchange rates under free trade. Nevertheless, these models carried an air of authority that convinced many people to ignore the naysayers and doomsdayers and support free trade as a creator of jobs and prosperity for Canadians. Ironically, as the destructive impact on jobs became increasingly apparent, proponents reversed themselves, saying that one could not say with any degree of certainty what role the FTA was playing, or that it was too early to determine its role.

Labor critics expect that NAFTA will exacerbate the so-called harmonization effect. The Conservative government and its corporate backers came into power with an agenda to dismantle the Canadian social contract (medicare, unemployment insurance, education, labor legislation, etc.) and the supporting tax structure, and remake it in the image of the leaner, meaner neighbor to the south. But Canadians generally supported their social contract and did not want it to meet the same fate as the weaker U.S. social contract, which had taken an enormous beating under Nixon and Reagan. The Conservative government therefore had no political mandate to change it.

Instead the Conservatives used the FTA as central tool to carry out their agenda through the back door. The integration of the two economies became a lever to reshape the Canadian economy in the U.S. image. The smaller economy must necessarily mirror the larger. This meant "forcing" the alignment of cost structures and social structures. It meant forcing down wages, labor laws, and union power, forcing down taxes especially on corporations and the wealthy, forcing down government spending on social programs. As one corporate head put it, "As we ask our companies to compete toe to toe with American industries we are forced to create the same conditions in Canada as exist in the United States."

During the free trade election campaign the Business Council on National Issues (BCNI), the big business lobby, denied in its advertising material that under the free trade big business would campaign to reduce social spending. However, once the FTA was safely passed, with indecent haste the BCNI ignored its promise and mounted a massive lobbying assault on the Canadian social contract, which the government is obligingly carrying out.

Proponents said that the exchange rate was the key safety valve that would protect against these harmonization pressures. A falling dollar would offset the pressure to level the playing field. Ironically almost from the day the trade deal was signed the Canadian dollar began to rise not fall. It has since risen 17 percent against the U.S. dollar. There is much circumstantial evidence pointing to a secret exchange rate deal but regardless, it is deliberate government policy and it has dramatically accelerated the harmonization and restructuring process in Canada.

It is not surprising that when NAFTA proponents say we need to further lock in what they euphemistically call the "market orientation" of the economy, or that we have to be at the bargaining table "to protect our hard won gains in the Canadian-U.S. round," critics are skeptical in the extreme. Hollow is the argument that says we have to protect vague or undefined gains for which we paid an extremely high price. (Are they talking about the illusory grail of secure market access, which we seem to keep paying for but never really get?)

The final lens, through which labor critics view the desirability of NAFTA, is the economic and political disintegration of Canada that is moving with great speed in the wake of free trade. The Canadian economy was created largely in defiance of the north-south market forces. With most of Canada's small population spread in clusters along the southern border, the creation of a distinct national economy integrated along an east-west axis was a major accomplishment. Canada accomplished this by building a transportation/ communication infrastructure; ribbons first of steel, then asphalt, then air and fiber optics. It created a national market through tariff and other policy tools. It created a system of agricultural supply management to achieve relative food security. It built a national public broadcasting network and other pathways of cultural expression as a counterweight to cultural onslaught from the south. It built a network of shared values embodied in a system of financial transfers to the poorer regions, and a social safety net comprising basic rights of citizenship. In all this, government as economic regulator and as a direct player in the economy has played a critical role.

The neoconservative governments' restrictive monetary policies, deregulation, privatization, and free trade have brought an unraveling of national economic and political structures. Conservative government brought the three fundamental recurring tensions in Canada to a covergence for the first time in the country's history: the lure of closer ties with the United States, rivalries and power struggles among the regions, and the long unresolved conflict between the English- and French-speaking "nations" of Canada.

The free trade debate itself created an extraordinary amount of rancor and even though in the end a majority of the population voted for parties opposing the FTA, the Conservatives were able to sneak through by splitting the opposition vote. Without a Conservative electoral sweep in Quebec, where both the business community and the independence party supported the FTA, it would never have come into effect.

Quebec separatist leaders and many Quebec nationalists on the left and right saw free trade as a mechanism to weaken Canada and facilitate the exit of Quebec from the Canadian federation. The bitterness toward Quebec voters left among many in the rest of the country was at least partly responsible for English Canada's opposition to Quebec's subsequent demands for constitutional reform to formally acknowledge its special place in Canada. The Quebec population in turn saw the constitutional collapse as a rejection by the rest of Canada, and the popular mood has shifted strongly in favor of sovereignty. The prospect of the Conservative government, now the most unpopular in Canadian history, being able to orchestrate a constitutional compromise that will reconcile Quebec and Canada, with the society divided and increasingly disconnected along regional lines, and with attitudes hardening, do look bleak indeed.

It is in this climate that Canadian labor critics see the extension of the free trade to NAFTA as a further destabilizing force, a move in the wrong direction.

4

The Canada-U.S. Free Trade Agreement: Lessons to Guide the Evolution of NAFTA

William H. Cavitt

On February 5, 1991, the presidents of the United States and Mexico and the prime minister of Canada announced their intention to begin negotiations on a North American Free Trade Agreement (NAFTA). Successful negotiation of such an agreement would create a free trade area comprising over 360 million people with a combined annual output in excess of $6 trillion.

Before discussing the prospects for a North American Free Trade Agreement, this chapter sets the stage by talking about the existing U.S.-Canada Free Trade Agreement (FTA) because its provisions and implementation set a precedent, if not a model, for NAFTA.

THE U.S.-CANADA FREE TRADE AGREEMENT

Canada is America's largest trading partner. Total bilateral trade in goods and services was $216 billion in 1992 up from $169 billion in 1988, or a $47 billion increase in four years. In 1992 the United States exported $91 billion worth of merchandise to 27 million Canadians and $103 billion to the 320 million people in the twelve nations of the European Community. Canadians bought over $3,355 worth of U.S. exports per person, compared to only $320 worth of U.S. exports per person in the European Community.

On January 1, 1989, a truly historic achievement was realized with the entry into force of the U.S.-Canada Free Trade Agreement. The FTA is a good deal for both countries—the proverbial win-win proposition. Both countries will enjoy greater economic growth, increased trade and investment, greater energy security, more jobs, lower prices, and greater competitiveness at home and abroad than they would without this agreement.

The FTA does not solve all bilateral problems. However, almost every problem is more amenable to solution with this agreement than without it.

While the U.S.-Canada Free Trade Agreement is the most comprehensive free trade arrangement ever negotiated, it seems more complex than it really is. The principle to remember is that the FTA is designed and intended to do three things: (1) to provide greater market access; (2) to provide more secure market access; and (3) to allow market forces to work. The FTA also takes account of sensitivities on both sides of the border. For example, Canada's concerns about its sovereignty, cultural heritage, social programs, and separate identity have been respected.

The CFTA means that the two countries are business partners—nothing more. It does not alter any other aspects of the bilateral relationship. The United States and Canada are and will remain separate, culturally distinct, sovereign countries.

The provisions of the agreement important to most people are these: All tariffs—without exception—are being eliminated over a ten-year period, thereby creating many new exporting opportunities. The FTA also provides periodic opportunities for requesting accelerated tariff elimination. The 1989 cycle was completed on April 1, 1990, when accelerated tariff elimination was effected on over 400 tariff line items, covering $6 billion in bilateral trade. The 1990 cycle was completed on July 1, 1991, when the governments of the United States and Canada accelerated tariff elimination on a further 250 tariff line items, plus 400 individual products, covering some $2 billion in bilateral trade.

A third and final round of negotiations was completed on April 2, 1993, when the two governments announced accelerated tariff elimination on 100 tariff line items covering $1 billion in bilateral trade. Those accelerated tariff eliminations represent an important vote of confidence by the business communities on both sides of the border in the efficacy of the agreement, because those changes were made at the request of business. Most nontariff barriers are being reduced or eliminated, thereby creating new marketing opportunities. The elimination of the Canadian embargo on imports of used aircraft and the phase-out of the embargo on used motor vehicles are two examples.

The investment agreement created a stable and predictable business environment essential to attracting and maintaining major capital investment. Cumulative direct investment in each other's economies totaled over $100 billion in 1992, up from $83 billion in 1987—a $17 billion increase in five years.

The energy agreement promotes further deregulation, removes almost all barriers, and assures buyers and sellers that they can make decisions on future energy supply relationships based on market considerations. Bilateral trade in energy and energy products exceeds $10 billion a year.

The services agreement covers over 150 services sectors and is the first comprehensive agreement in the world governing services trade. It embodies the principles of national treatment, the right of establishment, transparency, and the right to sell across borders. The services agreement assures that the already relatively open U.S. and Canadian markets will stay that way. Bilateral trade in business services was $26.4 billion in 1992, up from $15.8 billion in 1988.

Pursuant to the services chapter of the FTA, the U.S. and Canadian architectural professional organizations have developed mutually acceptable standards to allow architects to practice in both countries. The next step is for the two governments to review and ratify what the architects have done and to incorporate the agreed upon standards into the FTA, probably as a revision to the current annex covering architectural services.

New and improved border-crossing procedures and visa requirements for temporary business travel and tourism are facilitating travel back and forth across the border. This is important because improved trading opportunities are useless unless there is access to markets and customers. A bilateral border-crossing work group meets regularly to assure the smooth implementation of these commitments.

The standards agreement provides that standards-related measures and procedures will not be used to hinder trade unnecessarily and that both countries will work to harmonize such measures and procedures where appropriate. Some progress already has been made. For example, six Canadian and six U.S. heating and air conditioning standards have been combined into one binational standard. The big winners are the manufacturers in both countries who can now produce more efficiently to one standard, and consumers who have a wider selection at lower cost.

The government procurement agreement provides new, nondiscriminatory access to $500 million worth of annual Canadian federal procurements and to $3 billion of U.S. federal procurements. Since implementation of the FTA, over 591 Canadian government contracts, totaling over $33 million, have been awarded to U.S. companies of all sizes. Without the FTA, those tenders would not have been open to U.S. exporters.

Improved customs procedures and new rules of origin assure that the benefits of the FTA accrue only to the United States and Canada because they are the only countries that have undertaken its obligations. Two binational customs work groups—one on the rules of origin and the other on market access issues—are working to facilitate the movement of goods across the border. They also are working to assure that the new rules fulfill their designer's intentions to be transparent, predictable, simple to use, and easy to administer.

Binational panel review of final antidumping and countervailing duty determinations assures that the results of such unfair trade practice investigations were in accordance with domestic law and that the findings were fair and impartial. The binational secretariat, which administers the panel review process, continues to function smoothly. The efficacy of the panel review process has been widely praised by interested parties and panelists alike on both sides of the border.

A strong and expeditious dispute settlement mechanism assures that the resolution of disputes will be undertaken in a timely and orderly manner. This is important in any commercial relationship as large and as complex as that of the United States and Canada. Prior to the FTA, disputes were handled in an *ad hoc* manner, usually only after the two sides had become entrenched in their respective positions, from which compromise was difficult.

There have been some disputes about FTA implementation. This is neither surprising, nor a cause for alarm, given the magnitude of the agreement and of the bilateral trading relationship. These disputes account for only a tiny fraction of the overall trade and investment relationship, but typically they have gotten all the attention. It is unfortunate that disputes are considered "newsworthy" and get the press attention, whereas the large body of what is right and working is not considered newsworthy. Moreover, many of the disputes now associated with the FTA actually predate the agreement, fall outside of it, and are related to international obligations under the General Agreement on Tariffs and Trade (GATT). Hence, such disputes would exist in the absence of the FTA. Whatever the origin of the disputes, the FTA provides an orderly process to resolve them and is being used as intended.

Other FTA provisions include agriculture, fisheries, cultural industries, financial services, intellectual property, quantitative restrictions, telecommunications, safeguards, and wine and distilled spirits.

In summary, the U.S.-Canada Free Trade Agreement is a historic achievement that will create vast new trade and investment opportunities for business in both countries. However, the FTA can and will be an engine for further economic growth, new jobs, and lower prices only if the business community is aware of the changing commercial environment and adopts appropriate business strategies and marketing plans to take advantage of those opportunities. Over the long term, doing business across the border will be easier and more efficient because of the FTA. But in the short term, many laws, rules, and regulations with which the business community is familiar, have changed or will be changing.

NORTH AMERICAN FREE TRADE NEGOTIATIONS

When Canada and the United States began negotiating their free trade agreement, the idea of a NAFTA was inconceivable. Today, it makes excellent sense. First, a free trade agreement would contribute to long-term economic prosperity, stability, and growth in Mexico. An economically prosperous Mexico is important because the lack of economic opportunity is at the root of such bilateral problems as illegal immigration, drugs, and pollution. Second, NAFTA will advance the cause of economic reform in Latin

America. The eyes of the region are on Mexico, which is a leader among the Latin American nations. Its success could serve as a model for market-oriented policies and reforms elsewhere in the hemisphere. The United States' Enterprise for the Americas Initiative has as its goal the negotiation of a free trade zone from the Arctic to Antarctica. Successful ratification and implementation of NAFTA would be a milestone on the road toward the goal of a western hemisphere free trade area. Finally, a U.S.-Mexican FTA makes good business sense. U.S. business sees major trade and investment opportunities in Mexico and wants assured access to the rapidly growing Mexican market of 85 million consumers. Indeed, many business leaders believe that Mexico has the potential to become the economic miracle of the 1990s—the next newly industrialized country. Mexico is the United States' third largest trading partner, with two-way merchandise trade totaling $76 billion in 1992. Mexico also is America's fastest growing export market.

Exports are the key to U.S. economic growth. Since 1986 exports have grown at a faster rate than the economy as a whole. It is estimated that every $1 billion of U.S. exports supports more than 20,000 U.S. jobs. U.S. exports to Mexico have more then tripled from $12.4 billion in 1986 to $40.6 billion in 1992. That means U.S. jobs dependent on exports to Mexico have increased from about 250,000 in 1986 to 800,000 in 1992. Put simply: freer trade means more trade; more trade means more jobs. The importance of exports to American jobs and prosperity was a prime factor in the United States' decision to pursue a free trade agreement with Mexico and Canada.

The Impetus for Negotiations

In 1986 Mexico joined the General Agreement on Tariffs and Trade (GATT) and began a process of reform that continues today. President Salinas, building on the foundation laid by President de la Madrid, has implemented dramatic economic reforms. Included among those are the following:

- *Tariffs* were reduced to a maximum of 20 percent *ad valorem*, well below the 50 percent maximum of Mexico's GATT accession agreement. Many tariffs used to be as high as 100 percent. Today, on a trade-weighted basis, Mexico's average tariff on imports from the United States is about 10 percent—the same as Canada before the FTA cuts began to be made.

- *Import licenses*, which were universal as recently as 1983, are no longer required for all but 230 tariff lines, representing about 7 percent by value of U.S. exports to Mexico.

- *Investment regulations* were revamped in May 1989 to create a business climate more conducive to foreign direct investment.

- *Intellectual property rights laws* have been enacted, which have greatly improved Mexico's levels of protection for patents, trademarks, and copyrights.

- *Privatization of government-owned enterprises* has been completed or announced in many sectors. Of the 1,155 state-owned enterprises in 1982, 801 have been authorized for divestment and over 600 actually have been privatized. Banking, airlines, copper mining, telecommunications, insurance and steel are some of the sectors and industries being reprivatized.

- *External debt restructuring* has been tackled aggressively. Following debt rene-gotiation under the Salinas administration, Mexico's debt-servicing burden has declined, leading to heightened business confidence and increased capital inflows.

These reforms, and others in the offing, when coupled with a free trade agreement, can be a powerful engine for further economic growth, increased trade and investment, more jobs, lower prices, and greater competitiveness at home and abroad.

Indeed, the reforms enacted to date already are bearing fruit. The general economic climate in Mexico has improved substantially:

- Real economic growth was 1.4 percent in 1988, 2.9 percent in 1989, 3.9 percent in 1990, 3.6 percent in 1991, and 3.5 percent in 1992.
- Economic growth has exceeded population growth in each of the past four years.
- Inflation was reduced from 160 percent in 1987, to just 12 percent in 1992.
- External debt as a percentage of gross domestic product (GDP) was reduced from 60 percent in 1985 to 34 percent in 1992.
- Foreign direct investments approved by the government of Mexico increased from $3.5 billion in 1991 to $5.7 billion in 1992.
- As a direct result of tariff reductions and removal of import licenses, U.S. mer-chandise exports to Mexico more than tripled from $12.4 billion in 1986 to $40.6 billion in 1992.

These are some of the considerations that led President Bush to respond favorably to President Salinas' request of August 21, 1990, that the United States and Mexico enter into negotiations for a free trade agreement.

Subsequent to that decision, Prime Minister Mulroney asked Presidents Bush and Salinas to include Canada as a full participant in negotiation of a North American Free Trade Agreement.

Goals of NAFTA Negotiations

U.S., Mexican, and Canadian goals in NAFTA were similar to those the United States and Canada had. Stated broadly they are greater market access; more secure market access; and allowing market forces to work.

The negotiators have carefully examined the provisions of the U.S.-Canada FTA and the issues in the ongoing Uruguay Round of multilateral negotia-tions, to see which issues are applicable to North American trade and in-vestment.

The U.S. Department of Commerce also has been and is continuing to consult extensively with Congress and the U.S. private sector—business, industry, labor, and agriculture—seeking their views on what specific negotiating goals should be. Based on their advice, principal U.S. negotiating objectives include the following:

- Phased elimination of all tariffs.
- Rules-of-origin that are predictable, transparent, and simple to administer. Such rules assure that the benefits of the agreement accrue principally to those undertaking its obligations—sometimes known as the "no free riders" provision.
- Elimination of duty remission, duty drawback, and duty avoidance programs within the free trade area; maintenance of such programs would unfairly confer a competitive advantage on one partner country over another.
- Improved customs procedures and border infrastructure to facilitate the flow of goods among the partner countries.
- Elimination of nontariff barriers and performance requirements, such as import licenses and local content and export requirements.
- An investment agreement that will create a stable and predictable business environment essential to attracting and holding major capital investment.
- Comprehensive intellectual property rights protection, including well-developed standards of protection for patents, trademarks, copyrights, computer software, and trade secrets.
- A globally competitive North American automotive industry free of government-imposed trade and investment restrictions.
- Increased access to each other's government procurement markets, defined to include federal, state/provincial, local/municipal, federal/Crown corporations, and government-controlled/-regulated enterprises.
- A services agreement that embodies the principles of national treatment, the right of establishment, transparency, and the right to sell across borders. Such an agreement would enhance market access and export opportunities for U.S. service providers.
- Improved border-crossing procedures to facilitate the movement of temporary business travelers, shoppers, and tourists.
- Harmonization of standards related measures and procedures to preclude their being used as trade barriers, to increase trading opportunities, and to promote greater manufacturing efficiency.
- An effective dispute settlement mechanism that will increase certainty and predictability for exporters.
- Safeguards to assure that firms and workers have adequate time to adjust to changing competitive conditions and that the transition to free trade is gradual, with no abrupt or dramatic changes in existing patterns of employment, investment, production, or trade.

These are some of the goals that business, industry, labor, and agriculture would like to see the three governments achieve. Their suggestions closely track the provisions of the U.S.-Canada Free Trade Agreement.

Negotiating Process and Timetable

The United States is negotiating under the so-called fast-track procedures provided by Congress. The fast track is important because it means that Congress must approve or disapprove any resulting agreement by a single up or down vote within a defined time frame. Amendments are not permitted.

Without fast track, the president cannot assure negotiating partners that the deal they strike will be the one voted on by Congress. Indeed, both Mexico and Canada told the United States that without that assurance, they would not negotiate on NAFTA.

Congress gave its blessing to the NAFTA negotiations in May 1991, when it extended its delegation of authority to the president to negotiate under the fast-track provisions. NAFTA negotiations formally began on June 12, 1991, when the trade ministers of the three countries met in Toronto, Ontario, and agreed upon the modalities of the negotiations. The negotiations ended 14 months later, when the same trade ministers announced the successful conclusion of NAFTA on August 12, 1992.

President Clinton supports NAFTA and is expected to formally submit NAFTA to Congress for ratification and passage of all necessary implementing legislation once the parallel agreements on the environment, labor standards, and import surges have been concluded. Those negotiations began March 17, 1993. The day NAFTA and its implementing legislation is submitted to Congress begins a 90 legislative day period during which Congress will hold hearings, debate and, ultimately, vote on the agreement. The final vote is expected in time for NAFTA to enter into force on January 1, 1994, as envisioned in the agreement. While there have been, are, and will continue to be spirited debates in the United States and Canada about the wisdom of NAFTA, it is reasonable and realistic to expect that it will be approved by the U.S. Congress and by the Canadian Parliament.

CONCLUSION

This is an exciting time to be involved in trade in the western hemisphere. The U.S.-Canada Free Trade Agreement is a landmark achievement, which is guiding the way for others to growth through free trade and market-oriented policies and programs. As one FTA takes root and its members prosper, the example provides the momentum and gives the courage to others to follow. Changes are taking place in Mexico, and its desire for a free trade agreement is a historic window of opportunity that economics, geography, and history compel the United States to pursue. NAFTA offers an unparalleled opportunity to capture the energies of the three economies and to propel them into the vanguard of global competitiveness.

5

Reaction Panel Remarks Made at the Conference on North American Free Trade: Labor, Industry, and Government Policy Perspectives

William H. Cavitt

Why is the United States involved in NAFTA? Why did the president start this whole process? Why did he respond positively to President Salinas' requests? There were some broad, sweeping economic reasons for that. They are certainly valid, but let me give you a slightly different perspective. In fact, I would suggest three specific reasons why a U.S.-Mexican Free Trade Agreement makes good sense. (I will talk about this as though it were bilateral, because I do not think it is appropriate for me to be speaking on behalf of the Canadian government, inasmuch as I work for the U.S. government.)

First, a free trade agreement with Mexico would contribute to long-term economic prosperity, stability, and growth in Mexico. And an economically prosperous Mexico is important to us, because the lack of economic opportunity is the root of such bilateral problems as illegal immigration, drugs, and pollution.

Second, a U.S.-Mexican Free Trade Agreement would advance the cause of economic reform in Latin America. The eyes of the region are on Mexico. It is a leader among the Latin American nations and its success could serve as a model for market-oriented policies and reforms elsewhere in the hemisphere.

Now, I'm referring here to the President's Enterprise for the Americas Initiative, which has as its goal the negotiation of a free trade agreement for the entire western hemisphere. Successful negotiation of a free trade agreement with Mexico would be a milestone on the road toward hemisphere-wide free trade. Already quite a number of countries have expressed interest: Chile, Venezuela, Argentina, Brazil, Uruguay, Paraguay, and others.

Finally, a U.S.-Mexican Free Trade Agreement makes good business sense. U.S. business sees major trade and investment opportunities in Mexico and wants assured access to that market. Mexico is our third largest trading partner, with two-way merchandise trade totaling some $76 billion in 1992. And, Mexico is also our fastest growing export market. Mexico has a very high potential to consume U.S. goods. "Made in the USA" is a sign and mark of quality in Mexico. And Mexicans want those goods. About 70 percent of their imports come from the United States.

I was recently down along the border, in McAllen, Texas, on a day when a Mexican apparel manufacturer together with the local economic development group announced that the Mexican manufacturer was going to open an apparel plant on the U.S. side of the border. Not in Reynosa, where all those maquilas are, but on the U.S. side of the border. And the question was, why in the world would a Mexican manufacturer of apparel be opening a plant on the U.S. side of the border and paying our wages and all the other things that go with it, when he could go just a few miles across the border and have the same things for less? He wanted to be able to affix a label that said, "made in the USA." Because "Made in the USA" has market value in Mexico. The same good produced across the border would not have the commercial advantage, the commercial cachet that "Made in the USA" would have.

So, a lot of U.S. businesses have looked at the Mexican market, at those 85 million people. They have looked at the demographics on this continent and they see that our birth rates and the Canadian birth rates are relatively flat. Our populations are going to be pretty much the same in the year 2000 as they are now. But in Mexico they are growing at such a rapid rate, that they could easily be at a 100 million by the year 2000. Those are people who obviously want to be able to raise their standards of living, they want to be able to consume, among other things, U.S. goods, and U.S. business has taken a very serious, hard-nosed look at that kind of opportunity and said, "We want a piece of the action."

Now, it is important to note that exports are also key to U.S. economic growth. Since 1986 exports have accounted for more than 40 percent of U.S. economic growth measured by the gross national product. In 1990 alone exports accounted for 88 percent, or almost all of the growth portion of GNP. It is estimated that every $1 billion of U.S. exports supports over 20,000 U.S. jobs. U.S. exports to Mexico more than tripled from $12.4 billion in 1986, to $40.6 billion in 1992. That means that U.S. jobs dependent on exports to Mexico also tripled, from approximately 250,000 to 800,000. Put simply, freer trade means more trade and more trade means more jobs. And the importance of exports to American jobs and prosperity was a prime factor in Bush's decision to pursue a free trade agreement with Mexico and Canada.

What about the maquilas? I have had some involvement with the maquilas, dating back to 1970, when as a young officer I started following it as an import policy issue. And one of the first jobs I had in that role was to review a study that was done at the time by the U.S. International Trade Commission of the likely economic consequences on the United States if old item 807 of the Tariff Schedules of the United States was eliminated. I have been following the issue in various capacities for the past twenty-one years. I have also had occasion in the last few months to visit ten border cities and spend quite a bit of time talking with both U.S. and other maquiladora managers and updating my knowledge base and understanding of what is going on down there. And, from that background, I will present my perspective on the relationship of the maquilas to NAFTA. In some ways the maquiladora program is a sort of paradigm for free trade.

One of the questions I am often asked is, "Will a free trade agreement with Mexico result in a massive shift of U.S. jobs and plants to Mexico?" I think the answer is, no. I do not foresee any sudden or dramatic shifts of jobs to Mexico resulting from a free trade agreement. Let me give you six reasons.

First, any plant that could benefit from virtually free trade with Mexico could have moved there any time in the past 27 years under the maquiladora plan. NAFTA is not necessary in that context.

Second, total production and marketing costs are what matters, not wages alone. If wages alone were what mattered, then places like Bangladesh and Haiti would be economic power houses rather than economic basket cases.

Third, Mexican wages reflect Mexican productivity. Output per worker in the United States is five to six times that of Mexico. Moreover, since 1980 output per person employed in U.S. manufacturing has grown 2.5 times faster than Mexico.

Fourth, most exports from Mexico are already duty-free or virtually duty-free—some under the Generalized System of Preferences, some under the old 807 program now called 9802. And the average U.S. tariff on dutiable goods from Mexico is only 4 percent. Therefore, the elimination of those tariffs, in many areas, will be insignificant. There are exceptions where U.S. tariffs are very high, and certainly textiles and apparel is one of those.

Fifth, there is a shortage of skilled labor in Mexico. Technical school graduates are too few to meet the demand. Supply and demand studies by the University of Texas at El Paso show that Mexican engineers, technicians, supervisors, and managers in Ciudad Juárez earn salaries very close to that of their American counterparts in El Paso, somewhere in the range of 60 to 90 percent. In other words, if the American was making $20,000, the Mexican would be making somewhere between $12,000 and $18,000.

Finally, in many places throughout Mexico the social infrastructure is inadequate to meet current basic needs, never mind an influx of new plants and workers. Inadequacies include roads, bridges, border crossings, municipal transit, housing, health care, child care facilities, and even basic sewage disposal.

So for all these reasons and more, it is unrealistic to expect that a free trade agreement with Mexico would result in a sudden or dramatic movement of U.S. plants and jobs to Mexico.

Many people see the maquiladora program as a paradigm for free trade. There are a lot of lessons that could be learned from it. The program through the years has been criticized by labor and others on grounds that it results in the export of U.S. plants and jobs.

The U.S. International Trade Commission has studied the maquiladora program four times since 1970. In each instance, they found that the likely economic effects of the elimination of "production sharing," which is basically what the maquilas are all about, would be the most of the products of the maquilas would continue to be imported, but they would likely be of wholly foreign origin, and most likely from the Far East. Under those circumstances, U.S. and Mexican exporters would lose out to the benefit of Far Eastern exporters. There would be no U.S. jobs producing the components and no Mexican jobs assembling those components—in essence, a lose-lose strategy.

In a worst case scenario, the United States would lose the 154,000 jobs estimated currently producing components for assembly in Mexico and Mexico would lose the 438,000 jobs doing the assembly. Now, remember the difference earlier, between the relationship between productivity in the two countries. And if U.S. productivity is running five to six times that of Mexico, do a little bit of math and the productivity of that 154,000 U.S. jobs relative to the 438,000 jobs in Mexico comes out looking pretty good on our side of things.

Many U.S. manufacturers have testified that production sharing, contrary to popular myth, has saved thousands of U.S. jobs and also created many new ones. A study done for the McAllen, Texas Economic Development Corporation is instructive. Entitled "The Economic Impact of Maquiladora on the McAllen Hidalgo County Area," the study documents that in 1989, 20,691 maquila jobs in Reynosa, the sister city just across the river, supported 23,415 jobs in Hidalgo County, Texas. The study also showed that the economic activity generated by the maquilas added $428 million to the local economy of Hidalgo County. And that represents 15 percent of personal income and 16 percent of the jobs in what is statistically the poorest county in the United States. And those numbers do not include the thousands of jobs all over the United States that are producing the components that are shipped through Hidalgo County to Reynosa for assembly in those maquila plants.

In summary, studies have shown that production sharing is an economically sound concept that has proven to be good for both the United States and for Mexico over the past 27 years. I know for many "them's fightin' words." Yet NAFTA will help keep jobs in the United States and strengthen international competitiveness by harnessing the complementary strengths of three North American economies.

6

The Impact of Free Trade on Industry

Calman J. Cohen

The Emergency Committee for American Trade, better known as ECAT, is an organization of the heads of over sixty U.S. firms with extensive overseas business activities. Their worldwide sales last year totaled over $1 trillion, and they employed over 5 million persons. With major investments in Canada and Mexico, they have a keen interest in the ongoing talks on the creation of a North American Free Trade Area.

ECAT firms were among the principal supporters of the U.S.-Canada Free Trade Agreement and are strong supporters of the current efforts to negotiate a North American Free Trade Agreement. They view positively the economic liberalization measures being implemented in Mexico, making it a more attractive market for firms headquartered in the United States and Canada.

The transformation under way in Mexico can be illustrated by the recent decision of a major corporation based in Monterey to slash its staff in Mexico City. Most of its Mexico City staff had not been part of its salesforce but had been among its phalanx of "fixers" who had responsibility for finding ways around the reams of red tape generated by the government. However, with the government having followed through on its commitment to eliminate many of the structural impediments to commerce, the firm had begun to find its "fixers" to be costly and, more to the point, redundant.

Mexico now has a government committed to transforming the country into a modern industrial state through unleashing the forces of economic competition. The changes continue to spur the development of the autochthonous private sector and to lower Mexican barriers to the manufacturers, agricultural products, and services of U.S. and Canadian workers.

The changes in Mexico's economy that are under way are truly epochal and will lead its restructuring along the lines of the U.S. and Canadian economies. Most important, they will facilitate cross-border trade and investment flows with the United States and Canada. It is only prudent to recognize, however, that the changes are fully reversible if they fail to receive the support of Mexico's wealthier continental partners.

It is in the interest of the United States and Canada to see that the changes are preserved. Working with Mexico to form a regional free trade agreement will help ensure that these changes will survive the Salinas presidency and contribute to the economic growth in Mexico, Canada, and the United States into the twenty-first century.

Will elected officials in the United States and Canada support a free trade agreement that eventually may be worked out? Their support or opposition will be based on their reading of the effects of the agreement on their respective economies. Those who believe that it will provide an economic boost will be among its supporters; those who believe that it will cause harm will be among its opponents. Judgment day may, however, be delayed because it does not appear that the agreement itself will be completed any time soon.

Meanwhile, a debate rages in the United States over a basic issue: the effect of free trade on industry. In large part, the response to the question comes down to whether one sees an eventual North American Free Trade Agreement as a threat or an opportunity. There are many who view it as a threat, despite the recent International Trade Commission study that concluded that it would benefit the U.S. economy overall. There are several basic strands to their argument as heard in the corridors of power in Washington.

Some are fearful that U.S. industry will be unable to compete with Mexican industry and its low-wage workers. They forecast that manufacturing enterprises will shift production to Mexico from the United States for the primary purpose of reducing labor costs. They point to the maquiladora plants on the Mexican side of the U.S.-Mexican border as bellwethers of the impact of the free trade agreement.

This argument that U.S. industry will be unable to compete with lower-wage Mexican industry does not take into account that U.S. industry is a low-cost producer in many sectors. It would more easily be able to supply the Mexican market from expansive U.S. facilities—in some cases with underutilized capacity—were it not for trade barriers maintained by the government of Mexico. U.S. firms have frequently established manufacturing facilities in Mexico to leap over these barriers and sell to Mexican consumers.

A free trade agreement will encourage U.S. firms manufacturing in Mexico and the United States to find ways to rationalize production and become more competitive. It will not lead to the wholesale shift to Mexico of U.S. industry, most of which will continue to choose to locate facilities in the United States to ensure proximity to transportation networks, centers of advanced learning and research, and, most important, skilled labor.

In maquiladora plants on the Mexican side of the U.S.-Mexican border, Mexican workers assemble parts and components manufactured in the United States—largely not for sale in Mexico but for reexport to the United States. They are not symbols of the inability of U.S. industry to compete with Mexican industry. They are products of an inefficient Mexican economy. A North American Free Trade Agreement should lead to the obsolescence of maquiladoras.

The competitiveness of U.S. industry should not be underestimated. In a number of sectors, such as aircraft, computers, and chemicals, the United States remains the world leader. In other areas, such as apparel and textiles and steel, the United States has had a positive trade balance with Mexico. And more recent trade statistics indicate that the United States is currently running an overall trade surplus with Mexico.

Another strand to the argument of those who view a North American Free Trade Agreement as a threat is the belief that industry will shift from the United States to Mexico in order to escape from having to comply with U.S. environmental laws and regulations. The assumption is that Mexico's laws and regulations on the environment are weak or unenforced.

The reality is that environmental laws in Mexico mirror those in the United States. While the enforcement of those laws is not up to the level achieved in the United States, the government of Mexico has committed to steadily improve its monitoring of corporate compliance. In addition, negotiations between the United States and Mexico on ways to improve the environment are proceeding in parallel with the free trade talks. The talks increase the leverage the United States has to gain more rapid improvement on environmental protection in Mexico.

Stricter enforcement of environmental law in Mexico will safeguard the competitive position of U.S. firms, many of which as a matter of policy would require their facilities in Mexico to comply with U.S. environmental standards. The firms in Mexico that are not U.S.-owned but compete with U.S. firms will be forced to move to comply with U.S. standards. Furthermore, to the extent that the Mexican economy prospers under a free trade agreement, Mexico will acquire additional resources to upgrade its program of environmental protection.

Another strand to the argument of those who view a North American Free Trade Agreement as a threat is the fear that any lowering of tariff and nontariff barriers to Mexican products in the United States will eliminate the jobs of American workers. While many Mexican products enter the United States on a duty-free or a virtual duty-free basis, there are certain sectors of the U.S. economy provided with a relatively high level of protection. Some worker dislocation can be expected in these sectors as tariff and nontariff barriers are phased out over time. Workers who lose their jobs will need in most instances to acquire new skills and education. It will be essential that a variety of retraining programs be available to them to ensure that they do not have to bear alone the cost arising from an intergovernmental agreement to liberalize trade.

At the same time that some U.S. jobs will be lost, the lowering or elimination of many high Mexican tariff and nontariff barriers to U.S. products will generate over time new jobs in the comparatively open industrial and agricultural sectors of the United States. Currently, Mexico imposes greater restriction on U.S. exports than the United States imposes, on Mexican exports; accordingly, the United States stands to benefit as Mexico drops those restrictions. In addition, given that the negotiations with Mexico cover services and investment—two areas that have long been highly protected in Mexico—there is potential for further U.S. job creation as Mexico's barriers in those sectors fall.

ECAT members see the negotiation of a North American Free Trade Agreement as representing anything but a threat to the U.S. economy. Rather than a threat, it is an opportunity that if spurned by Mexico's hemispheric partners may be lost to our generation and future generations.

Narrowly defined, the North American Free Trade Agreement is an opportunity to redefine in three countries what is called the "home market." For the United States and Canada, it is an opportunity to add at one swoop some 80 million consumers to their home market. The restructuring that would take place in industry and agriculture to supply this new home market should improve the economic welfare of the population of all three countries.

Broadly defined, the successful negotiation of a North American Free Trade Agreement would provide support for the U.S. and Canadian approach to international trade, one driven by market principles. The establishment of a North American Free Trade Area would strengthen the ability of the United States and Canada to move the world trading system in the same liberal direction.

It is too early to tell whether the three governments will be successful in reaching an accord. it appears that they are making slow but steady progress. Industry will judge any accord on its merits; it will support an accord it believes to be in the commercial interest of the United States.

If a good agreement is reached, U.S. political leaders should endorse it and industry and labor should work together to make it a success. The alternative, for political leaders to walk away from a good agreement, would represent fear of change and rejection of a new path for the hemisphere that could contribute greatly to the prosperity of industry, labor, and agriculture in years to come.

7

Estimating the Impact of the U.S.-Mexican Free Trade Agreement on Industrial Labor

James M. Cypher

This chapter is concerned with only one aspect of an extremely complex issue—the labor market effects of the U.S.-Mexican Free Trade Agreement. It is the hypothesis of this chapter that the U.S.-Mexican FTA will be a "bad" agreement for working people in the United States and a "bad" agreement for their counterparts in Mexico. Within the context of a "bad" agreement for labor on both sides of the border it will be "relatively worse" for U.S. workers and "relatively better" for Mexican workers. U.S. workers will feel the effects primarily as a major force continuing to push down wages in the manufacturing sector, particularly where unions still maintain a foothold. By 1997, for reasons detailed below, approximately 220,000 high-wage, skilled and semiskilled U.S. manufacturing jobs will be lost due to the FTA—excluding the apparel and textile industries. These lost jobs, many in the Midwest region, will lead to a reduction in local, state, and federal tax revenues, which will, in turn, lead to a subsequent round of job losses.

For Mexican workers roughly five-hundred thousand new jobs may be created.[1] Since these jobs will primarily arise due to a surge in direct foreign investment (DFI), and since this DFI carries with it a transnational corporate culture that tends to pay above the prevailing wages in Mexico while offering relatively better working conditions, it might appear that the FTA is the miracle-to-come so avidly sought since the collapse of the oil boom midway in 1981.

The increase in jobs in Mexico—many in the manufacturing sector—should be placed in the context of the new doctrine of "modernization." Modernization means many things, among them that capital-labor relations will be utterly transformed. The neoliberal theory guiding Mexican policymakers in this area insists on the breakup or weakening of Mexican unions, along with the removal of all inhibitions to a "free" labor market. While the past practices of the Mexican unions have certainly revealed their manifold weaknesses, the swerve toward modernization—particularly since 1987—has ushered in a new era of antilabor policymaking that has been avidly implemented by union leadership. At the same time, following neoliberal principles, the state has actively sought to undercut the social wage arising from state-supported programs such as Social Security.

Labor, then, finds its capacity to achieve wage gains undercut by the increasing tendency of union leadership to contain wage increases within the context of a *pacto social* designed to use low wages as leverage to increase exports. At the same time the state has utilized the neoliberal doctrine of thinning down state expenditures and programs in order to attack the social wage.

Downsizing the state sector has and will have an important impact on both the industrial labor force and state sector employees. Until recently, the Mexican state utilized the state-owned firms as "employers-of-last-resort." However, since 1982 the 1,155 state-owned firms have been reduced to 269, with major firms such as Fertimex now undergoing privatization. PEMEX alone has cut 42,000 jobs since 1988, and is presently considering additional cuts of 43,000.[2] It is entirely possible that most of the new jobs created by the FTA in Mexico will simply replace jobs lost in the public sector.

Given this context, while Mexico's labor market might tighten modestly with the FTA—particularly in the manufacturing sector—and while wages may well rise a bit, wage gains will be severely constrained by the imposition of neoliberal policies and the need to utilize cheap labor as the underlying basis of the export platform strategy. In other words, relative to the 1940–81 period, the wage gains to be anticipated will be meager. Market forces will be constrained by even more powerful political-economic forces, at least where wages are concerned. Meanwhile, in a nation that needs an estimated eight-hundred thousand new jobs per year merely to satisfy the new entrants into the labor market, the FTA can fulfill neither Mexico's labor market needs nor its human needs.

BASIC FORCES BEHIND THE FTA

The FTA will be a "good" agreement for many if not most U.S. transnational corporations and for the *grupos nacional de poder* (conglomerates) in Mexico. These groups, above all other elements, have orchestrated the FTA, with the Business Roundtable leading the way in the United States, and COECE (Cordinator Empresarial para el Acuerdo de Libre Comercio), backed by the Business Coordinating Council (CCE) and other elite groups in Mexico.

Behind the recent wave of enthusiasm voiced by the governments of the United States and Mexico are four forces:

- A shared enthusiasm for the ideological constructs and assumptions of economic liberalism

- The need of the largest U.S.-based transnational corporations to bolster their profit rate through a drastic restructuring of U.S.-Mexican economic relationships

- The need for Mexico to consolidate its modernization program through a sizable increase in direct foreign investment, international borrowing from the transnational banks, and multilateral aid

- An attempt to reposition the U.S. economy and revive U.S. hegemony by strengthening its home base—now expanded to include Canada and Mexico

Both governments acknowledge and even champion the first force—enjoying the benefits of comparative advantage. The second and fourth forces are virtually never acknowledged at the official level. The key to the FTA is this second force—transnationalization. Originally, the FTA negotiations were termed "trade and investment talks," but investment was dropped from the title as discussions between the two nations proceeded.

If the FTA is to have important economic and social effects on the two nations it will largely be because: (1) U.S. corporations will find that the Mexican government has conceded to most of their demands regarding the elimination of various laws and rules that have heretofore limited and constrained the freedom of foreign capital; and (2) the Mexican government will open up virtually all areas of the economy previously reserved to either the state (the oil industry is of particular importance here), Mexican nationals, or joint-venture Mexican-foreign firms.

The fourth force behind the FTA is more problematic. Will the United States be able to increase its leverage in the global economy because it operates from a wider and stronger economic base? Or will that economic base within the NAFTA area be weakened by "polarizing" growth, as only a relatively few corporations and a relatively elite section of the U.S. economy benefits from the FTA? Will the trade blocs in the process of formation in Europe and Asia engage in benign or hostile relationships? There are few clues at this point in time that would allow for a definitive answer to these pressing questions.

In manufacturing consent for the FTA, models have played a prominent role on both sides of the border. These models basically attempt to support what Juan Gallardo of COECE and Carla Hills, U.S. trade representative, have repeatedly termed a "win-win" situation. Below, we present data and analysis normally not included in the models built under the sponsorship or influence of either the two governments or the powerful business organizations that represent the transnationals in the policymaking process.

U.S. INVESTMENT IN MEXICO: THE LABOR IMPACT

For the major participants involved—U.S. corporations, the Mexican government, U.S. and Mexican business organizations, U.S. government trade officials—the key purpose of the FTA is to resolve all remaining questions pertaining to the authority of the Mexican government to rescind or change the laws governing direct foreign investment (DFI). (Of course, there are other matters—intellectual property rights and nontariff barriers, for example, but they are not at the epicenter of the trade talks.) The fact that neither of the two "models" used to compute the effects of trade alone—the ITC and the Almon/MIMEX studies—shows any momentous changes for either country, when trade alone is considered, should come as little surprise.[3]

After all, Mexico now has ready access to the U.S. market, and vice versa. Of course, there are some important exceptions where high tariffs and restrictive quotas are involved, but trade alone is clearly not what the FTA policy debate is about.

Several studies have tried to model the effects of an investment surge into Mexico as a result of an FTA. The idea of a surge follows simple economic analysis—the rate of profit is substantially higher in Mexico than in the United States. If the FTA tends to resolve several significant issues that have placed a risk premium on foreign investments in Mexico, perfectly mobile international capital should flow to Mexico. This is not debatable. The issue is, how much? No one really knows, but the range, considered in five separate models, runs from a low of $12.5 billion (permitting a one-year jump in investment) to a high of $46 billion spread over a ten-year period.[4] An average estimate, then, would be roughly $30 billion. Usually the ten years from 1992 to 2002 are taken as the relevant time frame. The amount of investment is that which is assumed to equalize the risk and rate of return (profit rate on invested capital) between the two countries. Estimating such a process can be complex, since data on the overall rate of return in Mexico are difficult to ascertain, and computing the spread in risk after an FTA is, in effect, no simple matter. In any case, the published results of the studies cited in this section offer the reader scant details regarding precisely how this calculation was made, and what the conceivable weaknesses in the estimating techniques were. It is worth repeating, then, that no one knows how much U.S. capital will flow into Mexico, yet the probability of an investment surge is high.

President Salinas has stated on several occasions that he would hope to see annual direct foreign investment increase to $6 billion per year—roughly doubling that achieved over his predecessor. While no one can state for sure that Salinas' expectations will be realized, given what is known about the future intentions of the auto sector and about the profound disagreements U.S. corporations have with Mexico's foreign investment law, a change in the investment law—sure to be negotiated by the United States—would likely bring a surge in investments. (The auto sector firms have announced planned investments of $4.25 billion through 1996—see Appendix 7.1.)[5] This expectation is buttressed by the fact that there is a high probability that U.S. corporations in autos and auto parts, computers, and electronic equipment have reached a point on their learning curve where a surge should be anticipated.

In the event that investment jumped up to an average of $6 billion per year for the five-year period 1992–97, how would such a change impact the U.S. economy? Equalizing the risk, or one important factor determining the risk of DFI in Mexico (by eliminating the ambiguities in the foreign investment law and by eliminating the discretionary power the government holds over foreign investors, as well as by eliminating most of the strategic areas reserved to the state or to Mexican nationals and eliminating the performance requirements and domestic content requirements) should, according to all economic theory, draw investment funds into Mexico and out of the United States. Based on past investment patterns, roughly 63 percent of all new investment would come from the United States.

An FTA, then, would have an "investment shifting effect" wherein $30 billion × .63 = $18.9 billion of capital goods, plants, and equipment that would otherwise have been created in the United States will occur in Mexico. Using aggregative U.S. data for the year 1990 (the latest available) it can be demonstrated that every $1 billion in economic activity (value added) creates (or sustains) 20,135 jobs, the lost investment would eliminate 380,552 jobs in the building trades and the capital goods industries in a five-year period. Since this is a cumulative number the actual job loss in any one year is much smaller: 380,552/5 = 76,110.

This job loss should be balanced off against job gains in the capital goods industries, since part of the new equipment utilized in Mexico will be imported from the United States. The ratio of capital goods imported in relation to investment in Mexico, however, is not high. In 1988, the last year data were available to make such calculations, the ratio was $3.2 billion/$38.4 billion = 8.3 percent, with the U.S. share only 5.3 percent.[6] On the basis of this data, then, of the $30 billion of new DFI in the 1992–97 period, the United States should expect to provide via capital goods exports only $1.59 billion—creating 32,015 jobs in five years, or 6,402 jobs per year, primarily in the machine-tool and heavy equipment sectors. On an annualized basis, then, the job loss should be − 76,110 + 6,402 = − 69,708.

Once the capital has shifted south, however, it will be in a position to be used to produce products that will have as their objective the global market. (We are deliberately leaving out of account the growth of the internal market, on the premise that Mexico is attracting foreign capital for the purpose of functioning as an export platform. This is the premise of the Mexican government.) The historical capital/output should provide an indication of how many new products can be produced with the new capital entering Mexico. The private sector capital output ratio in Mexico is 1.2/1.[7] Thus, every $1.28 billion in capital stock generates the flow of $1 billion of new goods. Therefore, the $30 billion of new private investment will create a flow of output of $25 billion at the end of the five-year period. (The amount will build up year after year; in the first year it will be $5 billion in output, with $5 billion added each subsequent year.) At the end of five years $16 billion of the $25 billion in new output will be exported to the U.S. market. (The United States currently buys 64 percent of all Mexican exports.)

Some economists have assumed that an increase in imports from Mexico may occur as a result of the FTA, but that such imports will only replace other imports, primarily from Asia. In this approach, import penetration from Mexico will be exactly counterbalanced by a decline in Asian imports. This result is possible, but somewhat remote given recent history. The United States is experiencing a growth in imports in relation to its GNP. If past trends continue it is possible that all, or almost all, of the new imports coming from Mexico will be added to imports from elsewhere in the world. Should that be the case, by 1997 the FTA will have exported 322,160 manufacturing jobs to Mexico. That is, the U.S. O/L ratio determines that for each $1 billion in output 20,135 jobs are sustained. Therefore, with $16 billion in new capital in place aimed at exporting to the U.S. market the calculation is as follows: $16 billion of new imports × 20,135 jobs (per $1 billion in output) = 322,160 jobs. To this should be added the 69,708 jobs lost in 1997 due to the "investment shift effect"—roughly 400,000 jobs. Such an impact would be very difficult for the manufacturing sector to absorb.

By 1997 roughly 2 percent of all U.S. manufacturing jobs could be eliminated by an investment surge into Mexico. Expressed in aggregate percentage terms this may seem relatively minor, but such a drop in manufacturing employment should be understood within the broader context of the loss of nearly 1.5 million manufacturing jobs since 1979. Furthermore, the impact of the U.S.-Mexican FTA will be (most likely) one of many as the United States is presently negotiating twenty-nine FTAs in Latin American under the Enterprise for the Americas Initiative.

NET JOBS LOST OVER THE BASELINE YEAR OF 1990 DUE TO THE FTA

The above figures are aggregate estimates based on a zero baseline figure for foreign investment. In fact, the baseline figure for DFI should be $2.613 billion. Thus, without the FTA in the period of 1992–97 $2.6 billion × 5 = $13 billion of new DFI should flow to Mexico. The FTA is worth an additional $17 billion in net new DFI. Of this amount some $10.71 billion will have come from U.S. corporations. After five years this $10.71 billion of new capital in Mexico will create an annual flow of .833 × $10.71 billion

Table 7.1
U.S. Employment Impact of the FTA, 1992–97

Effect/Sector	Per Year	1992-97	Emp. in 1997
Displaced Investment	$5B	$30B (x. 63)	-76,110
Investment Displaced over Baseline	$3.4	$17B (x .63)	-43,129
Capital Goods Exports		$1.59B	+6,402
Capital Goods Exports over Baseline		$1.09	+4,389
Increased Output Exported to United States	$168. in 1997		-322,160
Increased Output Exported to United States over Baseline	$8.92B in 1997		-179,640
Total Jobs Lost to FTA			-391,868
Total Jobs Lost to FTA over Baseline			-218,840

= $8.92 billion of new output exported to the United States from Mexico. This reproducible capital stock, had it remained in the United States, would have supported 179,640 manufacturing jobs. Adding in the displaced workers who have lost their jobs in the investment sector $(43,129 - 4,389 = 38,840)$ the total expected job loss based upon the assumptions made above would be 218,840. In other words, over the baseline amounts (compiled using 1990 figures as the base) that would presumably flow to Mexico in any case, the net shift in investment caused by the FTA would result in the loss of 218,840 U.S. jobs in the manufacturing and investment sectors in 1997. Table 7.1 presents these data.

The dynamic effects of the FTA will not cease with the 218,840 displaced workers. In addition one must consider several other factors. First, the "job multiplier" measures the secondary and tertiary impacts of changes in employment. Job multipliers vary, given the intensity of labor in impacted sectors. As a general rule the multiplier has a value of 2 or a multiplier effect of 1. That is, for every worker unemployed by a change in the economy the "ripple effect" as the loss of income in one sector affects other sectors is generally found to be equal in magnitude to the original change. Therefore, one might anticipate $218,840 \times 2 = 437,680$ jobs lost from the FTA. (We have ignored the job multiplier effect in Table 7.1 because the growth in income in Mexico might result in the increase in U.S. exports of consumer and intermediate goods.[8])

Second, one must consider that whenever private sector investments are made a heavy commitment by the state is made to infrastructure, the legal system, and education. In brief, cutting investment in the United States results in a massive loss of government revenue and expenditures. Those expenditures now support nearly 30 percent of the economy (exempting military spending). State expenditures not made as production moves to Mexico translates into an erosion of the tax base, and consequently a shrinking of public outlays. This, in turn, translates into lost jobs in the public sector. In very crude terms each $1 of private sector capital in the United States is supported by 29 cents of public infrastructure. If $1 billion of private production is lost this means the loss of 19,920 jobs. Using this ratio it could be estimated—albeit in only a very approximate manner—that every $1 billion shift in private investment could result in the loss of 5,777 jobs in the public sector.[9] Shifting $10.94 billion of capital stock to Mexico ($2.19 billion per year for five years) could result in the annual loss of 12,640 jobs to workers who build government infrastructure. Here, the bulk of the impact would be felt by the construction unions. Once this capital is in place and producing in Mexico the social services that would have supported this production in the United States will not be needed. Consequently another, even larger, round of job losses could be estimated. The point here is neither to exaggerate the effects of the FTA nor to develop questionable estimates of job losses in the public sector. Rather, it is to emphasize that there will undoubtedly be some considerable job losses suffered in the public sector and to workers who provide equipment to that sector as a result of the FTA.

The dynamic effects of macroeconomic changes become difficult to trace and quantify when two (or more) effects can be anticipated from one change. In this case there are at least two effects to consider: (1) substantial increases in unemployment, and (2) strong downward pressure on prevailing wages. It is likely that, at the margin, the FTA will push wages down rather strongly. Not of course to, or near, Mexican wage levels—in accordance with the factor price equalization theory—but by substantial amounts because the impact of the FTA will be felt by highly unionized sectors such as autos, auto parts, machine-tools, capital goods, and electrical machinery and equipment. The FTA will have a considerable impact on the "labor aristrocracy" in manufacturing. This, in turn, will both pull down the percentage of unionized workers, and weaken pattern bargaining effects. The macroeconomic effect will be a lowering of the wage component in GNP, and therefore a decline in consumption. This will reduce economic growth and negatively impact investment. A minor plus might be that with wage costs declining U.S. exports might be more competitive. But this, of course, is the "low road," and many countries can beat the United States at this game.

While income and other tax revenues are shrinking because of wage reductions, the demands placed on the public sector to deal with the unemployed will increase. While the high-wage workers in autos and auto parts, capital goods, machine-tools, electrical machinery and equipment, and (quite possibly) the steel sector may have a fighting chance at retraining and reinsertion into the low-wage labor force, the impact on low-wage workers in apparel and computer assembly is likely to be quite pernicious. Here a relatively low-skilled, low-wage labor force will be faced with few alternatives aside from structural unemployment.

Thus polarizing growth (the increase in income disparities between various income groups) will accelerate. Concomitantly, homelessness, hopelessness, crime, and general civic disorder can only rise. Cities, states, and federal government will be pushed further toward deficits and cuts in social programs even as the need for such programs rises.

NOTES

1. Productivity in the new plants in Mexico will be close to the U.S. level (probably near 80 percent). Thus, the 220,000 jobs lost in the United States will translate into 275,000 jobs gained in Mexico. In addition the FTA will create opportunities for massive borrowing by the Mexican government in order to expand the infrastructure and certain state-owned firms such as PEMEX, and develop the tourism sector. Labor-intensive construction projects could nearly double the above figure for Mexico. However, under the best of assumptions, this is not a mere shifting of jobs. In addition, consider the fact that on average the Mexican workers will receive one-tenth the wage lost by the U.S. workers (see Appendix 7.2 for Mexican autoworker wages). Assume an average worker income of $29,000 in the United States $\times$ 220,000 = $6.4 billion of aggregate demand lost in the United States, compared to $2,900 $\times$ 500,000 = $1.5 billion. The net effect is that the NAFTA areas loses nearly $5 billion of demand.

2. *Mexico Business Monthly*, 1, 10 (Nov. 1991), p. 12. No data are available to gauge the extent of the layoffs due to privatization, but there can be no doubt that they are very large. Another example—small but telling—is the case of the famous Zacatepec sugar refinery in Zapata's heartland. This mill was declared bankrupt by the government in 1991, with 2,600 jobs lost. It will now be restructured with only 600 workers running the refinery. *Los Angeles Times*, Oct. 22, 1991, p. H6.

3. See C. Almon, *Industrial Effects of a Free Trade Agreement* (Washington, D.C.: U.S. Department of Labor/INFORUM, 1990); William Spriggs, "Potential Effects of Direct Foreign Investment Shifts Due to the FTA," testimony before the Subcommittee on Commerce, Consumer Protection and Competitiveness, U.S. House of Representatives, May 15, 1991; Clyde Prestowitz, et al., *The New North American Order* (Washington, D.C.: Economic Strategy Institute, 1991).

The employment impact calculated by these "trade only" models is small. Nonetheless, it is important to recall that these models suggest considerable intersectoral shifting (some sectors are impacted by import penetration, others expand their production and exports due to the increased demand coming from Mexico) which is costly both in terms of the workers and businesses affected, but also equally important is the impact on communities and public sector budgets. Even those areas that experience growth may have to make painful adjustments and undergo financial strain to provide the infrastructure and government services that should accompany growth. Even in the best of circumstances, good trade policy should be one wherein the "winners" compensate the "losers." This, in an ideal work, would open the way for considerable adjustments and transfer payments administered by the government. Trade adjustment costs are likely to be considerable.

4. See KMPK, Peat Marwick, *The Effects of a Free Trade Agreement Between the U.S. and Mexico*, Executive Summary, 1991; F. Gerard Adams, et al., *The Mexico-U.S. Free Trade and Investment Proposal*, University of Pennsylvania CIE-MEX/WEFA 1991; Clyde Prestowitz, *The New North American Order*, Economic Strategy Institute, 1991. The fourth study, by R. Hinojosa and R. McCleery, is discussed in William Spriggs, "Potential Effects of Direct Foreign Investment Shifts Due to Proposed FTA," testimony before U.S. House, Committee on Energy and Commerce Subcommittee on Commerce, Consumer Protection, and Competitiveness, 1991.

5. Clyde Prestowitz, et al., *The New North American Order* (Washington, D.C.: University Press of America, 1991), p. 80; *Mexico Business Monthly* (Aug. 1991), p. 2; *Mexico Business Monthly* (Nov. 1991), p. 12.

6. Bancomext, "Sumario Estadistico," *Comercio Exterior*, 39, 5 (Mayo 1988), p. 448.

7. INEGI, *Estatisticas Historicas de Mexico, II* (Mexico: INEGI, 1985), p. 611.

8. A rise in Mexico's income, brought on by increased investment in Mexico, should result in increased Mexican tourism to the United States, increased consumption of U.S.-produced consumer goods, and the purchase of some intermediate products. We have not attempted to take these matters into account, even though they are important to consider. It is doubtful that they would be strong enough to overcome all of the negative job multiplier effects.

9. See David Aschauer, "Infrastructure: America's Third Deficit," *Challenge* 34, 2 (Mar.–Apr. 1991), p. 41, for estimates of the public sector capital stock.

Appendix 7.1
Workers' Daily Wages in Mexican Auto Firms, March 1988 (in U.S. Dollars)

Company (Est.)	High Wage Position	Low-Wage Position	Average Wage Position
Chrysler Federal District	$11.83	$5.01	$9.30
Chrysler Toluca	$12.38	$4.35	$8.78
Chrysler Ramos Arizpe (1981)	$10.23	$3.95	$6,51
Ford Cuautitlan	$13.69	$6.41	$9.90
Ford Chihuahua (1983)	$10.88	$5.02	$7.48
Ford Hermosillo (1986)	$14.95	$8,31	$11.64
General Motors Federal District	$14.20	$7.45	$10.99
General Motors Toluca (1965)	$13.75	$4.66	$8.93
General Motors Ramos Arizpe (Autos) (1981)	$9.61	$3.94	$6.60
General Motors Ramos Arizpe (Engine Plant)(1981)	$9.38	$4.20	$6.50
Nissan Cuernavaca	$13.33	$6.36	$9.75
Nissan Aguascalientes (1981)	$7.44	$3.64	$5.68
Volkswagen Puebla	$15.53	$5.99	$10.01

Sources: Our computations are based upon auto industry labor contracts, materials of the Juanta Federal de Conciliacion y Arbitraje, and related data presented in Kevin Middlebrook, "The Politics of Industrial Restructuring," *Comparative Politics*, vol. 23, no. 3 (Apr. 1991).

Appendix 7.2
Projected Auto Sector Investments in Mexico

Company	Investment	Purpose	Export to U.S.
Nissan	$1 b. over 5 years	a. $400 m. for 200,000 autos per yr.	a. 32,000 new units by 1993; 64,000 by 1995.
		b. Shift component sourcing from Japan to Mexico	b. Ship $180 m. in new components by 1992 (up from $60 m. in 1990).
VW	$1.5 b. in Puebla Plant	a. Jump capacity from 220,000 to 300,000 in early 1990s.	Up to 70 percent exported to U.S. market. Reaching 315,000 units by 1993.
		b. Double production to 450,000 by 1993.	
Ford	$840 m. in early 1990s	Modernize and expand existing plant.	Increase production to 165,000 units by 1990.
GM	$50 m.	Production of wire harnesses.	n.a.
Mercedes-Benz	$40 m.	Joint venture in 1991-93 to produce buses.	n.a.
German Parts Co.	$165 m.	n.a.	n.a.
Kensworth	$65 m.	100 percent increase in truck output.	n.a.
TOTAL	$4.25 b.		

Sources: Clyde Prestowitz, et al., *The New North American Order* (Washington, D.C.: University Press of America, 1991), p. 80; *Mexico Business Monthly* (Aug. 1991), p. 2.

8

The Road to the North American Free Trade Agreement: Laissez-Faire or a Ladder Up?

Jeff Faux and Thea Lee

The ultimate objective in formulating and negotiating a North American Free Trade Agreement should not be the abstract or ideological goal of free trade. It should be to improve living standards for the 360 million people in the United States, Canada, and Mexico. If we are confident that the agreement produced by the trilateral negotiations will achieve this result, we should accept it. If not, it should be rejected.

The issue is not whether the United States should trade with Mexico and Canada or whether investment should be allowed to move among these countries. Canada, Mexico, and the United States are already important trading partners, and—as is evident in all three countries—investment is already quite mobile. The question is how such increased trade and investment should take place.

How the North American countries choose to integrate their economies will in some measure define their course of economic development during the next several decades. Two strategies confront us. One is modeled on the European path to integration, which was slow and gradual, sensitive to the disparities of income and social institutions between countries, and committed to achieving integration without penalizing workers. The other is the model implicit in the proposals of the Bush-Salinas-Mulroney administrations—to rapidly remove all remaining barriers to the flow of capital, goods, and services across borders, deviating from laissez faire only to the extent necessary to bribe the most powerful of domestic special interests.

From their onset the NAFTA negotiations have been cloaked in a shroud of secrecy, with even the U.S. Congress excluded from the process, contrary to the promises made during the fast-track debate. Clearly, the trilateral synchronizing of special interest bribery is turning out to be more difficult than the negotiators originally imagined.

This chapter will explore the probable outcomes for the U.S. labor force of a laissez-faire trade agreement with Mexico, as defined by the proposals and statements of U.S. and Mexican officials. We will then suggest what needs to be added in order to have any chance of achieving the ultimate goal of higher living standards for the vast majority of the population in the United States. To some degree, what is true for the U.S. workforce will be true for the Canadian workforce as well. We also believe that an integration strategy that maintains wages and living standards in the high-wage nations is the optimal path for the long-term prospects of the Mexican workforce as well.

THE IMPACT OF A LAISSEZ-FAIRE NAFTA ON THE UNITED STATES

As presently contemplated by the U.S. and Mexican governments, the proposed free trade agreement will harm the United States' long-term economic competitiveness and put in jeopardy the jobs of hundreds of thousands of American workers. It may also put downward pressure on the wages of millions more Americans working in sectors not directly affected by the agreement.

NAFTA proponents have argued that any dislocation caused by the agreement will ultimately benefit U.S. workers. MIT professor Rudiger Dornbusch claims, for example, that the free trade agreement with Mexico will focus trade policy on "creating *more* and *better* jobs."[1] The bad (low-wage) jobs will move to Mexico, he argues, while U.S. workers will move up the ladder to the high-paying, high-tech jobs that the agreement will create. No one could be against such a happy arrangement.

But all our past experience and all available data indicate that U.S. workers displaced by trade end up moving down the job ladder, to lower-paying jobs, or off the ladder to permanent unemployment, not up to better jobs than they started with. The Bureau of Labor Statistics has done a series of studies on displaced workers, starting in 1979 and continuing through 1990. BLS followed the same group of workers for a five-year period, recording changes in their industry or occupation, changes in income, and duration of unemployment spells. The results varied, depending on the time period and the industry involved. During recessions, the workers surveyed took bigger pay cuts and experienced much longer periods of unemployment; workers in relatively high-paying industries (such as steel or autos) took bigger percentage cuts than those whose wages were low to begin with. But even during the more prosperous period of the late 1980s, the average percent loss in weekly earnings was 10 percent for all manufacturing workers.[2]

And that loss covers only workers lucky enough to have gotten new jobs at all. A large number of displaced workers have not succeeded in finding new jobs by the survey date, sometimes as much as five years after they were first laid off. About half of these dropped out of the labor force altogether, while the others were officially unemployed. In apparel, for example, which tends to suffer disproportionately due to the geographic immobility and demographic makeup of its workers, 48 percent of the workers laid off in the previous five years had not found new jobs by January 1986. Of those who were not reemployed, 62 percent were no longer in the labor force.[3]

Nothing in the laissez-faire NAFTA strategy suggests that workers dislocated as a result of this new treaty will fare any better. Moreover, the consensus of long-range public and private forecasters is that growth in the U.S. economy will be considerably slower over the next decade than in the previous, suggesting that the fortunes of trade-dislocated workers in the United States will suffer more.

The public debate about NAFTA has been dominated by overoptimistic predictions of gains in income and employment over current trends for all three countries. These predictions rely heavily on economic models that are not well suited to the task assigned them. In its May 1 submission to Congress, the Bush administration cited the results of three economic models as evidence that the agreement would likely result in a net gain of "exports, output, and employment" for the United States. Two of the models (by the International Trade Commission and the accounting firm of KPMG Peat Marwick) are based on so-called computable general equilibrium (CGE) analysis of the U.S. economy, ostensibly constructed to be able to trace both the direct effects of an event and its repercussions. The third (Clopper-Almon-INFORUM-CIMAT) is based on a combination of input-output techniques and linear regression.

Yet, by construction, the models have assumed away many of the questions they purport to answer. Based on traditional economic models of international trade, the two CGE models are based on full employment. It is therefore impossible for them to find that the agreement will result in a net loss of U.S. jobs; they can only calculate sectoral shifts. Even more serious, all three models assume, contrary to all the evidence, that a free trade agreement will not facilitate a shift in productive investment from the United States to Mexico. This assumption about capital mobility is pivotal to the ongoing debate.

The Peat Marwick study does examine a scenario of increased investment in Mexico (an additional $25 billion), but the increase apparently materializes out of nowhere (what economists calls a "helicopter drop"). "The main assumption," the authors write in their executive summary, "is that [the increased investment] *does not replace any physical plant and equipment that otherwise would have been located in the United States*" (emphasis added). Given that the United States is by far the chief foreign investor in Mexico (accounting for 63 percent of direct foreign investment in 1989[4]), and that the past ten years have seen a massive shift in investment from the United States to Mexico, this is indeed a heroic assumption.

The ITC study acknowledges the possibility of capital flow from the United States to Mexico following the signing of an agreement, but refuses to factor such a possibility into its predictions about employment. Scattered throughout the ITC report are warnings (apparently remnants of the original analysis that slipped through a tight political edit) that if U.S. investment in Mexico increases substantially, job and income losses will be much higher than predicted. The report hints that those losses will affect even those U.S. industries that the ITC now assumes will be gainers from the free trade agreement, such as automobiles and machinery.

There are several reasons to believe that more investment will flow from the United States and Canada to Mexico after the signing of a free trade agreement. First, on a purely theoretical level, it makes sense that corporations seeking to maximize profits will locate production where overall costs—including wages, corporate taxes, and the costs incurred in complying with environmental or workplace safety regulations—are lowest. Of course, firms base production decisions on many less easily quantifiable factors as well: worker skills and reliability, quality of physical infrastructure, communications networks, and political stability, among others. And the likelihood of transplanting production depends also on the nature of the good produced. Even so, the vast disparity between U.S. and Mexican wages and the inconsistent enforcement of labor standards and workplace regulations in Mexico will combine to provide a powerful pull for multinational corporations currently producing (or contemplating production) in the United States.

That this pull was enough to lure many firms south is evidenced by past experience, both Canada's with the Canadian-U.S. Free Trade Agreement signed in 1989, and that of the United States with the Mexican maquiladora zone. In the case of Canada, a relatively small wage differential was sufficient to induce hundreds of firms—both American subsidiaries and Canadian companies—to relocate production from Canada to the United States. According to the *New York Times*,[5] eighty-seven Canadian firms had moved to Buffalo, N.Y., alone as of August 1991. Lower wages, lower taxes, and cheaper real estate in the United States, combined with practically unrestricted access to the Canadian market, apparently offered firms an irresistible temptation to relocate. According to Statistics Canada, 461,000 manufacturing jobs were lost between June 1989 and October 1991—almost a quarter of the manufacturing workforce.[6] The Mulroney administration blamed the loss of jobs on the overvalued Canadian dollar and the recession. Opponents claims that the appreciation of the Canadian dollar was negotiated as part of the free trade agreement with the United States. But wherever the truth lies on that question, it is indisputable that many jobs have been lost and that the confident predictions of job gains for Canadian workers have not been borne out.

Beyond the immediate job losses, the Canadian-U.S. Free Trade Agreement raises other broader economic issues. Canada's well-developed social insurance, safety net, and public investment policies are already being eroded by the trade agreement with the United States. According to Bruce Campbell, "The competitive pressure to level the playing field puts more pressure on government to relax social and environmental standards, lower taxes, etc., in other words, to tax less and spend less."[7] Extending the free trade agreement to include Mexico puts the Canadian public sector in even more jeopardy.

U.S. experience with Mexico's maquiladora export zone also reinforces the idea that investment decisions are quite sensitive to changes in trade policy. The rapid expansion of maquiladora production—in which goods assembled in Mexico from U.S.-made parts are reexported to the United States, paying tariff only on the value added in Mexico—has shifted hundreds of thousands of jobs from the United States to Mexico.[8] Currently, about five-hundred thousand Mexican workers are employed in maquiladoras, at an average wage approximately half that prevailing in the rest of Mexico's manufacturing sector.

A popular misconception about maquiladoras is that they produce only low-skill, labor-intensive goods. While this may have been true when the maquiladora zone was set up twenty years ago and the main activity was sewing garments, it is no longer the case. Today, apparel accounts for fewer than 10 percent of maquiladora workers; more than 40 percent work in electronics and 20 percent in transportation equipment.[9] Auto and electronics companies in particular have been increasingly willing to put sophisticated, state-of-the-art plants in Mexico, as skills, infrastructure, and corporate experience there have increased. In the future, we should expect Mexico's productive capabilities to continue to evolve and grow as they have done in the past.

Indeed, whatever advantages the U.S. economy received from the maquiladora system will disappear with the adoption of NAFTA. The U.S. tax code created an artificial incentive for maquiladora assembly plants to purchase U.S. components, so long as their products were exported to the United States.[10] With NAFTA, the maquiladoras will no longer be required to buy components in the United States in order to obtain duty-free access to the U.S. market.

Moreover, maquiladoras will no longer be required to export the goods they produce, as they are under current Mexican law. If maquiladora production for the Mexican market increases substantially, it could cut into the market for American-made goods that proponents of NAFTA predict will expand. Without a large jump in U.S. exports to Mexico as a result of the

FTA, even the fairly small employment gains forecast by the Bush administration's models will fail to materialize.

The real advantage of producing in the maquiladora zone in the 1980s lay not in avoiding tariffs, but in taking advantage of ultracheap wages and lax labor and environmental standards. Also, restrictive Mexican regulations on foreign investment did not apply to the maquiladora sector. Wages in the maquiladora sector are approximately one-fourteenth of U.S. manufacturing wages, and the Mexican government has lacked both the resources and the will to enforce even basic worker-safety provisions or environmental regulations.

Although the Mexican government has proclaimed its commitment to strengthening environmental and worker protection, it seems unlikely that under current political circumstances changes will go deep enough to close the yawning chasm between the two countries in these arenas. Indeed, whatever progress has been made so far, such as the highly publicized closing of the port of Veracruz, is a result of personal pressure from Salinas. He is engaged in a transparent campaign to win ratification for the trade agreement from the U.S. Congress. There is no serious independent political force in Mexico to maintain such pressure once the treaty is ratified. Thus, it is likely that the political factors attracting U.S. investment to the maquiladora zone during the past ten or twenty years will continue to play a role, and perhaps an increasingly important one, in the post-NAFTA business climate.

NAFTA is likely to make Mexico a more attractive prospect for foreign investment, both from the United States and elsewhere for several reasons. First, it will guarantee firms secure and permanent access to U.S. and Canadian markets. Even though most of the tariffs between the United States and Mexico have been removed or reduced since Mexico joined GATT in 1986, many nontariff barriers remain. NAFTA would likely eliminate most of these, including the Multi-Fiber Arrangement, which sets quotas for textiles and apparel.

Second, in the past multinational corporations have been reluctant to make the massive long-term investment in plant and equipment needed to take full advantage of cheaper costs in Mexico because of concern over the political climate. Specifically, they fear a return of popular hostility to foreign investment and the threat of nationalization. NAFTA would put the rights of foreign investors into an international treaty that future Mexican governments would find difficult or impossible to change. The International Trade Commission report notes that "By codifying liberal trade and investment policies in an international agreement, . . . a United States-Mexico FTA would increase the confidence of investors in Mexico's economy."[11] Thus, the attraction of Mexico for U.S. manufacturers is not Mexico's small consumer economy; it is the labor force of almost 30 million willing to work for a tiny fraction of U.S. wages.

Contrary to the assertions in former President Bush's May 1 submission to Congress, the wage differentials between the United States and Mexico are not due to productivity differentials between the two countries. Harley Shaiken, of the University of California at San Diego, found that though a Mexican Ford engine plant was 80 percent as efficient as a U.S. plant, workers were paid only 6 percent of U.S. wages.[12] Similar wage-productivity gaps have been found in other industries, such as telecommunications, as well.[13]

Nor are these wage gaps necessarily likely to narrow in the near future with or without a free trade agreement. At a business briefing session in Los Angeles in October 1990, Commerce Secretary Mosbacher distributed materials forecasting an increase in the "gap between the U.S. minimum wage and the Mexican direct wage . . . as labor shortages in the U.S. increase demand."[14]

In addition to guaranteeing access to U.S. and Canadian markets, NAFTA may also encourage investment by removing Mexico's remaining investment regulations in critical areas such as oil, for example, and regularizing Mexico's intellectual property laws. Reform of Mexico's intellectual property laws was a key demand of the U.S. business community during the early stages of negotiation. American firms have complained that Mexico's past failure to protect patents and copyrights has deterred investment there, especially by pharmaceutical and computer software companies who feared "knockoffs" and piracy by Mexican firms.[15] After fast track passed in the United States, Mexican lawmakers did in fact enact more stringent patent and copyright laws. Cuauhtémoc Cárdenas's opposition party, the Democratic Revolutionary party (PRD), criticized both the patent/trademark and copyright laws because they would raise prices, especially for the poor, who have benefited in the past from the relatively low price of medicine.

The pressure from the U.S. business community on Mexico to amend its unacceptably weak intellectual property laws highlights the hypocrisy underlying the debate over NAFTA. Congressman Ron Wyden (D-Oreg.) wrote to Kay Whitmore of the Business Roundtable: "The contradiction I see that greatly concerns me is that, while the Roundtable believes that the United States should require Mexico to raise its standards on intellectual property and investment to our level, I have been told that it does not believe that Mexico and the United States should raise their standards on environmental and labor safety to the higher level in either country. I do not understand the rationale for that distinction."

Unfortunately, the rationale is fairly simple: as it stands, the agreement's purpose is to facilitate the mobility of capital while deliberately preserving the relative immobility of labor. U.S., Mexican, and Canadian workers will be thrown into competition with each other to attract investment by offering the lowest wages and the least restrictive regulations. The threat of moving

production abroad is already a weapon many businesses can use to oppose
wage demands, environmental restrictions, higher corporate taxes, or stricter
health and safety regulations.

Zenith Electronics Corps. announced in October 1991 that it will move
the remainder of its television assembly operations to Mexico, resulting in
the loss of about 1,200 jobs in Springfield, Missouri. Zenith is the last major
American-owned maker of color televisions.[16] It will join the other 1,800
firms, most of which are U.S.-owned, currently producing in Mexico's maquiladora sector.

MEASURING THE EFFECT OF CAPITAL FLOWS ON JOB LOSS

The conventional studies that have attempted to quantify NAFTA's impact
on the U.S. economy have claimed that it is impossible to know how much
capital will flow from the United States to Mexico after NAFTA is signed.
The ITC asserts, for example, that the competitive strategy (for locating
plants) of the Big Three automakers is "unknown" and "difficult to assess."[17]
Rather than attempting to resolve this issue in order to come up with an
accurate estimate, however, the ITC study simply assumes that *no* capital
will flow. The other studies reflect similarly bizarre methodologies.

Estimating the magnitude of capital flows is no more inherently problematic than estimating migration flows or sectoral shifts. Three recent studies
have estimated the impact on the domestic labor market of a shift of investment from the United States to Mexico, employing different methodologies. Their results give a range of estimates that expand the limits of
the debate.

An EPI briefing paper reported the dramatic results of modifying one
standard computable general equilibrium model of U.S.-Mexican relations
to allow for a modest shift of capital between the United States and Mexico.
The analysis, by economists Raul Hinojosa and Robert McCleery, involved
reducing the risk premium for U.S. firms investing in Mexico. Free trade
was modeled as an elimination of tariffs between the two countries over ten
years beginning in 1992. The differential in returns to capital between the
United States and Mexico was allowed to fall by 2 percent the first year of
the agreement, and 1 percent each additional year until the year 2000, for
a 10 percent overall decline in the risk premium.

This scenario results in a movement of $44 billion in capital from the
United States to Mexico over the decade. As a consequence, during the first
ten years of the agreement 550,000 fewer high-wage jobs are created in the
United States than would have been the case in the absence of the agreement, and the U.S. gross domestic product falls by $36 billion relative to
the no-FTA scenario. Because the model assumes full employment, these
workers do get jobs, but they take a 50 percent wage cut. Some of this

employment-shifting effect is due to reduced immigration from Mexico, since the model finds that real wages in Mexico rise as a result of the increased investment.

James Cypher, in a report he is preparing for EPI, estimates that 358,000 U.S. jobs will move to Mexico over the next five years as a result of investment shifts brought about by NAFTA. Cypher assumes that Salinas will achieve his stated goal of $6 billion foreign direct investment a year (compared to the present level of $2.6 billion). Although it is not automatically true that direct foreign investment will in fact rise to $6 billion, as Salinas would like, if it *does not* rise by that amount, Salinas may be forced to devalue the peso substantially in order to keep making payments on the debt. A devaluation would further increase the gap between U.S. and Mexican wages. Of the increase in foreign direct investment, Cypher assumes that 63 percent comes from the United States, with the rest coming from other countries (preserving the current ratio). Cypher nets out the increase in capital goods exported from the United States to Mexico in order to come up with his final figure.

Economists Sam Bowles, Gerald Epstein, Timothy Koechlin, and Mehrene Larudee have also developed an estimate of job displacement, using a similar method. They find that 290,000 to 490,000 U.S. jobs will be lost over the next ten years, as U.S. and foreign investors build new capacity in Mexico, rather than in the United States, attracted by improved access to the U.S. market and a more stable investment climate in Mexico. They base their estimate on historical examples of the increases in U.S. direct foreign investment that took place when Ireland and Spain joined the European Community. Koechlin argues that there are parallels to be drawn between Ireland's joining the European Economic Community and Mexico joining the North American free trade area. Since both are relatively low wage areas and both joined markets many times their size, it is plausible that U.S. investment in Mexico will also take off as a result of its joining the much larger U.S. market.[18]

All the above models assume that increased investment in Mexico directly reduces investment in the United States by an equivalent amount. Critics say this new investment in Mexico would otherwise have gone to Asia, not to the United States. The critics are not on strong ground. First, Mexican wages are even lower than wages in the Asian newly industrializing countries, yet productivity is comparable in many sectors. Second, some foreign investors who—in the absence of a free trade agreement—would have invested in the United States in order to sell in the U.S. market may now choose to invest in Mexico. The other NICs cannot offer equivalent access to the big U.S. and Canadian markets that Mexico can offer. This further reduces investment in the United States beyond what these models have accounted for. Third, the supposed advantage to the United States of capital moving to Mexico instead of to Asia is that Mexicans buy more U.S. goods, and

Mexican-based firms buy more U.S. capital goods and components than do Asian firms. But Mexican consumers' buying power is tiny relative to the U.S. market, and—absent strict rules of origin in the final agreement—there is no guarantee that Mexican-based firms will not buy Asian components.

Another danger of a laissez-faire agreement is that Mexico may become an export platform from which European or Asian firms can produce for the U.S. market. While the U.S. business and labor communities are in agreement that NAFTA should include some rules of origin limiting trade concessions to products with a set percentage of North American components, Salinas seems less willing to limit his options. Mexico needs to attract as much foreign capital as possible in order to repay its debt; it is not in Mexico's interest to keep out willing investors. In fact, press reports from the first few NAFTA sessions identify rules of origin as a sticking point in the negotiations. Meanwhile, Nissan Mexico has announced plans to more than double its investment in Mexico with a new $1 billion state-of-the-art plant in Aguascalientes all the while protesting that doing business in Mexico is vastly overrated.[19]

A SOCIAL CONTRACT FOR NORTH AMERICA?

The central economic objection to the laissez-faire NAFTA is that it provides an incentive for U.S. producers to respond to market competition with a low-wage strategy, which will lower incomes and productivity over the long run, rather than the more difficult path of producing quality products more efficiently. This concern is serious enough to justify rejecting the treaty. Overcoming this objection will require a significant redirection of U.S. labor market and industrial policies.

One of the conceptual problems in the NAFTA debate has been the assumption on the part of NAFTA proponents that the benefits of the agreement will be permanent, while the costs will occur only once. This betrays a misunderstanding both of NAFTA itself and of its place in the long-term strategy of the United States. Whether we choose to see NAFTA as an event or a process will also influence the social and labor adjustment policies we think will be needed to accompany it.

Clearly, it was the intention of the Bush-Salinas-Mulroney strategy that NAFTA would be a dynamic, ongoing process, not a one-time event. Mexico has already climbed several rungs up the production ladder since the maquiladora program got started. If our economies are going to be tightly linked for the indefinite future, it makes more sense to consider what their industry, infrastructure, and workforce will look like in ten years, rather than to dismiss Mexico's productive potential on the basis of its current abilities.

Mexico's labor force is currently growing at a rate of one million per year, while only about three-hundred thousand to four-hundred thousand jobs per year are being created in the formal economy.[20] Even at an extremely high rate of future growth of 5 or 6 percent, the Mexican economy will not be able to generate enough jobs to reduce unemployment significantly from its current rate of about 20 percent.

Until Mexico has more meaningful democratic institutions and strong and independent labor unions, we cannot assume that wages will rise to reflect productivity gains. Protections against environmental exploitation and labor abuse in America are not achieved simply by the laws enacted by government, but by the strength of independent institutions, such as environmental organizations, civil rights groups, and labor unions. Their ability to monitor, to expose, to sue in court, and to defeat candidates who are indifferent to their concerns is the rock upon which such protections are founded. Mexico's one-party system, with its interconnections among business, labor, and political institutions, does not yet provide the culture to nurture the necessary independent advocacy, membership, and pressure groups.[21]

After taking power in a heavily contested and hotly disputed election in 1988, Salinas had every reason to want Mexico's federal elections to appear above reproach. Nonetheless, both Mexican and international journalists criticized polling irregularities and some abuse of the power of incumbency by the ruling Institutional Revolutionary party (PRI) in the August 1991 elections. The PRI swept the congressional elections and won all six governorships. Yet mass protests forced Salinas to cede the statehouses in Guanajuato and San Luis Potosí to opposition candidates after the election. He did so, however, without admitting that irregularities had occurred—an action that only reinforced the PRI's image as arbitrary and high-handed.[22]

Of additional concern was former President Bush's clear indication that the implementation of a free trade agreement with Mexico is only the first step toward developing similar agreements with other Latin American countries. Indeed, such discussions are already taking place under the rubric of the Enterprise for the Americas Initiative, which would promote trade and investment, eventually culminating in the "designation of a hemispheric free-trade zone." It would include some debt reduction, as in the Brady plan, in exchange for agreements by participating countries to "pursue viable economic reform programs and regularize their external financial obligations."

If this longer-term plan is undertaken, the employment issues raised in the U.S.-Mexican context will be magnified many times by the incorporation into a free-trade bloc of countries more similar to Mexico than to the United States. The U.S. economy may take decades to absorb the impact of formal integration with the economies of the entire western hemisphere. Thus, policies that go far beyond the limited and inadequately funded trade adjustment programs of the past will be needed.

Unprecedented and rapid moves toward global integration of the U.S. economy call for unprecedented changes in labor-market policies. If NAFTA is to have any chance of working for the benefit of U.S., Canadian, and

Mexican workers, it will have to incorporate a Social Dimension, similar to that embodied in the European Community's progress toward integration. The Social Dimensions has two aspects: (1) the Social Charter, which establishes the principle that trade should not be based on "social dumping," where poorer countries follow low-wage, low-regulation strategies in order to increase exports; and (2) the Structural Funds, which help redistribute resources within the Community to poorer countries, regions, and disadvantaged groups. The Structural Funds in turn are made up of two components: the regional fund, which provides financing to help narrow the gap between the levels of infrastructure in the poorer and the more developed EC countries;[23] and the social fund, which is used to address problems of long-term or youth unemployment at the level of the individual firm or industry. Employee and employer organizations can apply for these funds when they need financing for a specified project.

The German Trade Union Confederation vice president has warned that "In the absence of 'social rules of the game,' the battle of [European] Community-wide competition would be fought on the backs of the workers." This principle has not yet been accepted in the United States.[24]

The U.S. ideological commitment to free trade has translated into a presumption that free trade alone is sufficient to raise incomes and employment levels. Proponents argue that the best way to end child labor and environmental degradation in Mexico is to pass a free trade agreement. They reason that the higher incomes associated with freer trade will automatically allow stricter regulation and enforcement of environmental and labor standards. But this confuses correlation with causality. Higher incomes may be a necessary, but not sufficient, precondition for keeping children out of factories and the air we breathe clean. Democracy and citizen input into the government decision-making process is also crucial, and at the moment, these are lacking in Mexico.

The European attitude toward free trade, in contrast, is more pragmatic. If ending child labor is the goal, the Europeans are not content with enacting a broad free trade agreement and then sitting back for a few decades waiting for it to work. They have written specific standards into EC-wide law in the areas of greatest concern.

Existing European law in the areas of health care, child development, worker training, and adjustment assistance is much more extensive than comparable U.S. laws even before the Social Charter is fully implemented. In the area of unemployment insurance, for example, France provides benefits equal to 50 percent of lost earnings for up to two years. Germany is even more generous, paying 66 percent of normal wages for up to eighteen months, and 58 percent for an unlimited time after that. In contrast, U.S. unemployment benefits average only one-third of lost pay, and in all but three states, benefits are exhausted after six months. U.S. government expenditures on worker retraining also lag behind those in France, Germany, and the United Kingdom. The United States spends only $1,800 per participant on training, while Germany spends four times that amount, on average.[25] This higher European baseline makes their task of adapting the economy to the needs of increased economic integration easier than ours.

To meet the challenge of increasing global economic integration—of which NAFTA is only one element—the United States must embark on a permanent and continuous upgrading of its labor force in conjunction with trade and industrial policies that provide support for high-wage job creation. Only if such policies become conscious national goals is there any realistic chance to build the ladder that will make the difference between displaced U.S. workers sliding downwards toward higher unemployment and lower-paying jobs or climbing up to the next rung.

Without a skilled, well-paid, and adaptable labor force, the United States will find it virtually impossible to compete in global markets for anything but standardized, mass-produced goods. The need to invest in the U.S. labor force goes beyond aid to workers displaced by trade. The United States should be looking to the future, and toward a whole new labor-market process that starts in childhood and extends beyond retirement. To this end, we should fully fund child health and nutrition programs, including WIC (Women, Infants, and Children Supplemental Food Program); restore funding to Head Start, whose effectiveness has been shown time and again; and fund long-term paid training programs for displaced workers. (If these training programs do not include income support, then only workers with private income sources can afford to take advantage of them.) Any trade adjustment assistance should also include a continuation of medical benefits for displaced workers, as well as a bridge benefit for workers within four years of retirement age.

One example of the broader vision necessary for the United States to absorb the shock of the free trade agreement can be found in the proposals outlined in *America's Choice: High Skills or Low Wages*, the 1990 report of the Commission on the Skills of the American Workforce, led by Ira Magaziner, William Brock, and Ray Marshall. The commission recommends giving all employers "incentives and assistance to invest in the further education and training of their workers and to pursue high productivity forms of work organization." In particular, employers would be required to spend at least 1 percent of their payroll on employee education and training programs, or to contribute the same amount to a state-administered general training fund. Public grants would be available to assist firms in moving to higher performance work organizations. The states would also be responsible, with federal assistance, for assuring that all students met a higher national standard of educational excellence by age sixteen. Local employment and training boards would create and fund alternative learning environments for students who were unable to meet that higher standard in regular schools. In order to help prepare non-college bound students for the workplace, the commission recommends creating a system of technical and professional certificates and associates' degrees to be earned through completion of two- or four-year courses of combined study and work, modeled on the formal apprenticeship programs in other countries.

Yet far from rising to meet the challenge of global competition, federal spending on education and training has fallen in the past fifteen years as a percentage of GNP. In 1976 the federal government spent 0.8 percent of GNP on education and training; by 1990 this figure was only 0.5 percent. This decrease in spending has real consequences for workers whose skills need upgrading: the primary federally supported training program, the Jobs Training and Partnership Act, currently serves only 6 percent of a narrowly defined eligible population.[26] During a period when the U.S. trade deficit increased nearly fivefold (from the late 1970s to the late 1980s), the Trade Adjustment Assistance Program reduced the number of applicants it served from 199,000 to 37,000. It now serves only one out of four eligible workers.[27]

Government, business, professional commissions, and other researchers have attempted to estimate how much money would be necessary in order to fully fund human resource investments, including education and training and some child health and nutrition programs. Their estimates range from $29 billion to $58 billion annually. The total investment gap—including physical capital and research and development in addition to human resources—ranges from $63 billion to $126 billion. Robert Heilbroner has argued that the United States needs to quadruple its expenditures on public investment just to catch up with our principal competitors, Germany and Japan.

Finally, the government needs to take some responsibility for targeted job creation. Training and educating workers is essential, but it does not guarantee that the jobs will be there when they are needed. Sheldon Friedman of the AFL-CIO advocates using economic conversion proposals, including planning grants and subsidized loans, to bolster employment in affected regions or localities. The government could also create jobs related to commercial technologies that meet national needs, such as mass transit/ high-speed rail or high-definition television.[28] There is also a place for the less glamorous jobs as well. Richard Rothstein has laid out the case that the apparel industry, for example, is critical to the economic health of the United States.[29]

A treaty should not be signed until the administration and Congress have agreed to a credible and comprehensive strategy for worker training and job creation—and are committed to fully funding such a strategy. The major provisions of a free trade agreement should not be implemented until such a system is in place. The onus is on those who advocate a North American free trade agreement to develop a plan for providing American workers with a ladder of upward mobility. They need to convince the rest of us why the pattern we have seen so often and so clearly in the past—of workers displaced by trade bearing most of the burden of adjustment—will not repeat itself in the future. And in this case, there is reason to believe that more than those individuals who actually lose their jobs as a result of trade and investment will suffer: every worker whose average wage is bid down by the threat of corporate mobility, every community whose environmental standards are weakened, and everyone whose community is disrupted by the large-scale loss of jobs will pay part of the price.

The principle underlying the EC's "activist labor-market policy" is that good trade adjustment policies are neither optional nor do they constitute "charity." By their nature, freer trade and investment flows cause disruption and dislocation, as economies adjust to new sources of production and attempt to find their niches. By easing the process of change, and by protecting workers from the worst effects of this disruption, adjustment policies make change possible.[30]

Over the long term, failure to invest in its workforce will disadvantage North American producers when competing with the Europeans and the Japanese in the production of customized, high-quality goods and services. At the same time, North American producers will be equally disadvantaged in competing with low-wage Asian producers in markets for standardized, price-competitive goods. The United States cannot win an international contest based on cutting wages—nor is it in its long-term interest to be a victor in such a contest.

MEXICO'S LADDER

Will a laissez-faire NAFTA help Mexico continue to grow and develop its economy? For Mexico, even more than for the United States and Canada, a free trade agreement can be one element of a development strategy, but it is far from sufficient.

The most important single action the United States could take to spur development in Mexico would be to relieve it of its crushing debt burden. But any hopes that NAFTA would achieve this were dashed when the negotiators announced that debt relief for Mexico was "off the table" from the beginning of the talks.

Short of debt relief, strict standards written into NAFTA itself can help assure that the agreement does not simply exploit Mexico's relative poverty. A coalition of labor, environmental, and development groups (the Mobilization on Development, Trade, Labor and the Environment) has formulated a set of criteria that provides a framework for a more enlightened approach to this critical question. Among others, the MODTLE criteria include:

1. Fair labor practice enforcement mechanism. The agreement must incorporate a mechanism whereby trade unions or individuals can challenge any infraction of

labor rights or workplace standards in export-producing industries, bringing such infractions to reasonably swift adjudication before an international body.

2. Enforcement of the rights of free association and collective bargaining.

3. Harmonization of workplace health and safety standards. Regional standards must in no case be lower than those in any of the three countries.

4. Social infrastructure investment. Companies that invest in each of the countries could contribute to a fund to support social infrastructure in the communities in which they operate, including medical care, community development, and education.

5. Environmental assessment of NAFTA's impact prior to and during its planning. This procedure would be carried out by each of the three governments and should be open to citizen input at every stage.

6. Preservation of strong environmental standards. Nothing in NAFTA should require or encourage state, local, or national governments to loosen restrictive environmental or consumer protection laws. The recent GATT ruling in Mexico's favor on the issue of dolphin-killing tuna fishing sets an ominous precedent for trade agreements to undermine progressive national legislation when that legislation restricts trade.

7. Prevention of environmental dumping. In order to prevent corporations from locating production where environmental regulations are weakest, a countervailing duty should be imposed on industries that do not meet pollution control standards in the countries to which they are exporting. The duty would be equivalent to the corporation's savings from noncompliance, thus eliminating the economic advantage of such behavior.

8. Commitment to internationally recognized human rights, with strengthened redress procedures. NAFTA signatories should agree to adhere to the American Declaration of the Rights of Man, the Charter of the Organization of American States, and the American Convention on Human Rights, if they have not already done so. Parties should recognize the jurisdiction of the Inter-American Court of Human Rights, in cases where national judicial procedures are questioned.

Electoral, political, social, and cultural rights should also be acknowledged as crucial to the success of a free trade agreement. Even if not included in the body of NAFTA, these rights could be ratified in a parallel trinational agreement.

It also seems important to explore the possibility of raising and enforcing the minimum wage in Mexico, perhaps as a condition of signing the agreement. The growing divergence in Mexico between productivity growth and real wage increases signals a market failure of some sort in that country, perhaps reflecting the political imbalance of power there or the downward pressure on wages from the large informal sector and the large numbers of underemployed workers. As Walter Russell Mead has argued, "low wages in developing countries contribute to a weakness of global demand and . . . this weakness in turn undermines political support for the multilateral free trade system."[31] A higher enforced minimum wage in Mexico that better reflected productivity growth would serve two purposes: it would give Mexican workers more purchasing power, so that Mexican growth did not have to rely solely on exports; and it would relieve some of the pressure on U.S. and Canadian workers to accept deep wage cuts.

NAFTA essentially amounts to a Social Contract among the governments of the United States, Canada, and Mexico. But until democracy in Mexico is strong enough and functional enough to give its citizens an effective voice in this process, we cannot be sure exactly whom we are signing this contract with, or whose interests it will serve. The EC waited until Spain and Portugal had established civilian democracies before allowing them to join the Common Market. We should give Mexico the same opportunity before rushing to link our economy, and by extension, our political system with theirs.

THE BOTTOM LINE

If the NAFTA cheerleaders are right, and incomes and employment levels rise in all three countries as a result of the agreement, then stringent standards and adjustment programs will be at worst an inconvenience. They also will not impede positive change. For example, if income growth in Mexico actually does lead firms to act more environmentally responsible, then they will not mind having to abide by stricter standards. And if few workers are displaced by the free trade agreement, then the training and adjustment program will not cost very much to run.

But if the cheerleaders are wrong, then their policy prescription—to barrel ahead with an "unencumbered" agreement and desultory adjustment assistance—could have disastrous short-term consequences for hundreds of thousands of U.S. working people and negative long-term effects on the nation's living standards and competitiveness.

NOTES

Different versions of this chapter have been published by the Economic Policy Institute, as a briefing paper entitled "The Effect of George Bush's NAFTA on American Workers: Ladder Up or Ladder Down?" July 1992; and by St. Martin's Press in a forthcoming edited volume.

1. Rudiger Dornbusch, "U.S.-Mexico Free Trade: Good Jobs at Good Wages," testimony before the Subcommittee on Labor-Management Relations and Employment Opportunities, Committee on Education and Labor, U.S. House of Representatives, Apr. 30, 1991.

2. Tabulations on BLS Displaced Workers Surveys by Michael Podgursky, University of Massachusetts at Amherst.

3. Displaced Workers, 1981–85, BLS Bulletin #2289, Sept. 1987, p. 3. The sample includes only those workers who had worked at their jobs for three or more years before being laid off due to plant closings or moves, slack work, or the abolishment of their positions or shifts.

4. As cited in James Cypher, "Confronting Globalization: The U.S.-Mexico Free Trade Agreement," manuscript, Aug. 1991, p. 78.

5. *New York Times*, Aug. 9,1991.

6. Bruce Campbell, *Canada Under Siege: Three Years into the Free Trade Era* (Ottawa, Ontario: Canadian Centre for Policy Alternatives, Jan. 1992).

7. *Canadian Dimension*, Jan.–Feb. 1991.

8. Steve Beckman, UAW economist, testimony before the Trade Policy Staff, Sept. 4, 1991.

9. Gregory K. Schoepfle, "U.S.-Mexico Free Trade Agreement: The Maquilazation of Mexico?" Bureau of International Labor Affairs, U.S. Department of Labor, Apr. 18, 1990.

10. U.S. tariff code item 807, now know as item 9802, grants items assembled abroad from U.S. components easier access to the U.S. market.

11. TC (1991), p. viii.

12. As cited in Walter Russell Mead, *The Low-Wage Challenge to Global Growth: The Labor Cost-Productivity Imbalance in Newly Industrialized Countries* (Washington, D.C.: Economic Policy Institute, 1991).

13. See Kim Moody and Mary McGinn, "From the Yukon to the Yucatan," *Dollars & Sense*, Nov. 1991, p. 12.

14. *A Partnership for Growth: Investing and Manufacturing in Mexico*, briefing book distributed by Commerce Department to U.S. business executives in Los Angeles, Oct. 26, 1990; see also "Fast Track-Fast Shuffle," p. 13.

15. *U.S.-Mexico Free Trade Reporter*, vol. 1, no. 2, July 12, 1991.

16. *Washington Post*, Oct. 30, 1991.

17. ITC (1991, pp. 4–18).

18. Timothy Koechlin and Mehrene Larudee, "The High Cost of NAFTA," *Challenge*, Sept./Oct. 1992.

19. "Nissan Plans $1B Plant," *Financial Times*, Oct. 25, 1991.

20. *Mexico: Trade and Industry Report*, Office of Trade and Initiatives, Trade Analysis Division, Nov. 1990, p. 9.

21. Faux and Rothstein, "Fast Track-Fast Shuffle."

22. "Mexico: Country Shifts Course," *Los Angeles Times*, Oct. 22, 1991, p. H2.

23. *New York Times*, Oct. 7, 1991.

24. Gerd Muhr, "1992: The Social Aspects," *Labour and Society*, vol. 15, no. 1, 1990.

25. "European Worker Benefits," *AFL-CIO Reviews the Issues*, Report No. 55, Sept. 1991.

26. Jeff Faux and Todd Schafer, "Increasing Public Investment: New Budget Priorities for Economic Growth in the Post-Cold War World," Washington, D.C., Economic Policy Institute, 1991.

27. Sheldon Friedman, "Trade Adjustment Assistance: Time for Action, Not False Promises," *AFL-CIO Reviews the Issues*, Report No. 53, Sept. 1991.

28. Friedman (Sept. 1991); Robert B. Cohen and Kenneth Donow, *Telecommunications Policy, High Definition Television, and U.S. Competitiveness*, EPI, 1989; Susan Walsh Sanderson, *The Consumer Electronics Industry and the Future of American Manufacturing*, EPI, 1989.

29. Richard Rothstein, Keeping Jobs in Fashion: Alternatives to the Euthanasia of the U.S. Apparel Industry, EPI, 1989.

30. Doreen Collins, *The Operation of the European Social Fund* (London: Croom Helm, 1983), p. 3.

31. Mead (1991, p. 37).

9

Impact of the Potential Free Trade Agreement Between the United States and Mexico on Collective Bargaining from the Point of View of U.S. Companies

Manfred Fiedler

There are significant differences between U.S. and Mexican labor laws, in relation to blue-collar as well as white-collar employees. Mexican labor laws are generally tailored to protect the employee from the employer. The employee is traditionally perceived as the weaker of the two labor relation partners. Therefore, the employee is seen as vulnerable and in need of protection. This perception is fully shared by the Mexican administration.

In this respect Mexican labor laws raise some critical issues regarding a potential free trade agreement. First, there is a certain lack of flexibility. Mexican labor laws reflect a bureaucratic and traditional attitude in labor relations. There are only certain specific ways to negotiate with unions. Once an agreement has been reached it is binding, and nobody can change or adjust this agreement, even when the situation on which it was based has completely changed. In a modern economy, more flexibility is absolutely critical. Second, Mexican labor laws are very supportive of employees. This aspect is, at times, overemphasized. Especially when you want to terminate an employee or even go out of business, the law kicks in with some drastic regulations in terms of what is requested as severance pay or service pay. Such payments can have a devastating effect on any employer. The Mexican authorities have acknowledged that such populist regulations are hardly favorable for attracting investors. It also has a negative impact on competitiveness, because this kind of protection creates economic complacency. Therefore, we see a certain tendency in the attitude of the administration and even also on the part of the unions to apply more moderate rules.

The normal wage negotiations process with the union in Mexico consists of the following basic steps:

- The Collective Labor Union advises the employer that maturity of the labor contract is coming to the revision process (usually thirty days' advance notice, at a minimum).
- Advance notice includes a clause with a firm date for going on strike, if the revision or negotiation process fails to reach an agreement by both parties.
- The requested new conditions are negotiated (usually, wage increases once a year and increases in other benefits *[prestaciones]* once every two years). This negotiation requires participation of the employer's representative, union representative, and workmen representatives, as well as employer's law counselor, workmen's counselor, and representative of Mexican labor authorities.
- Upon agreement, a document signed by all participants is issued and then registered and authenticized at the Mexican Department of Labor. A copy of the authorized document goes to the employer.

It is not a very sophisticated process, but it determines very clearly what both sides are supposed to do. Representative of all parties concerned are involved, even a representative from the Mexican labor authorities. It is a rather large community and this seems to make it more time-consuming to reach consensus. But, once you come to an agreement everybody accepts that result and there is no doubt about what has been agreed upon.

Larger industries, like oil refinery (Pemex), power generation (CFE), sugar refining, and steel, arrive at *country-wide* agreements that include a mix of wage increases and other compensation usually every year. Negotiations are held at the headquarters of a participating company or the association of major employers.

Usually, benefits obtained by such collective bargaining are higher than those obtained by individual companies. Since the companies are generally quite large and economically influential, they tend to establish trustful relations to the unions and can afford to pay slightly higher wages that will retain their skilled workforce.

What are the experiences of U.S. companies currently operating manufacturing plants (maquiladoras) in Mexico? Since Mexican labor is comparatively inexpensive, U.S. companies generally offer better wages and overall compensation as comparable local peer companies. They tend to conform with Mexican labor laws and practices and entertain positive relations with the unions. Even for the Japanese, Mexican labor offers an attractive cost advantage. Foreign companies, in general, have learned to value the positive aspects of cooperative labor relations. Under such circumstances the employees do not see any need for being unionized.[1] The experience gained in the maquiladoras has shown that Mexican labor laws do not have the negative impact that was perceived at first, and U.S. companies have adjusted well to it.

The situation in Mexico is changing; the new government wants to become internationally competitive. With or without the free trade agreement there will be some reforms and a modernization of Mexican labor laws. Already in 1987 some new regulations were introduced to support and promote efficiency, quality, and productivity. But there is no doubt NAFTA will expedite the development and generate a positive effect in terms of labor relations. While it is always difficult to predict results in the future, NAFTA should have a harmonizing effect on the labor relation practices of both countries. Since collective bargaining has proven to be less controversial in Mexican than individual negotiations, this cooperative method to reach labor agreements might receive increasing consideration also in the United States. The overall attitude will focus on achieving balanced results for both sides. As a result, the relations between employers and the unions will become less stringent by mutual respect. Such an environment might lead to having the unions assume a different macroeconomic role and consequently a change in the perception of the employers as a "kind of an enemy."

SUMMARY

- Mexico will establish labor rules that promote the principle of pay for productivity and performance and that are easy to adopt by foreign enterprises operating plants in the country.
- The potential foreign trade agreement between the United States and Mexico will strongly support a gradual homologation between the labor laws in both countries.
- Collective bargaining will potentially gain momentum also in the United States as a proven means to establish improved labor relations.

APPENDIX 9.1

Ten Recommendations for Dealing with Unions in Mexico

1. Keep all negotiations courteous and friendly.
2. Always remember that a union is only as strong as the workers behind it.
3. Do not underestimate competence.
4. Be informed; do not let the union surprise you.
5. Double check facts before making any statements.
6. Remember that a union is always a negotiation partner; do not think of it as a "good" or "bad" union.
7. Never lose your temper with union leaders or with representatives of the union (culturally seen as weakness).
8. Do not let your pride get in the way.
9. Always seek local legal counsel.
10. Only what you have in writing can be assumed to be binding.

NOTE

1. In case of unionized plants in Mexico, see recommendations for negotiations in Appendix 9.1.

10

Free Trade, Globalization, and U.S. Labor: What Are the Long-Run Dynamics?

William C. Gruben

Two of the most significant chapters on the North American Free Trade Agreement in this volume, those by Robert Z. Lawrence and by Jeff Faux and Thea Lee, contradict each other. Is one or the other correct? The purpose of this chapter is to explain how both Lawrence and Faux and Lee miss one of the most important lessons we can learn from the events that have led to NAFTA, because both authors take too narrow a perspective.

Although Lawrence concentrates on the manufacturing sector, he more generally argues that the effect of the North American Free Trade Agreement on the United States will be small, and that Mexico has already liberalized its trade more substantially than it will further under NAFTA. This argument has much to recommend it. The United States is already open to Mexico through the maquiladora program and the Generalized System of Preferences. Moreover, Mexico has already liberalized its foreign investment laws. Lawrence argues that the real function of NAFTA is simply to make credible Mexico's policy changes by nailing them into an international accord.

Faux and Lee respond by noting that other studies show much stronger effects when they fully consider the influences of investment in Mexico. Perhaps they are correct, but there are reasons to wonder how strong their case is. For example, one of the studies Faux and Lee use to argue their case was performed by Hinojosa-Ojeda and McCleery (1991). In a subsequent study, however, Hinojosa-Ojeda and Robinson (1991) offer scenarios under which NAFTA may have a rather small effect.[1] Moreover, in a later paper (Hinojosa and Robinson, 1992) these authors find considerable fault with the very work that Faux and Lee extol, including that of Faux.[2] But if the agreement will, in fact, have a small effect then does this collection of essays really have a purpose?[3]

In fact, most analysts do think NAFTA will make some differences. Lawrence thinks it will increase U.S. sales of investment goods. Faux and Lee think it means a massive shift of physical capital investment from the United States to Mexico.[4]

I argue not only that Lawrence, and Faux and Lee have missed the most important lessons of NAFTA, but that they missed them by focusing on manufacturing and by taking too short-sighted a perspective. Of course, the short and middle run are important. Those are the runs that occupy us most in our daily lives. But it is at least as important to address broader and longer-term issues.

A consideration of the short- and medium-run effects of NAFTA have important implications for long-run changes in the global economy—and for what those changes mean to American workers. First, the U.S. industries that will benefit most from NAFTA in the short and medium run tend to use most intensely the types of inputs that the United States has in most abundance—that is, physical capital (plant and equipment) and human capital (a high-skilled labor force). That is why virtually every econometric model that studies industry impacts finds that the chemical industry and the plastics industry will benefit.[5] Those are capital-intensive industries. Most studies find that the instruments and machinery industries, and business services, benefit, which are high-skill and labor-intensive.

Conversely, the largest forecasted U.S. decreases in employment—as a result of NAFTA—tend to be concentrated in industries in which job skill requirements are low or in which production requires low concentrations of capital. Those are the areas where Mexico can compete right now. The other general class of industries that will lose employment are those that are heavily protected and whose products are sold at artificially high prices in the United States compared to the world price.

Among the most widely agreed upon U.S. losers from NAFTA is apparel. This industry uses low-skilled labor and benefits from high trade protection. So does footwear, another anticipated loser.

A consideration of occupational or job categories tells a similar story. Many types of high-skill employment are estimated to increase, while some less-skilled jobs are likely to disappear. According to some estimates, U.S. engineers and engineering and science-related technical workers will gain employment. Jobs in metal-working and machine-building occupations will increase.

Here we have consistency with Lawrence's capital-exporting story. Meanwhile, the decline in the apparel industry motivates a reduction in jobs from sewers and stitchers. It is interesting that this latter category of jobs has been shrinking even without the North American Free Trade Agreement. This detail brings me to my principal theme, which is long-run dynamics.

Despite my criticism of the Lawrence, and Faux and Lee chapters, I want to begin with an issue that was raised in them. But I then want to add a twist to it. The issue is the product cycle. Recall that the idea of the product cycle is that different skill levels are required to produce a good at different stages of its market life. When a product is first invented, bugs have to be worked out. At that time, and for some time thereafter, high-skilled labor may be required to produce this good or service. But after a while, the production process will turn it into a routine. The production process is deskilled. That is, it can now be performed by lower-skilled laborers.

In the United States, this process used to involve development in the Northeast because that is where the high-skilled labor was. Once the routine was established, businessmen moved the plant to the South, where the workers did not have many skills. But, for what the company now wanted workers to do, they did not need many skills. Moreover, wages were low in the South.

When we think of deskilling and of product cycles, it is common to think of assembly operations, or of cutting and sewing. But in the second half of the twentieth century, deskilling is not limited to assembly. For example, in the early 1960s virtually all computer programming was a highly complex task because programmers had to write code that could be directly understood by the computer. Now, with the development of a plethora of computing languages and compilers, teenagers who have not yet graduated from high school, and some children in elementary school, can program computers. It is not for nothing that, even as early as the 1970s, there appeared in wide use a programming language with the appropriate name of *Basic*.

What do these claims have to do with my quibble about the Lawrence and the Faux and Lee chapters? To answer this question, consider the principal concerns expressed in this volume. Among the phenomena mentioned in other chapters are maquiladoras. Authors of chapters in this volume are concerned that Japanese and other foreign companies will use Mexico as a back door to get their products into the United States. The problem, for U.S. workers, of cheap labor in Mexico has been raised. Behind all of these issues is a phenomenon that has been on the rise for the past twenty-five years—the globalization of manufacturing. That is, production sharing.

Recall the details of this phenomenon. U.S. firms or Japanese firms or European firms manufacture some components of a product in their home countries. But other components of the same product can be produced more cheaply in Singapore, so these companies make them there. Some components can be made more cheaply in Korea, so they make those parts there. Mexico finds its way into the process as well.

Why can these companies production share so much more now than, say, in the 1950s? Part of the reason involves a decline in shipping costs per unit. Part of the reason involves declines in the costs of communication. But one of the other large parts is the accelerated process of deskilling.

These points bring us to a second issue. While part of the explanation for the globalization of manufacturing involves deskilling, that is clearly not the only reason why manufacturing has globalized. To address another, as yet undiscovered cause of this phenomenon, it is useful to offer another anecdote.

Texas Instruments is a multinational company whose products involve extremely high levels of technology. Texas Instruments operates in a highly competitive environment, so the company is motivated to get its high-tech work done on the cheap. Texas Instruments discovered a highly skilled labor force that would work for much less than high-skilled workers in the United States usually will. In India, there are computer programmers and systems analysts with advanced degrees whose skills are underutilized in that country. So Texas Instruments hired such people in India, has them do their work there, and then beams the work back to Dallas.

The foregoing descriptions of globalization raise at least two issues. The first is that less developed countries, where wages are low, are increasingly able to do work formerly done in developed countries because of the increasing perfection of the process of deskilling. Second, these countries in many cases have upgraded their skill levels. This means that, with a given level of demand for workers with a given high level of education, the return to that level of education is going down because there are more people who have it.

I noted that I would add a twist to the traditional product cycle story, and it is at this point that I shall make the twist. To make it, I shall offer another anecdote. A recent article by management consultant Peter F. Drucker (1991) addresses a new long-term strategy—a collective strategy of Japanese corporations. The basis for this strategy is that—because of factors like those I have discussed—the return that future Japanese workers are likely to derive from working in manufacturing production is not consistent with the expenditures the Japanese are making on their educational system. Only more highly skilled work than is likely to take place in such production would be consistent with such high educational spending. The Japanese do not want to reduce spending on education.

The Japanese solution—and this is the twist I said I would add—is to get Japan ultimately out of manufacturing. There will still be Japanese manufacturing companies, but their production operations will not be in Japan. The return to education will not be enough. The Japanese will leave manufacturing production to Thailand, Singapore, and other developing countries.

This anecdote brings me back to my argument that the Lawrence, and Faux and Lee, articles are too narrowly focused on manufacturing and do not sufficiently consider the long run. The history of the United States in the twentieth century is a history of shifts in labor demand. Above all, it is a history of shifts from work in goods-producing industries to work in the service-producing sector. That is the sector in which—despite their expressed concerns about manufacturing—Lawrence, Faux and Lee, happen to work.

The first such shift was out of agriculture. Technology shocks in agriculture made farmers so productive that there was no need for so many of them. After all, people can eat only so much. This increased productivity also held down the cost of agricultural products, so people could now spend their incomes on other things. The other things they spent their incomes on included services. And workers who once would have been farmers went into the service-producing industries (Phillips and Fox, 1992).

The next shift also involved technological shocks. But this time, the share of employment in manufacturing fell because of technology shocks. While I was earlier discussing agriculture, and I am now addressing manufacturing, the story is similar. Labor productivity in manufacturing rose more rapidly than product demand, so manufacturing's share of the workforce fell while the service-producing sector's share rose.

If these long-term patterns of labor demand-change continue, a consideration of them yields conclusions and policy implications that differ not only from what Lawrence, and Faux and Lee focus upon, but the overall focus of this volume. It is to these conclusions and implications that I now turn.

CONCLUSIONS AND IMPLICATIONS

A great deal of what has been addressed at this conference involves what we are going to do to keep American workers in manufacturing. But the same factors that have led to the globalization of production—lower shipping costs per unit, cheaper and easier communication, deskilling, rising educational levels in some developing countries—are unlikely to abate. Technological change is behind these factors, and there is no hint that we are likely to see any less of it in the future. International competition in manufacturing is going to intensify. Moreover, the history of manufacturing is a history of technological advance that has lowered the relative share of labor in manufacturing. It is important to note that this is not simply a U.S. phenomenon. It is a world phenomenon. The largest increases in labor demand are in service-producing industries, not goods-production industries. While a principal question addressed in this volume involves what we are going to do to keep American workers in manufacturing, the more important question is what are we going to do so that they can get out of it?

NOTES

Opinions expressed in this chapter do not reflect the opinions or positions of the Federal Reserve Bank of Dallas or of the Federal Reserve System.

1. Hinojosa-Ojeda (the same author cited by Faux) and Robinson (1991) state that "The short-term downside economic risk for the U.S. is very small since our empirical results indicate that the impact of the creation of an FTA on the U.S. economy, assuming no other changes in Mexico, is tiny. In the longer run, however, if Mexico fails to achieve a transition to an open development strategy, the economic risks for the U.S. are greater." It is useful to recall that Mexico has already liberalized its investment laws.

2. Hinojosa-Ojeda and Robinson (1992) criticize models advocated by Faux and Lee, in part, because such models offer the following questionable chain of causation. (1) NAFTA will stimulate increased foreign investment in Mexico; (2) much of the increased investment will come from the United States; (3) increased U.S. investment in Mexico will reduce aggregate investment in the United States; (4) given fixed U.S. capital-labor ratios, the fall in U.S. investments will lead to a decline in aggregate employment. Hinojosa-Ojeda and Robinson note that "whereas steps 1 and 2 . . . seem plausible, steps 3 and 4 are highly questionable." They argue that such models' typical estimates of U.S. investment in Mexico due to NAFTA ($3 billion to $6 billion) are a "tiny fraction of aggregate U.S. investment and even a small fraction of the current U.S. trade deficit" (Hinojosa-Ojeda and Robinson, 1992; 85). More to the point, they note, these changes are tiny compared with likely macroeconomic adjustments in the United States over the next decade. Additionally, Hinojosa-Ojeda and Robinson argue that "the changes in U.S. investment in Mexico postulated by Koechlein and others represent a tiny part of the U.S. capital market and should have a negligible effect on interest rates or returns to capital in the United States. There is no theoretical or empirical reason to think that these investment changes will have any effect at all on aggregate investment. In fact, EC experience after Spanish and Irish accession suggests that NAFTA should increase direct foreign investment into the United States" (Hinojosa-Ojeda and Robinson, 1992; 85). Additionally, Hinojosa-Ojeda and Robinson (1992) offer reasons why such models' typical assumption of a fixed aggregate capital-labor ratio is suspicious in the short run and unsupportable in the long run. They argue that "Even though changes in the sectoral structure of employment are to be expected as a result of changes in trade and investment policy, the argument . . . that, in the aggregate, jobs will 'relocate' from the United States to Mexico with an increase in commodity trade and investment flows is theoretically and empirically unsustainable" (Hinojosa-Ojeda and Robinson, 1992: 85). In sum, Hinojosa-Ojeda and Robinson suggest that the work that Faux and Lee extol suffers from at least as many faults as those they criticize.

3. Even if the net impact of NAFTA proves positive for U.S. employment, as a number of studies suggest it will, there is evidence that any long-lived redistribution of labor demand may temporarily raise the natural rate of unemployment. That is, an expansion in U.S. employment due to NAFTA may still result in a temporary increase in the unemployment rate during the time it takes for workers to move from shrinking to expanding industries. See Loungani, Rush, and Tave (1990) and Loungani and Rogerson (1989).

4. For a further development of these arguments, see Chapter 7. However, Meade (1991) notes that "some business organizations have noted that the relaxation of Mexican laws on foreign investment may do little more than divert U.S. direct investment abroad from other low-wage developing countries (particularly Asia) to

Mexico." Gruben (1990a, 1990b) offers some indirect evidence to suggest that this argument is partially but not totally correct.

5. For a list of papers containing such models, see the references. In this context, it is interesting to note that a study by Brown, Deardorff, and Stern (1991) shows that, because of the degree to which NAFTA improves the United States' terms of trade, it increases the inflation-adjusted return to labor by 0.2 percent, even though trade liberalization reduces the protection of labor. In the same model, Canada's terms of trade decline slightly.

REFERENCES

Almon, Klopper, et al. "Industrial Effects of a Free Trade Agreement Between Mexico and the USA." Prepared by the Interindustry Economic Research Fund for the United States Department of Labor, NTIS Accession Number PB 91–110627. Sept. 1990.

Brown, Drusilla K., Alan V. Deardorff, and Robert M. Stern. "A Computational Analysis of a U.S.-Mexico-Canada Free Trade Agreement." Presented at the 30th Annual Meetings of the Western Regional Science Association, Monterey, Calif., Feb. 1991.

Cypher, James M. "Estimating the Impact of the U.S.-Mexico Free Trade Agreement on Industrial Labor." Paper Presented at the Conference "North American Free Trade: Labor, Business, and Government Policy Perspectives," University of Minnesota Industrial Relations Center and Twin City Area Labor Management Council, Minneapolis, Nov. 19, 1991.

Drucker, Peter F. "Japan: New Strategies for a New Reality." *Wall Street Journal*, Oct. 2, 1991, p. A12.

Faux, Jeff and Thea Lee. "The Road to the North American Free Trade Agreement: Laissez-Faire, or a Ladder Up?" Paper Presented at the Conference "North American Free Trade: Labor, Business, and Government Policy Perspectives," University of Minnesota Industrial Relations Center and Twin City Area Labor Management Council, Minneapolis, Nov. 19, 1991.

Gruben, William C. "Mexican Maquiladora Growth: Does It Cost U.S. Jobs?" Federal Reserve Bank of Dallas *Economic Review*. Jan. 1990a, 15–29.

———. "Do Maquiladoras Take American Jobs? Some Tentative Econometric Results." *Journal of Borderline Studies*, 5, 1, Spring 1990b, 31–46.

Hinojosa-Ojeda, Raul, and Robert K. McCleery. "U.S.-Mexico Interdependence, Social Pacts, and Policy Alternatives: A Computable General Equilibrium Approach." *Estudios Economicos*, vol. 5, no. 1, 1992, 69–68.

Hinojosa-Ojeda, Raul, and Sherman Robinson. "Alternative Scenarios of U.S.-Mexico Integration: A Computable General Equilibrium Approach." Department of Agricultural and Resource Economics, Division of Agriculture and Natural Resources, University of California, Working Paper No. 609, Apr. 1991.

———. "Labor Issues in a North American Free Trade Agreement," in Nora Lusting, Barry P. Bosworth and Robert Z. Lawrence (eds.), *Assessing the Impact of North American Free Trade*, (Brookings, Washington, D.C.: 1992).

Hunter, Linda, James R. Markusen, and Thomas F. Rutherford. "U.S.-Mexico Free Trade and the North American Auto Industry: A Theoretical and Applied General Equilibrium Analysis." Unpublished, Fraser Institute, 1991.

Lawrence, Robert A. "International Competition and the Evolution of a North American Free Trade Area." Paper presented at the Conference "North American Free Trade: Labor, Business, and Government Policy Perspectives," University of Minnesota Industrial Relations Center and Twin City Area Labor Management Council, Minneapolis, Nov. 19, 1991.

Loungani, Prakash, and Richard Rogerson. "Cyclical Fluctuations and Sectoral Reallocation: Evidence from PSID." *Journal of Monetary Economics*, 23, 2, Mar. 1989, 259–73.

Loungani, Prakash, Mark Rush, and William Tave. "Stock Market Dispersion and Unemployment." *Journal of Monetary Economics*, 25, 3, July 1990, 367–88.

Meade, Ellen E. 'The Implications of a Free Trade Agreement with Mexico." Unpublished, Federal Reserve Board of Governors, Washington, D.C., May 1991.

Peat Marwick Policy Economic Group. "The Effects of a Free Trade Agreement Between the U.S. and Mexico," Feb. 1991.

Phillips, Keith R., and Beverly Fox. "The Texas Economy: Beyond the Boom and Bust." Federal Reserve Bank of Dallas, *Southwest Economy*, Jan.–Feb. 1992, 7–8.

United States International Trade Commission. *Review of Trade and Investment Liberalization Measures by Mexico and Prospects for Future United States-Mexican Relations, Phase I: Recent Trade and Investment Reforms Undertaken by Mexico and Implications for the United States*, Investigation No. 332–282, USITC Publication 2275, Apr. 1990.

———. *Review of Trade and Investment Liberalization Measures by Mexico and Prospects for Future United States-Mexican Relations, Phase II: Summary of Views on Prospects for Future United States-Mexican Relations*, Investigation No. 332–282, USITC Publication 2326, Oct. 1990.

———. *The Likely Impact on the United States of a Free Trade Agreement with Mexico*. Report to the Committee on Ways and Means of the United States House of Representatives and the Committee on Finance of the United States Senate on Investigation No. 332–297 Under Section 332 of the Tariff Act of 1930, USITC Publication 2353, Feb. 1991.

11

The Impact of Free Trade on the Collective Agreement

Morley Gunderson and Anil Verma

Systematic analysis of the impact of free trade on labor issues has not received the attention that has been given to other areas of the impact of free trade. When there is discussion of labor issues it tends to focus on labor market impacts pertaining to worker displacement and the effects on wages and employment (Gunderson and Hamermesh, 1990). There has been little systematic analyses of the impact of free trade on the broader area of labor relations in general or on the collective bargaining agreement in particular.

Some studies have discussed the potential impact of Canadian U.S. free trade on broader labor relations issues. For example, George Adams (1990) deals with some legal issues pertaining to specific provisions of the Canadian-U.S. Free Trade Agreement (FTA). Roy Adams and Jerry White (1990) focus on the reasons that the FTA tends to be supported by business and opposed by organized labor. Beige (1986) discusses the possible impact on labor-management relations, emphasizing productivity and managerial efficiency and the need for a humane adjustment strategy. Belous (1988) emphasizes how differences in labor costs and unionization rates will become more important under the competitive pressures of free trade. Betcherman and Gunderson (1990) outline the positions taken by labor, management, and government, as well as the expected impact on training, compensation, and human resource management practices at the workplace. Block (1989) emphasizes how business, as opposed to labor interests, seems to be disproportionately served by the various aspects of the FTA. Gunderson (1990) emphasizes the regional dimensions of the impact of free trade on the labor market and on industrial relations. Gunderson and Verma (1992) deal with Canadian-U.S. comparisons in areas like labor cost, productivity, unionization, and strike activity, as well as the positions of labor, management, and government on the question of global competitiveness. Randall (1986) focuses on the detrimental impact of free trade on labor, emphasizing the competitive pressures placed on bargaining outcomes as well on social programs.

The purpose of this chapter is to discuss the impact of free trade on one specific area: collective agreement provisions. The theoretically expected impacts are discussed and then some illustrative evidence is presented based on Canadian collective agreements over the period 1981 to 1991, a period that encompasses the FTA that began January 1, 1989. Prior to that analysis, however, there is a discussion of some basic background points that have implications for the collective bargaining response and are not always brought out in the debate.

SOME BACKGROUND ISSUES

Pressures from free trade are part and parcel of the broader set of inter-related changes that are occurring, and it is difficult if not impossible to disentangle the separate impact of free trade. On the supply side of the labor market, pressures are emanating from the aging workforce, the continued labor force participation of women, the dominance of the two-earner family, and the growing ethnic diversity of the workforce. On the demand side of the labor market, other changes include global competition especially from the newly industrializing countries; industrial restructuring especially from manufacturing to services; deregulation and privatization; continuous pressures from technological change; and pressures for flexibility and adaptability associated with more flexible modes of production and just-in-time delivery systems. Usually the free trade pressures work in the same direction as these other forces, thereby exacerbating their adjustment consequences. While we tend to focus on the "downside" adjustment consequences (e.g., plant closings, permanent job loss), adjustment consequences also occur on the "upside" (e.g., skill shortages, retraining). The collective bargaining process will have to deal with both the upside as well as downside adjustment consequences.

The cumulative impact of these changes can be substantial especially in the unionized sector. This is illustrated by the fact that the adjustment consequences, especially from permanent job displacement, tend to be greatest for high-wage, unionized, blue-collar workers with considerable seniority (Gunderson and Hamermesh, 1990, p. 238). Clearly, more is to be gained or lost by bargaining over these issues in the collective bargaining arena.

The collective bargaining arena, however, is only one area for dealing with these adjustment issues. They will also be dealt with, in varying degrees, through the mechanisms of the private, unregulated labor market, as well as through government regulations, legislation, and programs. Responses from the collective bargaining arena cannot be viewed in isolation from how these other mechanisms will deal with the adjustment and other consequences of free trade. For example, the extent to which collective bargaining has to deal with the adjustment consequences of free trade (e.g., retraining needs) depends upon the extent to which government programs deal with the adjustment consequences for the workforce as a whole, both organized and unorganized.

In that vein, the legislative and regulatory mechanisms for dealing with the adjustment consequences of free trade will be affected in an indeterminate fashion. On the one hand, the adjustment consequences will increase the need for legislation and programs in such areas as advance notice, severance pay, successor rights, wage claims under bankruptcy, retraining, and relocation as well as income support programs like unemployment insurance. On the other hand, free trade can also make it more difficult to institute or expand such programs because it is more difficult to pass their cost on to employers who can more easily relocate to areas where there are minimal regulations, and export to the areas of more costly regulation.

This is part and parcel of the notion that competitive pressures on the product market side lead to a "forced harmonization" of laws and regulations in the labor market. This is so because under free trade, businesses can more easily invest and locate in areas of minimal regulatory cost, and export to the areas of more costly regulation. Jurisdictions will increasingly compete to attract and retain business by offering a regulatory climate that is conducive to business. This need not imply zero regulations, since some may be conducive to the functioning of business, but it likely will be minimalist regulations. In the policy debate over these issues, employers will likely be paid more attention to because of their greater threat with respect to investment and location decisions. Under the FTA, for example, Canadian employers increasingly argue that they are unable to compete with U.S. employers, especially in the Sun Belt where labor regulations are minimal. Of course, U.S. employers argue that Canadian employers have a competitive advantage because health and pension costs are lower since they are provided through the state.

While the pressures toward harmonization will be toward the lowest common denominator (i.e., the least regulatory environment) this need not always be the case. Some jurisdictions may seek to compete for business on the basis of providing a safety net or publicly supported training, even though there are costs. As well, political agreements across countries can lead to upward harmonization if that is the collective will. This is perhaps best illustrated by the European Economic Community, where there is considerable political pressure (e.g., through the Social Charter) to harmonize upwards to the *higher* standards of countries like Germany, to avoid the so-called social dumping of countries with low wages and labor standards. In the case of the EEC, however, this is greatly facilitated by the fact that the EEC is a common market with a common external tariff, which means that the regulatory costs are "protected" somewhat by the common tariff. Imports that are low-cost because they do not embed these regulatory costs are less of a threat because of the tariff on such imports. As well, high-cost countries can impose the higher-cost standards on the lower-cost countries as a condition of entry into the EEC.

The Canada-U.S. FTA, and a possible agreement to include Mexico, is a free trade agreement and not a common market agreement as is the case with the European Common Market. In addition to involving the free trade of goods and services, a common market has two further characteristics: the free mobility of labor and a common external tariff. Neither of the later two characteristics is involved with the FTA. This means that the collective bargaining response does not have to deal with issues pertaining to complete free labor mobility across the countries—an issue that obviously would be important under free trade with Mexico given that labor compensation in that country is roughly one-seventh that of Canada and the United States (Capdevielle, 1988). The absence of a common external tariff, however, means that the free trade countries could not agree to an upward harmonization of their labor legislative initiatives, with the cost consequences of those initiatives being protected by the common external tariff, as is the case with the EEC.

EXPECTED IMPACT OF FREE TRADE ON THE COLLECTIVE AGREEMENT

These background issues highlight a number of implications for the theoretically expected impact of free trade on the collective agreement. Free trade will create adjustment consequences on both the upside and the downside, and these will exacerbate the adjustment consequences that are emanating from various other sources. There will be pressure for the collective agreement to deal with such issues as advance notice, severance pay, seniority for layoffs and recalls, subcontracting, and retraining to deal with the downside adjustment consequences. There will be pressure to "downsize" through such mechanisms as early retirement, attrition, worksharing, and leaves of absence, perhaps in return for job security for incumbent workers. There will be continued pressure for wage concessions and breaks in traditional pattern-bargains to gear settlements to the ability-to-pay of particular situations. The upside adjustment consequences will put pressure on adaptability and flexibility to meet the rapidly changing needs and skill shortages. This could imply fewer and broader job categories, multiskilling for a variety of tasks, retraining provisions, and a deemphasis on seniority as the main criterion for promotion.

Parties to the collective agreement will also have to deal with the fundamental question of whether to follow a cooperative strategy or to continue in a mode that is often adversarial and confrontational. This is especially an issue for Canadian unions where there is often (but not always) the perception that cooperation and concessions started the "slippery slope" of declining unionization in the United States to levels that are less than half those in Canada. The FTA has highlighted that dilemma, whereby Canadian employers often argue that they cannot compete with their less unionized U.S. counterparts who not only do not have to pay a union wage premium but also have more flexibility in their workplace practices.

Parties to the collective agreement also increasingly have to deal with the extent to which they are prepared to adopt, or at least deal with, the new workplace practices that are increasingly being introduced, especially into the nonunion sector. Such practices include team production, quality circles, employee participation, multitasking, contingent compensation, and contingent workforces.

EVIDENCE OF CHANGING COLLECTIVE AGREEMENT PROVISIONS

The previous discussion highlighted numerous areas where collective agreement provisions will be subject to change from free trade pressures as well as the other interrelated pressures emanating from both the supply and demand side of the labor market. In this section, we illustrate those changes based on major collective agreements in Canada between 1981 and 1991. The evidence should be regarded as illustrative rather than definitive because data problems make comprehensive and accurate comparisons impossible.

Specifically, the coding of provisions changed substantially over time, a practice that is necessary to reflect the changing nature of collective agreements. The detailed footnotes of Table 11.1 are an attempt to reconcile some of those differences, but they are an imperfect reconciliation and in many cases comparisons are simply not possible. As well, the 1981 figures refer to collective agreements of two hundred or more employees, while the 1991 figures refer to two hundred or more employees in the federal jurisdiction, but five hundred or more in the provincial jurisdictions. Thus the 1981 data will include numerous mid-size collective agreements (200–500 employees) that are not included in the 1991 data.

Subject to these caveats, the comparisons over the ten-year period illustrate some of the changes that have occurred, in part in response to the pressures emanating from free trade and the other interrelated forces. As illustrated in Table 11.1, by 1991 almost half of all employees were covered by collective agreements that put some restrictions on contracting-out, compared to only one-quarter of employees in 1981. Worksharing as a means to deal with downsizing declined in importance, albeit here the definition changes likely account for much of the change. Perhaps the safest statement that can be made is that worksharing does not appear to be an important

Table 11.1

Collective Agreement[a] Provisions, Canada 1981, 1991 (Percentage of Employees Covered by Provision)[b]

Provision	1981	1991
Contracting-out restriction	25.5[e]	46.8
Worksharing	7.5[d]	1.8
Technological change		
Advance notice	38.5	53.5
Notice of lay-off	9.4	7.7
Retraining provision[e]	28.1	29.4
Joint committee	22.2	27.0
Relocation allowance	--	6.5
Wage and employment guarantee	.23.4[f]	31.8
Training, usually paid[g]		
On-the-job	--	43.9
Outside courses	--	33.7
Apprenticeship	--	29.4
Notice of lay-off		
1-5 days	21.4	10.3
6-15 days	15.6	15.3
16-22 days[f]	2.3	12.6
Over 22 days[f]	9.0	13.2
Other	4-9	3-5
No provision	46.8	45.1
Seniority used for		
Promotion	68.8	47.9
Lay-off	73.1	69.4
Recall	65.7	66.5
Retention of seniority during lay-off	65.4	63.6
Severance pay and S.U.B.	61.2	64.4
Pay guarantees		
Reporting pay	41.6	30.7
Stand-by pay	33.8	40.4
Call-back pay	78.2	69.9
Overtime in excess of time-and-one-half[h]		
After regular hours schedule[i]	12.1	13.3
After specified hours in day[j]	30.4	38.1
On Saturday, or 6th day worked	32.1	37.9
On Sunday, or 7th day worked	51.8	53.6
On holidays	48.2	57.0
Right-to-refuse overtime	34.7	32.7
Wage incentive plan		
Piece rate	4.4	4.3
Group incentive	0.4	0.4
Other	7.2	3.8
None	88.1	92.7
Leaves of absence		
Paid maternity[k]	18.1	48.4
Paid adoption	31.6	32.6
Education--job related	--	39.3
Education--general education	--	29.5
	--	2.4

Table 11.1 (continued)

Education--union		
Education--sabbatical	--	6.7
Paid bereavement	--	86.6
Paid jury duty	83.9	77.1
Paid witness duty	--	67.6
Illness in family	--	39.2
Paid marriage	19.1	33.9
Full-time union office	--	60.9
Union business	85.8	73.6
Extended parental leave	--	32.5
Extended paternity leave	--	34.1
Unpaid personal leave	--	44.8

[a]Major collective agreements covering all industries (except construction) with two hundred or more employees in 1981, and two hundred or more employees in the federal jurisdiction, and five hundred or more in the provincial jurisdiction in 1991.

[b]When there are a number of categories, they may not sum to 100 because the categories may not be mutually exclusive.

[c]Refers to prohibited, or prohibited if leads to lay-off in 1981; refers to "restrictions on contracting-out" in 1991.

[d]Refers to a provision on the "distribution of work" during slack periods in 1981, which could be more inclusive than the specific method of "worksharing" used in 1991.

[e]In 1991 the categories are "right to retraining" and "reference to retraining," with the later presumably being more all-inclusive, including the more specific right-to-retaining. In 1981 the categories were "on-the-job training in new equipment," "on-the-job training for another job," and "other," as well as "no provision." The category "retraining provision" used here is the all-inclusive "reference to retraining" in 1991, and any of the categories referring to retraining in 1981.

[f]Includes a small number (less than 1%) who were subject to provisions referring to wage and employment security being promoted through attrition or the distribution of work.

[g]Occasionally, the training is only partly paid, or it is not known whether it is paid.

[h]The 1981 figures may be slightly understated because the 1981 tabulations had a category for "other," some of which may have involved premiums in excess of time-and-a-half. Even if *all* of these were allocated to the category of providing overtime in excess of time-and-a-half, the proportion increased only slightly, usually by less than one percentage point.

[i]In 1981 refers to "after normal weekly hours."

[j]In 1982 refers to "after normal daily hours."

[k]In 1981 53.8 percent of employees had some form of maternity leave clause, with 35.7 percent specifying leave without pay and 18.1 percent specifying some form of pay or supplementation. The considerable differences in the categorization between 1981 and 1991 make this comparison especially fragile.

mechanism for dealing with downsizing, likely reflecting the union concern that worksharing deals with the symptoms and not the causes and it really amounts to "unemployment sharing."

Advance notice of the advent of technological change became more prominent, so that by 1991 over half of the employees were covered by such provisions. Retraining provisions, joint committees, and wage and employment guarantees in the advent of technological change exist for about one-quarter of employees. The proportions have increased slightly since 1981, especially for the wage and employment guarantees.

Unfortunately, the definition and coding changes preclude comparisons of training provisions. However, in 1991 about 44 percent of employees were covered by provisions that provided for on-the-job training. The numbers were smaller for outside courses and apprenticeship training.

Slightly over one-half of the employees were covered by provisions providing for notice of layoff. The proportions were fairly similar in 1981 and 1991, albeit the proportions with lengthier periods increased in 1991.

While seniority remained a prime criterion for layoff and recall, its importance declined substantially for promotion. Changes in pay guarantees do not seem consistent in that reporting pay and call-back pay declined, but standby pay increased. The use of overtime premiums in excess of time-and-a-half increased slightly in most categories. Wage incentive plans remained uncommon. Paid maternity leave increased substantially, so that by 1991 almost half of the employees were covered by such a provision.

CONCLUDING OBSERVATIONS

Unfortunately, definitional and coding changes make it difficult if not impossible to determine the extent to which collective agreement provisions have changed in the last decade in response to free trade and other interrelated pressures. There appears to be some increase in worker protection as evidenced by more restrictions on contracting-out and increased use of advanced notice of technological change and longer notice periods in the case of layoffs. Seniority appears to have declined as a criterion for promotion but not for layoff or recall. This evidence does not appear strong enough, however, to draw the conclusion that a degree of worker protection was provided in return for greater managerial discretion in areas like promotion.

In general, most provisions (at least those for which comparisons could be made over time) did not change substantially over the decade. To the extent that this is a generalization that is true for provisions other than the small number here for which we have comparable data over time, it will suggest different things to different people. Some will view this as evidence of the inability of the collective agreement to deal with the rapid changes that are occurring in the workplace. Others will view this as evidence of the ability of the "classic" tried-and-true structure of existing provisions to deal with an ever changing environment. Is the glass half-full, or half-empty?

A more definitive answer to this question would require more information than we are able to muster in this chapter. Information is needed on a broader array of collective agreement provisions, as well as on how those provisions are applied in practice. Information is also needed on changes in pattern bargaining and on actual workplace practices at the shop-floor level, as well as joint initiatives outside of the collective agreement, such as sectoral adjustment committees. In the absence of such information, we are unable to provide a clear picture of whether the provisions in the collective agreement itself are a vehicle through which some of the transformation of industrial relations is occurring.

NOTE

Support for this paper was provided by the Social Sciences and Humanities Research Council Grant for the project on Structural Change in Canadian Industrial Relations at the University of Toronto. We are also grateful to Labour Canada for providing the special tabulations of the collective agreement provisions.

REFERENCES

Adams, George. "Impact of the Canada-United States Free Trade Agreement on Collective Bargaining." Paper presented at the Personnel Association of Toronto Industrial Relations Conference, Apr. 1990.

Adams, Roy, and Jerry White. "Labor and the Canada-U.S. Free Trade Agreement." *ILR Report* (Fall 1990) 15–21.

Beige, Carl. "The Implications of Free Trade for Canadian Labour-Management Relations: A Management View." *New Pressures on Canadian Industrial Relations*, Proceedings of the 34th Annual Conference of the Industrial Relations Centre, McGill University, 1986.

Belous, Richard. "The Impact of the U.S.-Canadian Free Trade Agreement on Labour-Management Relations." Paper presented at a conference on Flexibility and Labour Markets in Canada and the United States, Quebec City, Sept. 20, 1988.

Betcherman, Gordon, and Morley Gunderson. "Canada-U.S. Free Trade and Labour Relations." *Labor Law Journal* 41 (Aug. 1990) 454–60.

Block, Stephen. "The Free Trade Agreement as a Negotiated Settlement as Seen from a Canadian Industrial Relations Perspective." Proceedings of the 26th Conference of the Canadian Industrial Relations Association, June 4–6, 1989.

Capdevielle, P. "International Comparisons of Hourly Compensation Costs." *Monthly Labor Review* 112 (June 1989) 10–12.

Gunderson, Morley. "Regional Dimensions of the Labour Market Impact of Free Trade." *Canadian Journal of Regional Science*. 13 (Autumn 1990) 247–258.

Gunderson, Morley, and Daniel Hamermesh. "The Effect of Free Trade on the North American Labour Market." In *The Dynamics of North American Trade and Investment: Canada, Mexico and the United States*, edited by C. Reynolds, L. Waverman, and G. Bueno. Stanford, Calif.: Stanford University Press, 1990.

Gunderson, Morley, and Anil Verma. "Canadian Labour Policies and Global Competition." *Canadian Business Law Journal*. 20 (March 1992) 63–89.

Randall, Murray. "Free Trade and Canadian Industrial Relations: A Union View." *New Pressures in Canadian Industrial Relations*, Proceedings of the 34th Annual Conference of the Industrial Relations Centre, McGill University, 1986.

12

Transnational Collective Bargaining and NAFTA

Pharis Harvey

The North American Free Trade Agreement debate has brought to the surface questions within and about the labor movement that have been dead, or at least dormant, for decades. Whatever happens to NAFTA, there is already much gain to the labor movement by the stirring of these age-old questions about the nature of international solidarity, the basis for joint strategies, the importance of central coordination of the trade union movement, and the strategic significance of broader social coalitions between labor and other social sectors.

Certainly NAFTA is not the only reason these questions have resurfaced; the collapse of communism in Eastern Europe has also vastly shifted the political and ideological context in which these questions are raised. With ideological fear and polarization at least at a temporary standstill, perhaps the issue of internationalism can be raised anew in a more pragmatic way, without immediately involving the specter of international conspiracies or subversion. It might, in a few years, even be possible to overcome the legacy of Gomperism with its anticommunist overlay of the postwar world, and reinsert the labor movement into the political mainstream as a clear and independent political actor.

The question of a central North American labor body is both premature, and the wrong place to begin this inquiry. The official, central labor bodies are not, with limited exceptions, where the new world is breaking out. As is generally true in history, innovations and challenges to old, tried, and wanting ways of doing things are most often and effectively challenged at the perimeter, not the center. People and organizations at the margins, whom power does not serve, are much more likely to conceive of new power arrangements. People and organizations at the center, or those who have for some time been central and are becoming marginalized, are much less likely to imagine different schemes for recovering imbalances. The old adage of the frog in the slowly heated pot is true of labor centrals as well: by the time they realize that the pot has been warming, it is too late to jump out. They are cooked.

BUILDING SOLIDARITY AND MEMBERSHIP

What can the labor movement do to foster solidarity and membership growth across the borders? First, it seems important to recognize that the labor movement is not fully encompassed under the rubric of the organized trade union federations. The labor movement is broader, and potentially, also includes would-be organized workers in states and industries where organizing is very difficult, workers who resist unionization out of a bad history or because of particularly effective antiunion corporate policies, immigrants and other minority groups employed in marginal work, the unemployed, self-employed farmers and small businesspeople, part-time workers, displaced homemakers, pieceworkers at home assembling simple manufactured goods or doing data entry, technicians and professionals not currently involved in any workplace collectivity. While unionization may not be the rubric under which all these unite, all are affected by and are potentially part of a broad movement around economic and social issues that affect people in their work lives.

Second, it is important to recognize that the issues the labor movement faces are also faced by other sectors and issue groups, such as environmentalists, community development organizations, alternative political groups, religious groups, consumer advocates, in ways that make new linkages natural and strategic.

Third, we should remember that such concepts as the "international division of labor" and "comparative advantage" are floating, constantly changing justifications for international business to shift the factors of production, but that they do not signify a permanent zero-sum relationship between workers in the United States and other countries. Points of advantage, of competition, and of solidarity are influenced by constantly shifting technologies, markets, finances, and methods of production. Strategies for international labor solidarity have to be built on broadly defined common goals to resist the erosion caused by these changes.

These are truisms, but perhaps it is useful to state them baldly, for the failure to recognize them can lead to truncated strategies, needless antagonisms, and unnecessarily narrowly defined alliances.

The experiences that have shaped my own involvement in this arena for the past couple decades bear this out. And especially, during the past year, as the labor movement, environmentalists, consumers, religionists, human rights groups, farmers, and development advocates have learned to work together on the North American Free Trade agenda, we are rediscovering the importance of these truisms.

We have formed a genuinely motley group of interests, which took the name MODTLE (Mobilization on Development, Trade, Labor and Environment) after its variegated character was disparaged repeatedly by the *Wall Street Journal.* For what the journal saw as its weakness, we recognized as its strength. MODTLE has been able to open up a debate in this country about the nature of the economic integration that is being urged on us, and has succeeded in finding and building on the points in common of interests and groups that had only occasionally worked together before. We also have found common ground with Mexican and Canadian groups in similar coalitions, so that we have begun the process of forging an alternative regional agenda for development that attempts to build on the strengths of each of the three countries, rather than exploiting the weaknesses and vulnerabilities.

As we joined forces to criticize and challenge the proposed U.S.-Mexican free trade agreement, we realized that what we had in common was much more than a tactical need for each other and the coincidence of opposition to a flawed process. We shared, across these several special interests, a common vision, broadly put, of democratic process on economic affairs, of practices in the workplace that were both safe for workers and the communities in which they live, for standards of safety and health that protected consumers and workers alike, for wages and social protection, health care, education, cultural respect, and integrity of communities. It was this broader agenda, not our several points of tactical need for alliance, that kept the coalition together, and growing.

What we learned about this in the United States influenced the way in which we developed work with Mexicans and Canadians. There is evolving a similar coalition in Mexico, as has already developed with greater success in Canada, and the principles that hold it together are these broader ones, not the narrower, but equally important lines of sectoral interests. And for this reason, we are finding it possible to work as three national coalitions, from three very different countries, to build a common vision of a regional future. We have begun the process of forging an alternative regional agenda for development that attempts to build on the strengths of each of the three countries, rather than exploiting the weaknesses and vulnerabilities.

In order to build a movement across the northern and southern borders to protect and advance the cause of working people we must think in broad terms and build on the basis of quite broadly defined goals.

THE ROLE OF INDEPENDENT UNIONS

It is within this broader framework that the question of the role of independent unions becomes important. If the AFL-CIO, for example, is working with a broader social movement in Canada and Mexico than is defined by its formal relations with the Canadian Labor Congress or the CTM (Confederacion de los Trabajadores de Mexico) the fact that the Mexican movement also includes nonofficial unions, independent unions with which the AFL-CIO has no ties becomes much less important, much less a stumbling block, than it would be if the AFL-CIO were being asked to relate primarily to these non-CTM unions directly or in just a labor-based coalition. The CTM, an official union in Mexico, which means it is closely tied to the government and ruling party, also can join at whatever level it feels comfortable. This happened recently in Zacatecas, Mexico, when several CTM leaders joined in a forum sponsored by a broad band of social organizations. Unfortunately the AFL-CIO was not able to participate at the national level, although some regional labor federation officials joined.

A similar effort is taking place within the Coalition for Justice in the maquiladoras, which is a multisectoral effort to develop a code of conduct for American firms working in the border region of Mexico, supported by organized labor, religious, community, and development groups in the United States and, to a lesser extent, in Mexico.

DIALOGUE AND JOINT RESEARCH

Within this framework of broadened social coalitions, the second level of engagement becomes important: dialogue and information sharing by unions in the same industry or engaged with the same multinational companies. This trinational process is already underway, with the communication workers in the lead, and with a number of other unions making significant progress. Auto workers at the local and regional levels have held several conferences together, as have electricians and safety and health specialists.

The difference in the structures of the unions between the United States and Mexico makes this dialogue somewhat more difficult to plan at a national level, since, for example, there is no Mexican auto workers union to serve as a counterpart to the UAW. So perhaps it is wise for the internationals to foster and encourage company-level dialogue, sharing information and building up a level of trust and mutual interests before attempting the next level. That could either be to hold national union level talks about specific sectors or to attempt to negotiate jointly or in parallel with some company with operations in two or three of the countries.

In order for this to become even thinkable, however, it would seem important that the three national union centers begin to develop joint research centers where collective bargaining agreements, labor statistics, company data, and other relevant information can be gathered, analyzed, and shared. Only when unions in each of the three countries are able to function on the basis of the same facts will they be able to build common strategies.

COPING WITH WAGE COMPETITION AND CHEAP WAGE STRATEGIES

Wage competition, and the vast shortage of jobs in all three countries, will make common action difficult at best, if steps are not also taken to lessen the level of disparity in wages and benefits. This calls for a multipronged effort, which goes far beyond what can be done by labor unions, even working together in the closest harmony. For it involves the deliberate choice of a different set of government priorities and policies than those chosen by the Bush and Salinas administrations. The meeting in Zacatecas, Mexico, began to examine this issue, and strongly endorsed a multipronged approach as the only way to cope with the possibility that Mexico's cheap wages would be sealed in as a point of comparative advantage long into the future, exerting a steady downward pressure on U.S. and Canadian wages and labor rights protection. This approach includes at least two essential elements:

- Debt relief for Mexico, coupled with a schedule for raising the minimum wage and a program for minimum wage enforcement. The Mexican debt burden, however one assigns the blame for it, has been the primary culprit in the downwardly spiraling wage system in Mexico during the past decade. Without sufficient capital to address social needs, repair the damage done to the agricultural economy that is causing a flood of out-migrants to the cities and northward into the United States, and to shore up the minimum wage levels, Mexico can hardly expect to staunch the flow.

- Enforcement of workplace health and safety standards through several mechanisms:
  —endorsement of relevant International Labor Organization (ILO) conventions and passage of necessary legislation for compliance by all three countries as a basis for bringing standards up to an internationally accepted norm
  —increased budgets for enforcement, perhaps funded by revenues from cross-border transactions
  —trade sanctions against companies that cut costs by producing for export in areas of lax enforcement or loose laws
  —access for complaints on these matters to the courts of any of the countries involved in cross-border transactions affected by the practice at issue

Clearly bringing about these steps is beyond the capability of the labor movement acting on its own or alone.

A SINGLE TRINATIONAL LABOR CENTER?

Finally, if many of these steps are taken, the question of forming a common labor center for the three countries may evolve as a natural step toward institutionalizing whatever progress has been made. However, it is not a necessary final step, and in fact, may not be desirable from a political and cultural perspective. It is hard to imagine that labor movements in any of the three countries are strong enough now, or will be in the near future, to sustain an attack on them launched by nationalistic forces that accuse them of being the running-dogs of foreign interests. Certainly the national policies of each of the countries will not allow for major involvement by a labor movement whose loyalty to the national polity can be called into question for some time.

Not until and unless the level of political integration of the region has advanced far beyond its present stage should the national identity of the labor movements be weakened, or an international or regional identity be substituted for the national one. Securing open dialogue and cooperation, common agendas, and shared strategies at the level of national labor centers will be quite sufficient a challenge for some time to come.

The United States, Mexico, and Canada are engaged in a historic effort to change their mutual relationship with each other in the context of a rapidly changing global political and economic environment. How labor participates in this will depend almost entirely on how willing labor is to reach beyond its traditional boundaries, form new alliances, and challenge old verities. To their credit, the labor movements in all three countries have begun this process already, but it remains to be seen whether they will be able to overcome the major stumbling blocks placed in their way not only by international capital and multinational business-oriented governments, but by their own histories and institutional problems as well.

13

The North American Free Trade Agreement as an Element of U.S. Trade Policy

Robert T. Kudrle

The consideration of mutual labor-management concerns can be viewed at least two ways: mutual concerns of those firms and employees most directly affected by the proposed liberalization and the mutual concerns of those touched only indirectly. In the first category, of course, fall those who will enjoy special gains as well as special difficulties. Even if these two groups are considered together, they leave out most of labor and management in the country whose interests are vitally affected by the North American Free Trade Agreement (NAFTA) as it shapes U.S. foreign economic policy. Exclusive attention to those most directly affected could lead to more of the special interest policies most Americans claim to be in revolt against. Moreover, as virtually all Americans are either labor or management (and a huge share are to some extent both) in a broad sense, the topic invites a consideration of the national interest more generally.

Most evaluations of the proposed NAFTA lack an explicit consideration of the appropriate criteria by which such an arrangement should be judged. Without such a discussion, alternative outcomes are evaluated by a confusing amalgam of gains and losses in such analytically distinct spheres as overall national gain, income distribution changes, and political viability.

Much modern writing argues that a country's foreign economic policy must concern itself with security and autonomy issues as well as the more obvious search for increased national prosperity.[1] Some NAFTA proponents have used security arguments in their cause: a more prosperous Mexico will reduce tensions between the two countries and hence the threat of future conflict. Skeptics might wonder just what kind of security threat to the United States Mexico could possibly present in a post–cold war world in any event, and a country with a national income of only a few percent of the United

States could not present a threat to U.S. autonomy under any plausible scenario.[2] Thus prosperity concerns have dominated the discussion of adding Mexico to the incipient trading area with Canada.

Economists have argued for free trade since the nineteenth century. And, in general, elite opinion worldwide is probably more convinced of the virtues of openness now than ever before. Yet countries still refer to their own liberalization measures as "concessions" and insist on a quid pro quo from their trading partners. Much has been written on this subject, but a large part of the economic argument boils down to two points: (1) liberalization more easily overcomes interests threatened by imports when it can be offset politically by identifiable exporting gainers, and (2) while unilateral liberalization almost always increases national income, simultaneous liberalization by trading partners provides another great source of gain. (For serious examination from different perspectives, see Destler, 1992; Williamson, 1983; Bhagwati, 1988, 1991.)

At the level of official doctrine, the United States has scarcely changed its basic posture since the end of the Second World War: the more open the world economy is, the better. For at least two decades, however, the public and policymakers alike have become increasingly convinced that trading partners have been yielding less than they ought to in return for access to the U.S. market (Destler, 1992). The United States has pursued a three-pronged attack on the problem: it has attempted to increase the range of issues dealt with at the currently stalled Uruguay Round talks in GATT; it has armed the president with authority to take unilateral action against trading partners maintaining "unreasonable" protection against American sellers (Gephardt, 1991; Williams, 1991); and it has established FTAs with Israel (1974) and Canada (1987). NAFTA, while quite distinct from the Canadian-U.S. agreement, will doubtless incorporate many of its features and is in many ways an extension of it.

TYPES OF FTA

Free trade agreements,[3] which allow for free exchange between signatories while maintaining each nation's separate commercial policy toward the rest of the world, are not new. The archetype of what some today call a "conventional" FTA was the European Free Trade Area,[4] which paid little attention to what went on inside the economies of its constituent states and mainly lowered formal trade barriers among them. A second type of FTA could be called a "liberalizing" FTA. It begins with economies that either are, or aspire to be, liberal in their own internal trading. In pure form, it would do two things: it would treat a partner's activities in its own economy as similarly as possible to its own, and, partly of necessity, it would make the maximum range of national practices similar or at least congruent to those of its partners. While not necessarily open to new members on the same terms as the original members for practical reasons, the hallmark of purely "liberalizing" FTA would be the accomplishment of a regime that would in principle be open to others on similar terms. The particulars of the agreement are minimally geared to special characteristics of the constituent economies and particularly to special problems in the relations between them. The Canada-U.S. FTA contains many features of this type, although it is at yet far from comprehensive even in conception.[5]

A third type of FTA could be called an "exclusive" FTA. Here complementarity between the two economies is stressed over the beneficial effects of increased competition between them. Moreover, such conceptions typically envision these complementary strengths as a source of economic power in facing the external world. Some schemes for North American integration foresee such a pact.

The three types should be thought of as extreme cases; they cannot be completely identified with real schemes. The European Free Trade Area engaged in considerable harmonization of policies beyond those narrowly connected with trading; the U.S.-Canada FTA was clearly geared in many dimensions to the precise character of the bilateral relation; and even those who advocate a U.S.-Mexican pact principally as a complementary alliance to confront the rest of the world do not typically exclude the accession of other states.

While free trade with Mexico must involve agreement about much more than border controls, the United States should bargain hard for the second kind of FTA and avoid the temptations of a kind of "strategic alliance" in which the countries give each other such benefits as assured access or assured supply over extended periods of time. Such agreements are profoundly illiberal. Assured access and assured supply, at least of nonstrategic goods, should be the province of private commercial agreement (when not anticompetitive) and not government accord.

NAFTA should support thoroughgoing liberalization of the Mexican economy. Commentators are surely right that Mexico has not by any means reached an adequate level of internal liberalization.[6] An effective agreement would not only contain assurances that future government policy will not be used to distort the Mexican price system in ways that affect its international trade but must also demonstrate a willingness to cooperate with the United States and Canada to guard against informal public and private discrimination. If the United States is not careful it could wind up with another political and economic "Japan" problem: the "immaculate rejection" of foreign goods through tacit collusion and the political firestorm that would result.

Carefully devised policies in this area could accomplish a number of valuable objectives at once. Overcoming U.S.-administered protection aimed at "fair trade" lay at the heart of Canadian ambitions for the FTA and ranks high among Mexican objectives as well.[7] Free trade between economies based firmly on market principles eliminates much of the rationale for such protection. Rules about permissible subsidies can be developed, and "dumping" can be attacked with conventional competition policy. Mexico thus has much to gain from assuring that its economy will be based on demonstrably effective competition. A pact assuring cooperation between nascent Mexican competition authorities and cognate authorities in Washington and Ottawa could provide important assurances to Mexico's partners while accelerating the development of the Mexican economy.

Second, policies to treat adjustment problems under NAFTA should be based insofar as possible on the principle that suffering from economic change should be equally relieved wherever it occurs in the economy. Ideally, NAFTA could be the occasion for an improved, comprehensive national program that matches workers with available jobs and provides improved opportunity for further training. This is very different, however, from essentially admitting a property right in protection. In particular, there is no reason the government should "buy off" specific industries that are negatively affected by increased trade.

This consistency principle relates to the issue of the phasing-in of liberalization. The Canada-U.S. FTA liberalized some trade at once, some over five years, and some over ten years.[8] All GATT rounds have introduced their liberalizations in less than a decade. Some have argued that the very different structures of the U.S. and Mexican economies justifies phasing in reductions over a period of up to twenty years. It is hard to make an equity argument for such an extended period of adjustment. No nonhuman capital losses realized from liberalization should be assigned to the taxpayer or consumer, and labor adjustment policies should work far more rapidly. The "tax" of protectionism should be lifted as quickly as is feasible from the U.S. consumer.

One approach to accelerating liberalization and improving worker adjustment at the same time might be to calculate the economic waste involved in the kind of extended protection that some propose and dedicate those resources to experimental worker relocation schemes. The schemes could be presented as genuine social experiments that might later be used more generally throughout the economy.

Third, NAFTA should avoid all guarantees of exclusive partnership. In particular, the United States should avoid entangling Mexico in a kind of industrial policy based on an implicit division of labor in which the two countries guarantee each other protected shares of particular markets for set periods of time. Instead the NAFTA should, where possible, encourage liberalization by third countries. For example, the use of rules of (national) origin is intrinsic to any FTA because its whole raison d'être turns on selective liberalization, leaving higher barriers to be faced by those outside the FTA. Yet GATT might be persuaded to permit countries to vary mandated local content under rules of origin based on the openness of the source countries of the major non-North American content. Mexico intends NAFTA to increase its attractiveness as a site for multinational corporations seeking to serve the entire North American market. All three countries might employ this very real attraction as a means of opening up other markets to the products of all traders and not just NAFTA members. Such varying stringency of rules of origin should be fully accepted by all three NAFTA members, however, and based insofar as possible on documented evidence of objectionable source country trading practices or their elimination.

Using rules of origin to encourage increase liberalization abroad should be contrasted with some suggested initiatives that blatantly increase protection over its present levels. For example, one recent analysis (Prestowitz, et al., 1991) suggests replacing the MFN duty on goods that are only lightly processed in a country of NAFTA (presumably Mexico) with a 20 percent tariff instead. Not only would such action almost certainly violate GATT but its very spirit is illiberal; extra protection is casually enshrined for alleged abuse instead of offering especially liberal treatment for liberal trading partners.

Fourth, the United States should avoid a bean-counting approach to NAFTA negotiations. Some proposals have suggested sector liberalization taking place such as to maintain a bilateral balance in sectoral trade or in the trade of complementary sectors. Economic reasoning rebels against any attempt to maintain overall bilateral national balances in a multilateral trading world.[9] How much less defensible are negotiations based on attaching a premium to bilateral sector balances, such as in textiles and apparel. They lack any significance for national economic welfare, and their superficially neutral effect on "jobs" is entirely illusory. For example, if, as some have proposed, U.S. apparel imports should be matched by U.S. textiles exports as a condition for further liberalization within NAFTA, the net impact on jobs is meaningless unless those released from one activity are immediately hired in the other. In fact, considerable uncertainty exists about changes in the structure of employment resulting from NAFTA largely because shifts in product demand by production site cannot be forecast with very much precision, even by the most sophisticated models. And the impact of the agreement on overall U.S. employment over any substantial period of time will be approximately nil because wages in various parts of the economy will adjust to changing supply and demand for various categories of labor.

Finally, concern with environmental issues abroad should be steadfast but honest. Conceptually, possible U.S. aims can be broken down into two groups: environmental problems that directly "spill over" into the United States and those that do not.[10] The United States must insist on effective amelioration of all environmental problems falling into the former category, at least insofar as it attends to the same problems from domestic sources. The second category, however, is doubtful. While its certainly true that environmental degradation everywhere is to be lamented, the United States typically does not presume to penalize its trading partners for 'local" environmental problems. In the second category the test of whether environmental concerns are being used as an excuse for protectionism would be whether the United States would consider trade retaliation if they occurred in other countries. This argument does not ignore the fact that such retaliation or conditionality might one day play a role in U.S. trade policy. The immediate question, however, concerns the propriety of singling Mexico out for especially stringent treatment.

In summary, future relations among the countries of North America should be as much as is feasible an extendable model of relations among nations that aim to maintain as much cultural and political distinction among themselves as possible while pursuing liberal economies at home and reciprocated liberalization in foreign economic policy. In particular, any agreement should avoid measures that seriously complicate the further liberalization of the world economy.

NOTES

1. National assertion can also be cited as a fundamental national goal. It relates, among other things, to the quest for relative status internationally. For a more complete discussion, see Kudrle, 1991.

2. Any form of trade dependency is virtually impossible, and even substantially increased foreign direct investment that might come to the United States from Mexico under NAFTA would pale by comparison with the stocks of other nationalities that are already here, and increased foreign direct investment (IFDI) as a whole can scarcely be regarded as an autonomy threat anyway (Kudrle, 1991). The only substantial autonomy threat from Mexico comes from immigration. Proponents argue that NAFTA could reduce illegal immigration by making Mexico a more attractive place to live. Those alarmed about the immigration question point to the possible evolution of a free trade area into a common market with free migration. See n. 3.

3. Free trade areas eliminate formal trade barriers among the participants but leave each with its own barriers against the rest of the world; customs unions go the next step and develop a common protection policy against nonmembers; common markets allow for movements of factors of production, most notably labor (because now most capital movements are not seriously controlled by most countries anyway). Economic union implies a full coordination and harmonization of fiscal, monetary, and socioeconomic policies. This rather standard typology appears in Caves and Jones, 1981: 257.

4. EFTA was born in 1957 as the "outer seven"; it was formed from countries not included in the six that formed the original core members of the European Economic Community (EEC). It dissolves as its members enter the EEC's successor, the European Community.

5. It should be kept in mind that the Canada-U.S. agreement is not a "done deal." Many key problems, including those on administered protection, were not solved but were put on an agenda for mutual discussion. If common ground cannot be found over the next few years, the entire agreement could fail.

6. Many commentators have suggested that if internal liberality were used as an

index of appropriateness for FTA partnership, Chile would dominate all other Latin American countries.

7. Mexico is particularly concerned about use by the United States of the "escape clause" sanctioned by national law and by GATT. Technically, this route to protection rests on excessive damage to a domestic industry and does not necessarily involve unfairness. See Destler, 1992.

8. After the FTA between the United States and Canada was signed many industries on both sides of the border began to petition for an acceleration of barrier removal. This is not surprising; once a strong and confident firm establishes its adjustment strategy, it may well find trade barriers merely an undesirable business expense.

9. An emphasis on bilateral balances largely discredited Congressman Gephardt's foreign economic policy ideas among professional economists. For a typical critique, see Williams, 1991.

10. This does not deny that the United States can be ultimately affected by "national" environmental degradation or degradation that most directly affects third countries; it may want to take a position on such degradation. But see text following.

REFERENCES

Bhagwati, Jagdish. 1988. *Protectionism*. Cambridge, Mass.: MIT press.
———. 1991. "Fair Trade, Reciprocity and Harmonization: The Novel Challenge to the Theory and Policy of Free Trade." Mimeographed.
Caves, Richard E., and Ronald W. Jones. 1981. *World Trade and Payments: An Introduction*. 3d ed. Boston: Little, Brown.
Destler, I. M. 1992. *American Trade Politics*. 2d ed. Washington: Institute for International Economics.
Gephardt, Richard. 1991. "Super 301: It's Time for Teeth." *International Economic Insights*, Nov.–Dec.
Kudrle, Robert T. 1991. "Good for the Gander?" *International Organization*, vol. 45, no. 3.
———. 1991. "The Challenge Within: Foreign Direct Investment in Europe in the Sixties and the United States in the Nineties." In *Investment in the North American Free Trade Area*. Edited by Earl Fry. Provo, Utah: Brigham Young University Press.
Prestowitz, Clyde V., Jr., and Robert B. Cohen (with Peter Morici and Alan Tonelson). 1991. *The New North American Order: A Win-Win Strategy for U.S. Mexico Trade*. Washington, D.C.: Economic Strategy Institute and University Press of America.
Williams, Lynn. 1991. "The Case Against Gephardt II." *International Economic Insights*, Nov.–Dec.
Williamson, John. 1983. *The Open Economy and the World Economy: A Textbook in International Economics*. New York: Basic Books.

14

International Competition and the Evolution of a North American Free Trade Area

Robert Z. Lawrence

The productivity growth in the United States between 1873 and 1973 grew at an annual rate of about 2 percent a year. Since 1973 it has been inching along at barely 1 percent. That sets a particular situation for the United States and it is not a good one. In the 1970s we avoided dealing with that slowdown in productivity growth, essentially by putting more people to work. We had an influx of women in the workforce and the baby boom generation moving into the labor force. And so, our economy was able to grow, not by increasing living standards per worker but simply by adding more workers to the workforce.

In the 1980s we came up with a second strategy: we simply spent more than we produced and borrowed the difference from the rest of the world. Spending in the U.S. economy was growing at around 3.5 percent a year and production at 2.5 percent a year with the difference being made up by foreign borrowing. What this meant in the 1980s was that the growth of points of our economy were essentially the parts of the economy that depended on domestic spending because domestic spending was booming along. And those were basically the services sector of our economy.

At the same time the manufacturing sector, the goods sector of the economy, was extremely hard hit, because those spending policies in turn drove interest rates up, led to a dollar that went sky high, and priced American products out of world markets, and so we had a much smaller growth in mining, in manufacturing, in farming—the "traded goods" sector of our economy.

The 1990s are going to be the mirror opposite of the 1980s. In fact, in the 1990s we have exhausted those two avenues for growth or for increasing our spending. First, the labor force is slowing down. It is not the baby boom generation anymore, but the baby bust generation. And female labor force participation is plateauing. The result is that we are having labor force growth only on the order of about 1 percent a year. If we take that 1 percent and add it to another 1 percent, which is the productivity performance we managed to record over the 1980s we get real GNP potential growing at only 2 percent a year. And if we then assume that we make some small headway in increasing our savings rates, in bringing down the government budget deficit and reducing the trade deficit, that will imply that domestic spending will be growing more slowly than 2 percent a year. Think about the change from an economy where spending was at 3.5 to just under 2 (and that is assuming away any recession). That is just assuming we grow at our full potential. What that implies is that for the services sector of our economy the growth prospects absent increase in productivity performance are rather dismal.

The locus of growth in the 1990s, therefore, has to be in the manufacturing sector and the sectors that can depend on international trade to stimulate the demand for their products. Absent that and an increase in productivity, our economy has severe long-term problems. So how we can stimulate economic growth and what kinds of policy initiatives we can come up with that can spur improvements in productivity and in performance are really the key questions. It is in that context that we have to think about the North American free trade area.

Traditionally, indeed, over the whole postwar period, the United States has advocated freer trade. But, for most of the postwar period we believed that this ought to be done in a multilateral setting. The strategy was to use GATT to bring down tariffs and to do so on a most favored nation basis.

For example, if the United States were to negotiate with France and use its power to persuade the French to lower a tariff rate, the lower French tariff rate would now be enjoyed by all of France's trading partners. Likewise, if France could persuade the United States to bring down a tariff, that lower tariff would be enjoyed by all of the members of the general agreement on trade and tariffs. This was a mechanism designed to use the power of the strong to negotiate, and to provide benefits to those weaker countries who could not come up with much. It reflected a view of the world that said, in a sense, that lowering tariff barriers was good and not simply those confronting American trading interests, but global interests. And so it was GATT that was remarkably successful under U.S. leadership in bringing down tariff rates all around the world.

GATT also provided four regional trading arrangements and the most important of those was clearly the European Community, which the United States supports. It is important to emphasize, of course, that when countries form a regional trading arrangement, they give the members of that arrangements preferential treatment. This is, therefore, a violation of the principle of "most favored nation" treatment, and a violation of the essence of GATT. But GATT, in Article 24, acceded to these agreements provided they were broad-based, not just a particular confined to one or two sectors, but had to deal with a larger number of goods, and provided no new barriers were erected against outsiders. That was the U.S. policy until the 1980s. Since that time, for a number of reasons, the U.S. policy has deviated from a sole dependence on this multilateral approach to achieving its freer trade objectives.

We can well understand why the U.S. economy was wrenched as a result of what happened to our currency in the early 1980s. In addition to the long-term competitiveness pressures that were felt by numerous American industries in the 1980s U.S. manufacturing was subject to severe problems. The result was an increasing impatience in the United States with relying on the speed at which GATT, the general agreement on trade and tariffs and international negotiations, could deliver what Americans sought.

In particular, the concern had to do with different practices, unfair practices in U.S. eyes, that prevailed in other parts of the world. In addition, what we also saw was a perception that GATT alone could not deal with the kind of problems that arise today in international economics. Basically, as tariffs have been brought down, the nontariff barriers remain. And it is not just those nontariff barriers that explicitly are devoted to trade; all kinds of institutional developments within economies, different practices that exist around the world, affect trade flows and once we move to a global economy, those divergent institutional trade practices become major issues of concern.

In U.S. discussions with the Japanese, it is not the border barriers that we are concerned about, but the very different institutional practices, some of which are not even related to international trade and investment but nonetheless inhibit international trade and investment. We have also seen an awareness of this in Europe with the formation of the European Community and the EC92 measures. The Europeans have concluded that it was not enough just to lower tariffs, indeed, to eliminate tariffs. There remain significant barriers to the free movement of goods, services, capital, and labor across the European market. They have sought to create a genuinely single market. And what they have realized is that it takes more than simply paying attention to border barriers. They are seeking where necessary to harmonize standards, in other cases to have mutual recognition of standards. But, it is a much more fundamental and deeper form of intereconomic integration.

This is also true of the North American area. We are not simply talking about traditional trade policy measures, but much deeper concerns. The United States embarked in the 1980s on a multitrack approach. The United States did not stop with the Uruguay Round of negotiations; indeed those looked like, at last, they might be coming to a successful conclusion. And there it brought up many issues, trying to broaden the purview of GATT to include some of these questions such as intellectual property rights, trade-related investment measures to improve the dispute settlements of GATT, to introduce services into GATT, to reform agriculture.

All these issues were taken up in that framework. But bilateral trade negotiations were also considered. Antidumping, and safeguards provisions, and voluntary restraint arrangements were all growing features of America's response to international trade in the 1980s. So we had unilateralism, mutlilateralism, and regionalism, beginning with the free trade area of Israel and then the Canadian free trade area.

As much as the United States may have sought to initiate free trade, when it came to a regional arrangement between the United States and another country, it was clear that the smaller country had to be a willing participant. Then in the mid–1980s it was on Canada's initiative that we saw a dramatic change. Historically, Canadians had sought to do everything they could to avoid becoming the fifty-first state of the United States. But in the 1980s many Canadians became aware that their avenues for growth in the traditional primary commodity areas did not look good. And they sought to enhance the competitiveness of their economy by proposing a free trade area with the United States. It was not a coincidence, of course, that a conservative government came to power in the mid–1980s and it too sought a free trade area with the United States as a way of introducing reforms in Canada that it believed would benefit the country. The MacDonald Commission also advocated that initiative. Canadians saw that a free trade area with the United States would give them numerous benefits.

In particular, Canada has suffered from the fact that its market is small by international standards, and Canadian firms, therefore, tend to be subscale by international standards. In addition, Canadian consumers pay higher prices because there is not as much competition in Canada as there is outside Canada. And so, when economists sat down and tried to figure out how Canada would be affected by a free trade area they came to the conclusion that there would be rather considerable benefits from a free trade area by increasing the potential for specialization within Canada by allowing Canadian firms to enjoy scale economies and by enhancing competition in Canada.

From the U.S. side, there was also benefits that were perceived from such an arrangement. Canada had higher protection than the United States. Canadian tariffs against American products were much higher, typically, in virtually every product category than American tariffs. And so a deal that lowered and eliminated those tariffs actually provided net benefits to the United States. The U.S.-Canada agreement was implemented in 1989.

Many people today in Canada would argue with and claim that this agreement has been a dismal failure. It is difficult to interpret what has happened in Canada today as being solely due to what has happened in the free trade area. Indeed, one of the problems of both free trade and protections is that frequently trade policies get the credit or the blame when they are not solely to blame. If we think back to the Great Depression, high tariffs may have been a contributing factor but they were certainly not the whole story. Likewise, liberalization that accompanied postwar economic growth is given a lot of credit it does not deserve. In Canada today one has to acknowledge that there have been some other economic policies that are extremely important in interpreting the current Canadian situation.

An extremely tight monetary policy is one. Essentially, in order to bring down inflation in Canada, the Bank of Canada has sent interest rates extremely high, and that has resulted in a dramatic appreciation of the Canadian dollar. Regardless of what is happening in the trade policy arena, Canadians have found themselves priced out of the American market as a result of those exchange rate changes. And the result has been a dramatic increase in unemployment in Canada. It has also been associated with a declining economy and with Canadians finding it much cheaper to go shopping in the United States. It is inappropriate to ascribe those changes to the free trade agreement that has yet to be implemented. It is in fact a win situation for Canada although it will take time to emerge and require a major adjustment in Canadian macroeconomic policy.

If it required a great change in Canada to move to negotiate a free trade agreement with the United States, it required a truly revolutionary change in Mexico. The Mexican economy in the 1980s was propelled, in fact, to the situation it found itself in by severe debt problems and by an economy that had developed around oil, which suddenly found in the early 1980s and then later again in 1985 a collapse in oil prices. The result was tremendous problems in the Mexican economy and development of a strategy that totally altered the pattern of Mexican development from an import-substituting, inward-oriented, government-dominated, highly regulated economy to an outward-oriented, trade-driven, export-driven economy, in which the private sector was given a much greater role.

We have seen truly dramatic changes in Mexico over the 1980s as they have moved to implement their new strategy. In the mid–1980s during GATT Mexico unilaterally lowered tariffs. They took import quotas that were protecting their market and removed them. They took tariffs, some of which were over 100 percent, and brought them down to levels where they were on average only around 10 percent. So what we had in addition to privatization and a lot of structural changes within Mexico was in fact a unilateral movement toward freer trade. But, it was not enough. It was perceived by the Mexicans as not enough, and they sought to have an export-oriented economy. And what they found was despite lower wage rates, despite the fact that tariffs between the United States and Mexico average only around 4 percent today, with many Mexican products getting into the United States duty-free through the so-called General System of Preferences (GSP), there was not the kind of response the Mexicans, perhaps, had expected initially. They also found that the rest of the world was not necessarily hospitable to Mexican exports. And they were not particularly concerned as the Canadians had been about the actions taken in the United States in the form of anti-dumping, countervailing duty, and other kinds of protective actions. They recognized that if they were to secure foreign investment they had to convince foreign investors and, indeed, Mexican investors, that these policy changes were permanent. They had to be credible and they had to be permanent. That is the essential element in what the Mexicans are seeking from a U.S.-Mexican free trade agreement. It is to make the changes they have already implemented, by and large, permanent, to convince outsiders that they will be so.

Developing countries pleaded in GATT for many years that they wanted special and differential treatment. And they go it. Yet once a developing country has become convinced that what it would like to do is liberalize, then joining GATT simply does not convince outsiders that it is serious because GATT has many escape routes for those developing countries.

What is the effect of this agreement, in particular, on the United States? On balance, particularly in the short run, it has rather small effects but they are positive. We know that Mexico has higher tariffs than the United States, around 10 percent average. The U.S. tariffs are 4 percent or less in some cases. Remove both of those and again what you provide on balance are net increases in the demand for American products. We have already seen, in fact, how liberalization in Mexico over the 1980s led to an improvement in the U.S. trade balance with Mexico. If we take out oil, there has been a rather significant improvement in the American balance of trade with Mexico over this period. We need to keep this in mind when we listen to those who argue that somehow, because of low wages, Americans cannot compete with Mexico, that somehow, the low wage advantage enables Mexicans to overcome and will lead to Mexicans overcoming American firms. There are some areas where labor costs are extremely important and cheap labor may be the most important ingredient in certain kinds of activities, but those are not all. And in many other areas it is the highest skill, technology, quality, and that is the basis on which the United States ought to compete and on which it does compete. And, as a result the U.S. trade balance with Mexico has improved.

There are also those who say the Mexicans are too poor to ever want to buy our products. There is no question that there is extreme poverty in Mexico, but again, when we see investment in Mexico it is not only consumers who buy American products, it is producers who buy investment goods: machinery and capital. And in fact, in addition to this effect of the two tariffs being lowered Mexicans tend to specialize in the labor-intensive activities and the Americans specialize in the technology-intensive activities. Not totally, and indeed, in some cases we find in certain industries it might not be what we expect. As a result of specialization the Mexicans are involved in the cheaper labor kinds of activities and the U.S. labor force is upgrading as it moves into other kinds of activities. So we have a specialization process

that is beneficial in providing better wages and better employment opportunities for American workers.

A third effect has to do with the fact that the agreement is not simply about
trade, but also about investment. If America increases its investments, if the
world increases its investments in Mexico, Mexico, which is borrowing from
the rest of the world, will by definition be running bigger and bigger trade
deficits. Countries that borrow from the world provide the world with fewer
goods than they get from it. That is how a country absorbs those savings from
the rest of the world into their economy. So, a Mexico that is able to borrow
is a Mexico that runs bigger trade deficits. Countries like Mexico do not take
the borrowings and hoard. They want to borrow in order to spend. And who
gets the benefits? Mexico's major trading partner, the United States, with
whom Mexico does roughly 70 percent of its trade. A Mexico that is absorbing
investment, therefore, is one with bigger and bigger trade deficits, and its
trading partners will have larger and larger trade surpluses. That is another
beneficial impact that comes as a result of increasing Mexico's potential as an
absorber of foreign investment. On balance, particularly in the short and medium terms, as those investment flows go to Mexico they will help create a
demand for American equipment with American capital goods. Therefore,
they more than upset the loss that would accrue as a result of American imports from Mexico. But, by and large these effects tend to be relatively small,
particularly when compared to the size of the U.S. economy. We have a situation where on balance they are favorable, but nonetheless they are small.
And that also implies that with the exception of certain key sectors, the adjustment problems are relatively small.

On balance the trade relationships with Mexico still today represent only
6 percent of U.S. international trade. Just to give an idea, therefore, they
are a very small share of the aggregate American economy. Nonetheless,
we should look at this as a down peg. We should look at the adjustment in
a much longer-term time horizon. There is potentially a population of 90 to
100 million people out there and as they develop it will naturally result in
spurts of growth back into the United States. A Mexico that is more affluent,
which increases its growth rates, will be one from which fewer immigrants
come to the United States. There are some who claim that if Mexicans raise
their wages they will tend to migrate more. The argument is somehow that
they are too poor to pay for the journey. And if they earn higher wages they
will tend to come in increasing droves to the United States. By and large,
however, people have a preference to live in their own countries and therefore, as living standards improve in Mexico, the tide of immigration will
cease.

There is a tendency to discuss the U.S.-Mexican free trade agreement as
if today's labor markets were not already highly integrated. People who live
in San Diego know and those border towns know only too well the ease with
which Mexican labor simply moves across the border. We already have an

integrated labor market. The damping effect on our wage structure is already being felt today.

Objections are also raised to the agreements from a global perspective. There are mutlilateralists who are concerned that this shift in American trade policy is really damaging to our overall global position, indeed, to the global economy. There are some who believe that the world is breaking up into regional blocs. Instead, we should ask whether the regional trading arrangements are building blocks or stumbling blocks. Some people argue that what is happening is a fragmentation of the world economy. But what is happening is a deeper integration of the world's economy. And indeed, if we look at this North America free trade area we can see some important signs in that regard. Most multilateralists and free traders would agree that if a country lowers the barriers with a second and in fact lowers its barriers with its other trading partners, that is something the international system should approve of. The Mexicans have actually paid up front; they have already lowered their barriers with respect to all their trading partners.

In addition, the changes that are going to take place in Mexico will bring benefits, not simply for Americans, but for all outsiders. If Mexico has new international property rights, those property rights will be given to all outsiders, not just the United States. If Mexico constrains its industrial policies, in various ways, those benefits will accrue to all outsiders. The same is true of the European Community. Harmonized standards across all of Europe make it easier for anyone who wants to sell in Europe.

It is surely more easy to negotiate with just a few key partners, and to ultimately whip together a global trading system, than with the hundred odd members that exist in GATT. These regional trading arrangements are important, particularly because the process will not end here. Former President Bush announced his Enterprise for the Americas Initiative. It was not simply a U.S.-Canada agreement; it was open to the Mexicans. There is a host of Latin American countries waiting in the sidelines, indeed, clamoring. Countries like Chile and others are going to be eventually a part of this arrangement. The U.S.-Canadian-Mexican arrangement is, therefore, going to be an open arrangement, just as we saw with Europe, which began with the six, went on to the twelve, and is now expanding to include the former East European countries and the Scandinavian and other countries. Regional arrangements in the world are not erecting barriers to outsiders, but contributing to a multilateral system.

Although this is a win-win situation there are losers. The United States has not had adequate policies to deal with those who are adversely affected by changes, which on balance will benefit the United States but, nonetheless, will hurt certain firms, certain workers, and certain communities. We need to do far more in this regard. The principle of trade adjustment assistance is a good one, but we have to change the mechanisms by which we implement. We need a much more generous emphasis on skill acquisition and training and a wage compensation program for displaced workers—not simply while they are unemployed but to compensate them once they get their new jobs for any loss of earnings they might have experienced as a result of their displacement.

We have to think about helping communities. Communities should be allowed to insure their tax basis. A tax base insurance policy would be a mechanism to offset some of the downward spirals that individual communities experience in the face of plant closure.

15

The Role of Trade in North American Integration

Sunder Magun

In June 1990 Mexico and the United States agreed in principle to negotiate a free trade agreement. At the same time both countries invited Canada to join in the forthcoming trade talks. In September 1990 Canada reluctantly accepted the offer to participate in the Mexican-U.S. trade talks. Although the U.S. administration is seeking fast-track authority for negotiating a trade deal with Mexico, all three countries have started to consult each other with the objective of preparing a negotiating agenda and a timetable for trilateral trade talks. Mexico and the United States aim to establish a North America free trade area that will remove trade and investment barriers and that will also provide protection for intellectual property rights.

Although Canada has accepted the offer to participate in the forthcoming trade negotiations, this decision appears to have been made with some hesitation. Canada is concerned that a bilateral free trade agreement (FTA) between Mexico and the United States would cause trade diversion from Canada to Mexico in the American market. Furthermore, the gains expected from the 1988 Canada-U.S. Free Trade Agreement (FTA) would not be realized in the future if the United States and Mexico sign a bilateral free trade agreement. Thus, Canada's motivation for agreeing to negotiate trilaterally is related in part to minimize the trade and investment diversion effects of a Mexican-U.S. free trade area (MUFTA). Canada is also concerned that a bilateral agreement would encourage Canadian companies that depend on exports to the American market to move to Mexico in order to benefit from lower Mexican wages. A further concern is that a North America Free Trade Agreement (NAFTA), based on a trilateral free trade agreement between Canada, the United States, and Mexico, would enhance import competition from Mexico in Canadian markets, especially for Canada's labor-intensive industries such as textile, clothing, knitting, and leather products.

CANADA'S TRADE FLOWS WITH MEXICO AND THE UNITED STATES

Canadian trade linkages with Mexico are limited but growing. In 1987 Canada exported US$418 million of goods to Mexico and imported US$882 million of goods from Mexico. Therefore, Canada has a negative trade balance. Although the United States ranks first, Mexico ranks roughly seventeenth among our trading partners. In 1987 Canada's trade with Mexico accounted for 0.4 percent of our total exports and 0.6 percent of our total imports (see Table 15.1). On the other hand, Mexico's trade with Canada accounted for 2.3 percent of Mexican total exports and 2.6 percent of Mexican total imports.

For both Canada and Mexico, the United States is their largest trading partner. It is also important to note that the American market is increasingly becoming more important for both Canada and Mexico. About three-quarters of Canadian exports go to the United States and almost the same share of Canadian imports comes from the United States. Similarly, Mexico has roughly same export and import shares with the United States.

Table 15.2 provides a detailed breakdown of trade flows among the three North American countries, disaggregated by seven broad commodity groups. Canada and Mexico have a distinct pattern of trade with each other. In 1987 about two-thirds of Canadian exports to Mexico belonged either to agricultural product groups or to resource-intensive commodity groups and the remaining one-third fell into the machinery and transportation equipment group. There have been large changes in the pattern of Canadian exports to Mexico over the past decade and a half. The share of agricultural products in Canadian exports to Mexico steadily increased from 30 percent in 1971 to 49 percent in 1989. On the contrary, the share of machinery and transportation equipment in our exports to Mexico steadily declined from 43 percent in 1971 to 32 percent in 1987.

There have also been large shifts over time in the structure of Mexican exports to Canada. Almost two-thirds of Mexican exports to Canada now belong to machinery and transportation equipment (M&E). A major portion of this commodity group relates to auto parts. The share of M&E in Mexican exports to Canada has been climbing very rapidly. The exports of M&E to Canada went up by 27-fold over the short period from 1981 to 1987. However, such large Mexican exports in M&E to Canada do not imply that Mexico is exporting more advanced goods than Canada. In fact, most of these exports contain a high component of low-skilled assembly labor. However, Mexico has started to raise the skill level of its workers and has indeed started to produce high-quality products in recent years. Like the structure

Table 15.1
Canadian and Mexican Export and Import Shares, 1971, 1979, and 1987

Part A	Canadian Exports		Canadian Imports	
Year	Percentage share of Canadian exports to Mexico	Percentage share of Canadian exports to the United States	Percentage share of Canadian imports from Mexico	Percentage of Canadian imports from the United States
1971	0.4	68.1	0.2	70.8
1979	0.4	65.9	0.4	71.8
1987	0.4	75.1	0.6	72.8

Part B	Mexican Exports		Mexican Imports	
Year	Percentage share of Mexican exports to Canada	Percentage share of Mexican exports to the United States	Percentage share of Mexican imports from Canada	Percentage share Mexican imports from the United States
1971	2.3	69.0	2.8	60.7
1979	1.6	71.2	1.7	67.5
1987	2.3	64.8	2.6	72.0

Table 15.2
Structure of Intra North American Trade, 1987

Commodity Group	Canada to Mexico		Mexico to Canada		Canada to United States		United States to Canada		United States to Mexico		Mexico to United States	
	Value	(%)	Value	(%)	Value	(%)	Value	(%)	Value	(%)	Value	(%)
Mineral fuels, lubricants, and related products	1.3	0.3	108.8	12.3	8,614.0	11.6	1,448.0	2.8	698.5	4.5	4,059.8	19.8
Agricultural products	203.2	48.6	87.3	9.9	12,696.1	17.0	3,902.8	7.5	1,609.6	10.4	2,393.1	11.7
Resource-intensive manufactured products	64.3	15.4	32.6	3.7	10,671.5	14.3	3,798.8	7.3	1227.5	7.9	1,798.3	8.8
Labor-intensive manufactured products	4.2	1.0	32.8	3.7	1,510.8	2.0	1,515.9	2.9	899.4	5.8	845.5	4.1
Chemicals and related products	6.7	1.6	11.1	1.3	3,209.0	4.3	3,246.4	6.3	1,424.8	9.2	416.0	2.0
Machinery and transportation equipment	132.5	31.7	567.9	64.4	34,783.1	46.6	33,773.5	65.3	7737.5	50.1	8,716.3	42.5
Miscellaneous manufactured equipment*	5.6	1.3	42.0	4.8	3,096.8	4.2	4,040.7	7.8	1,855.3	12.0	2,294.5	11.2
TOTAL	417.8	100.0	882.4	100.0	74,572.2	100.00	51,726.2	100.0	15,452.6	100.0	20,523.5	100.0

1. Values are in millions of U.S. dollars.
*Includes commodity groups not specified.
Source: Statistics Canada, The World Trade Date File 1987.

of Canada's exports and imports from Mexico, the M&E group dominates both on the import and export sides of American trade with Mexico. Around half of American exports to and imports from Mexico represent machinery and transportation equipment. This pattern of North American trade results largely from the intraindustry trade of large multinational enterprises (MNEs) which are very active in the three countries. The share of mineral fuels and agricultural products in Mexican exports to the United States is also significant (about 30 percent).

It is important to note that the Mexican economy is undergoing major structural reforms. These reforms were initiated by the Madrid administration (1982–88) and were speeded up by the Salinas administration. As a result of these economic reforms, the Mexican economy is becoming increasingly open to more international competition. Several public enterprises, related to steel production, copper mines, a national airline, telephone services, and commercial banking system, either have been privatized or are in the process of being sold to private investors. Furthermore, Mexico has reduced unilaterally its tariff and nontariff barriers to foreign trade. The average tariff rate declined from 23.5 percent in 1985 to 12.5 percent in 1989. Over the same period, Mexico also reduced the maximum tariff rate from 100 percent to 20 percent.[1] Nontariff barriers to imports have been reduced substantially as well. The number of tariff items subject to import license coverage have now been virtually reduced to zero (see Figure 15.1). Substantial structural economic reforms in Mexico will have profound effects on its future trade and investment patterns with Canada and the United States. Our foregoing trade analysis, which only extends to 1987, cannot capture the future influences of the Mexican reforms on the structure of North American trade. As Mexico develops industrially, Canadian and American trade relations with Mexico will increasingly become more intensive. The intraindustry trade among Mexico, Canada, and the United States will grow substantially.

PATTERN OF INTERNATIONAL SPECIALIZATION IN NORTH AMERICA

Each country in the North American market has a distinct comparative advantage. Each country's factor endowments determine its pattern of international specialization and its structure of North American trade in the long run. Canada has vast natural resources, a highly trained workforce, and a modern transportation and telecommunications network. The United States has a large population and a highly trained workforce, vast land resources, and a very large industrial and scientific infrastructure. Mexico is a developing country, with a large and rapidly growing population and with vast and rich natural resources, especially energy and mining resources. To improve its international competitiveness, Mexico is rapidly liberalizing its

Figure 15.1
Liberialization of Import Controls, Mexico, 1982 to June 1990

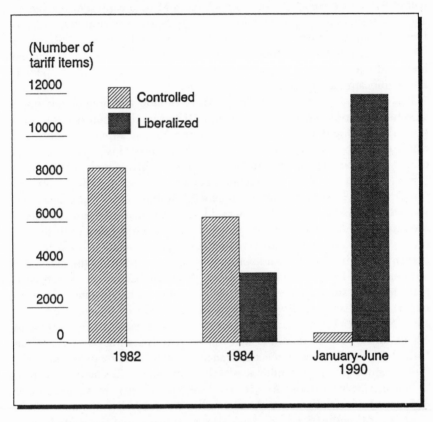

Source: Based on data from the Mexican ministry of commerce and industrial development.

domestic economy and foreign trade. Starting in 1986 the Mexican trade policy has shifted from import protection to more active export-led growth. As a result, like the Asian "Tigers" such as Korea, Taiwan, and Hong Kong, Mexico is becoming a Latin American "tiger" in the North American market.

In order to gauge the complementarity of the three North American economies, we can develop and analyze the indices of "revealed" comparative advantage (RCA, Balassa 1965). The RCA indices by commodity indicate the nature of comparative advantage each country possesses in its export basket, and the changes in the indices show the shifts in the pattern of international specialization over time. The Balassa index of RCA is defined as the ratio of the country's export share in a given commodity at the world level to the country's share in total merchandise export at the world level. Algebraically, the RCA is defined as:

$$(1) \quad RCA = \frac{x_{ij}}{\sum_j x_{ij}} \; / \; \frac{\sum_i x_{ij}}{\sum_i \sum_j x_{ij}}$$

where x stands for exports and the subscripts i and j refer to commodity category and country, respectively.

RCA > 1 indicates comparative advantage in a given commodity group.

RCA < 1 indicates comparative disadvantage in a given commodity group.

Tables 15.3, 15.4, and 15.5 show revealed comparative advantage indices for Canadian, Mexican, and American exports by selected commodity groups. The RCA indices have been calculated for all the two-digit SITC (Standard International Trade Classification) commodity groups for two years (1971–73[2] and 1986–87).[3] The data for RCA calculations have been derived from a large World Trade Data Base, which is maintained by Statistics Canada. The + and − in the tables show the direction of the shift in competitive advantage during the 1971–87 period.

Looking over Table 15.3 for Canada, Canada's comparative advantage lies in physical capital and resource-intensive products, such as pulp and waste paper; electric current; pulpwood and sawlogs; crude fertilizers and crude minerals; road vehicles; cork and wood manufacturers; and inorganic chemicals. In all these commodity groups, Canada's comparative advantages have improved over time. Furthermore, Canada does have comparative advantage in such commodities as paper and paper board; iron ores, nickel, copper, and aluminum; natural and manufactured gas; fish and fish products; oilseeds; and power-generating machinery and equipment. However, the country's comparative advantage is declining over time in all these products.

In general, the Mexican comparative advantage is significantly different from that of Canada. There are striking shifts over time in the Mexican RCA indices. Mexico's comparative advantage lies in those products that use low-skilled assembly labor, and in resource-intensive products. Mexico has comparative advantage in such commodity groups as petroleum and petroleum products; power-generating machinery and equipment; telecommunications and sound recording and reproducing apparatus and equipment; and electrical machinery apparatus and appliances not elsewhere specified (n.e.s.). The last two products are produced by the industries that are located in maquiladoras (in-bond border assembly factories). These industries in maquiladoras often use low-skilled assembly labor and benefit from lower wages

Table 15.3
Revealed Comparative Advantage for Exports, Canada, 1971–73 to 1986–87

SITC	Commodity Group	RCA's 1971-73	Ranked By 1986-87 RCA's
25	Pulp and waste paper +	6.77	7.66
35	Electric current +	3.66	5.41
24	Cork, pulpwood, and sawlogs +	3.78	5.40
64	Paper and paper board ˙	4.04	3.74
27	Crude fertilizers and crude minerals +	2.77	3.37
28	Iron ores, nickel, copper, aluminum ˉ	4.02	2.80
78	Road motor vehicles +	2.74	2.78
04	Cereals and ceral preparations +	2.32	2.54
56	Manufactured fertilizers ˙	2.46	2.46
34	Petroleum, petroleum products, and related materials ˙	5.54	2.25
32	Coal, coke and briquettes +	0.80	2.19
68	Nonferrous metals ˙	2.48	2.14
03	Fish and fish preparations ˙	2.23	2.04
63	Cork and wood manufactures (excluding furniture) +	1.51	1.70
22	Oilseeds ˙	1.71	1.51
71	Power generating machinery and equipment ˙	1.78	1.30
52	Inorganic chemicals +	1.06	1.30
41	Animal oils and fats +	0.85	1.27
62	Rubber manufactures (n.e.s.) +	0.36	1.11
23	Crude rubber (incl. synthetic) +	0.55	1.10
21	Hides, skins and furskins, raw +	0.80	1.04
00	Live animals chiefly for food +	0.90	1.03
11	Beverages ˙	1.38	0.84

Note: RCA values greater than (less than) 1 show comparative advantage (disadvantage in a given commodity group. The + and − show the direction of the shift in comparative advantage during the 1971–89 period. Not elsewhere specified (n.e.s.).

Table 15.4

Revealed Comparative Advantage for Exports, Mexico, 1971–73 to 1986–87

SITC	Commodity Group	RCA's 1971-73	Ranked By 1986-87 RCA's
27	Crude fertilizers and crude minerals (excluding coal, petroleum and precious stones) ⁻	6.64	4.65
00	Live animals chiefly for food ⁻	6.09	3.98
34	Petroleum, petroleum products, and related materials ⁺	0.16	3.63
07	Coffee, tea, cocos, spices, and manufactures thereof ⁻	4.79	2.84
71	Power generating machinery and equipment ⁺	0.69	2.74
05	Vegetables and fruits ⁻	5.12	2.51
76	Telecommunications and sound recording and reproducing apparatus and equipment ⁺	1.75	2.15
77	Electrical machinery, apparatus and appliances, (n.e.s.) ⁺	0.67	2.10
03	Fish and fish preparations ⁻	6.31	1.88
11	Beverages ⁺	0.64	1.65
82	Furniture and parts thereof ⁺	0.60	1.42
06	Sugar, sugar preparations ⁻	7.92	1.41
68	Nonferrous metals ⁻	3.08	1.24
01	Meat and meat preparations ⁻	1.69	0.11
29	Crude animals and vegetable materials ⁻	1.35	0.57
43	Animal and vegetable oils and fats ⁻ ˙	1.29	0.16
56	Fertilizers, manufactured ⁻	1.24	0.10
89	Miscellaneous manufactured articles, (n.e.s.) ⁻	1.21	0.55
59	Chemical materials and products, (n.e.s.) ⁻	1.14	0.11
63	Cork and wood manufactures (excluding furniture) ⁻	1.14	0.94
74	General industrial machinery and equipment, (n.e.s.) and machine parts, (n.e.s.) ⁻	1.08	0.44
65	Textile yarn, fabrics, made-up articles, (n.e.s.) and related products ⁻	1.03	0.32
84	Articles of apparel and clothing accessories ⁻	1.01	0.50
78	Road motor vehicles ⁻	1.21	0.93

Note: RCA values greater than (less than) 1 show comparative advantage (disadvantage in a given commodity group. The + and − show the direction of the shift in comparative advantage during the 1971–87 period. Not elsewhere specified (n.e.s.).

Table 15.5
Revealed Comparative Advantage for Exports, United States,
1971–73 to 1986–87

SITC	Commodity Group	RCA's 1971-73	Ranked By 1986-87 RCA's
22	Oilseeds +	4.68	4.98
41	Animal oils and fats ⁻	3.84	3.78
12	Tobacco and tobacco manufactures +	2.80	3.22
79	Other transport equipment +	2.32	2.88
04	Cereals and cereal preparations ⁻	3.35	2.52
21	Hides, skins and furskins, raw +	1.40	2.40
75	Office machines and automatic data processing equipment +	2.36	2.38
87	Professional, scientific and controlling instruments and apparatus, (n.e.s.) +	1.99	2.25
32	Coal, coke and briquettes +	2.23	2.24
09	Feeding stuff for animals (excluding unmilled cereals) +	2.06	2.24
56	Fertilizers, manufactured +	1.03	2.20
25	Pulp and waste paper +	1.17	2.07
73	Power generating machinery and equipment +	1.97	2.00
59	Chemical materials and products, (n.e.s.) +	1.43	1.57
54	Medicinal and pharmaceutical products +	0.98	1.40
79	Electrical machinery, apparatus and appliances, (n.e.s.) +	1.30	1.32
24	Cork, pulpwood and sawlogs +	0.98	1.31
52	Inorganic chemicals ⁻	1.45	1.31
72	Machinery specialized for particular industries ⁻	1.42	1.25
51	Organic chemicals ⁻	1.52	1.22
28	Iron ores, nickel, copper, aluminum +	0.69	1.17
26	Textile fibres +	1.00	1.17
23	Crude rubber (incl. synthetic) +	0.70	1.09
74	General industrial machinery and equipment n.e.s and machine parts, (n.e.s.) ⁻	1.46	1.02
78	Road motor vehicles ⁻	1.21	0.93

Note: RCA values greater than (less than) 1 show comparative advantage (disadvantage in a given commodity group. The + and − show the direction of the shift in comparative advantage during the 1971–87 period. Not elsewhere specified (n.e.s.).

in Mexico. Eventually, the location of such high-skilled industries would help raise the productivity and wages of the Mexican workforce.

It is important to note that Mexico's pattern of international specialization shifted significantly during the 1971–87 period. In a number of commodity groups, which are mostly unskilled labor-intensive or resource-intensive, Mexico has shifted from a position of comparative advantage to one of comparative disadvantage. These product groups include meat and meat preparations; crude animals and vegetable materials; animal and vegetable oils and fats; manufactured fertilizers; textile, yarn, fabrics; and articles of apparel and clothing accessories. It is interesting to note that Mexico is reducing its specialization in textiles and clothing.

Table 15.5 shows the RCA indices for the United States. It is evident that the American comparative advantage, which appears to be stable over time, lies in high-skill or human capital-intensive products and in natural resource-intensive commodities. The products with a rising comparative advantage include oilseeds; hides, skins, and fur skins; tobacco and tobacco manufactures; other transport equipment, which includes aircraft and parts; office machines and automatic data processing equipment; professional, scientific, and controlling instruments; manufactured fertilizers; electrical machinery; pulp and waste paper; and cork and wood. The three major industries that moved from a position of comparative disadvantage in 1971–73 to a position of comparative advantage in 1986–87 include medicinal and pharmaceutical products, metalliferous ores, and crude rubber products. It is also interesting to note that the American auto industry no longer has a comparative advantage in the global market: it moved from a position of comparative advantage in 1971–73 to a position of comparative disadvantage in 1986–87.

The above analysis of the RCA indices indicates that each country in North America has, in general, a unique and complementary pattern of specialization. As such, under a North America free trade area, each country will build upon its comparative advantage by doing what it already does well better. In the process of doing that, it will enrich and raise the economic well-being of the other two trading partners.

As we have pointed out earlier, Canada has reluctantly agreed to participate in Mexican-U.S. free trade negotiations. Canada, in fact, is very much concerned about losing its market share in the American market. Many Canadians believe that NAFTA, or MUFTA, would result in trade diversion effects, at least in the medium term: Canadian imports will be displaced by lower-cost Mexican imports in the U.S. market. It is feared that the expected gains from the Canada-U.S. Free Trade Agreement will not be realized by Canada under North American economic integration. The size of trade diversion effects depends upon the degree of "similarity" between Canadian and Mexican exports. The trade diversion effect would be significant if and only if Canadian exports "overlap" commodity-by-commodity with Mexican exports in the U.S. market. In order to measure the export similarity indices for Canada and Mexico, we have used the formula suggested by Finger and Kreinin (*Economic Journal*, Dec. 1979). The Finger–Kreinin export similarity measure can be defined algebraically as follows:

$$(2) \quad S(ab, c) = \{\Sigma_i \text{ Minimum } [x_i(ac), x_i(bc)]\} * 100,$$

where

countries "a" and "b" are exporting to country "c"

X_i (ac) is the share of commodity i in country a's exports to country c

X_i (bc) is the share of commodity i in country b's exports to country c

If the commodity distribution of a's and b's exports are totally similar, the similarity index $S(ab, c)$ is equal to 100. If a's and b's exports are totally dissimilar, the similarity index $S(ab, c)$ is equal to zero.

For calculating the similarity measure, we have again used the most disaggregated trade data from The World Trade Data Base, which contains detailed data on export flows by country for six hundred (4-digit SITC) commodity groups.

Table 15.6 presents the similarity indices in import markets for 1971 and 1987. An interesting result is that in 1987 one-third of Canadian value of exports to the United States is matched by Mexican exports in the same product classification. Furthermore, the similarity index increased from 16 percent in 1971 to 34 percent in 1987. This reflects that Mexico's economic structure is becoming more similar to that of Canada. Therefore, after the establishment of NAFTA, Canada would face relatively more competitive pressures from Mexico and would lose some market share, as a result of trade diversion, in the U.S. market. Under North American economic integration Canada would have to adjust to a new trading environment and thus would incur significant transitional adjustment costs.

In addition to these important trade diversion losses, Canada would suffer some losses because NAFTA would increase Mexican competition to Canadian industries in the domestic market. As a result of new competition, Canadian production losses would occur due to increased Mexican exports to Canada. Some industries, such as nonelectric machinery, paper products, wood products, printing and publishing, chemicals, and nonmetallic mineral products would face more competition from low-cost Mexican imports. Output and employment in these industries would fail. On the other hand, output and employment in leather products, nonferrous metals, rubber products, and footwear would increase significantly.

The positive effects are long-term and would come from direct export gains for Canada in Mexican markets, trade diversion gains for Canada in Mexican markets, and dynamic income (productivity) gains that would result

Table 15.6
Indices of Similarity* of Exports; Exporting Countries to Import Countries, 1971 and 1987

Exporting Countries	Importing Countries					
	Canada		Mexico		United States	
	1971	1987	1971	1987	1971	1987
	(per cent)					
Canada/Mexico	-	-	-	-	-	-
United States/Mexico	12	13	-	-	-	-
United States/Canada	-	-	21	21	-	-

*The total exports have been adjusted to remove the scale effect. See J. M. Finger and M. E. Kreinin [1979]. "A Measure of "Export Similarity" and Its Possible Uses." *The Economic Journal*, pp. 905–10 (Dec.).
Source: Statistics Canada, *The World Trade Data Base*, 1971–87.

from the rationalization of North American industries and from rising real incomes of Mexicans after the establishment of North American economic integration. With North American economic integration, the potential to expand Canadian exports and foreign direct investments in Mexico is expected to be very large. Futhermore, the Mexican population is expected to grow rapidly over the next four decades. As a consequence, the demand for foreign imports in Mexico would grow significantly. With North American economic integration, Canada can benefit substantially from expanding Mexican domestic demand. Such dynamic gains are expected to be large when real incomes of Mexicans expand under free trade.

SUMMARY AND CONCLUSION

Canada should participate actively in the forthcoming trade talks between Mexico and the United States. It should support the objective of establishing a North American free trade area, encompassing all three economies in North America. There will, of course, be some medium-term losses that could be directly attributed to the establishment of NAFTA. The transitional losses include trade diversion losses for Canada in the U.S. markets and Canadian production losses in domestic markets due to increased Mexican exports to Canada. The competitive pressures from Mexico to some labor-intensive or resource-based industries would increase under North American free trade. Thus, there would be important adjustment costs to Canadian labor and business. Canada may have to review its labor market adjustment policies, such as retraining and worker adjustment programs, with the objective of facilitating adjustment in the labor market. The U.S. administration has already committed itself to developing specific action plans for addressing labor market concerns of a North American free trade area.

However, in the long run, Canada would gain substantially from North American trade integration. Each country in North America has a unique pattern of international specialization. Each country would build upon its strengths. Canada would benefit from direct export gains in Mexican markets, trade diversion gains in Mexico, and dynamic income (productivity) gains that would result from industry rationalization across the three economies in North America. Such large dynamic gains would accrue to Canada when real incomes of Mexicans rise as a result of North American free trade. As a result of current structural economic reforms, the Mexican economy is growing rapidly and Mexico will become a "Latin American Tiger" within the next decade or so. Economic prosperity in Mexico, along with its rapid population growth, will stimulate the demand for foreign imports. As a consequence, Canada will benefit substantially from expanding demand in Mexico.

NOTES

The views expressed herein are the personal views of the author and should not be attributed to the Economic Council of Canada. I am grateful to Steve Long, a graduate student from Carleton University, and to my colleagues Someshwar Rao, Raynald Létourneau, Tony Lempriére, and Danielle Wright for their comments and assistance. This chapter is part of our larger, continuing study on Canada's Trade Prospects and International Competitiveness.

1. These tariff rates have been derived from a paper by Rudiger Dornbusch, "US-Mexican Trade Relations." Mimeo, p. 14 (July 1990).

2. The average of 1971 and 1973 exports by commodity is used in RCA calculations.

3. The average of 1986 and 1987 exports by commodity is used in RCA calculations.

REFERENCES

Balassa, B. [1977]. " 'Revealed' Comparative Advantage Revisited: An Analysis of Relative Export Shares of the Industrial Countries 1953–1971." *The Manchester School of Economic and Social Studies* vol. 45(4) (Dec.).

———. [1965]. "Trade Liberalization and 'Revealed' Comparative Advantage." *The Manchester School of Economic and Social Studies* vol. 33 (May).

Balassa, B., and Luc Bauwens. [1988]. *Changing Trade Patterns in Manufactured Goods: An Econometric Investigation.* Amsterdam: North Holland.

Cline, William R. [1989]. *United States External Adjustment and the World Economy.* Washington, D.C.: Institute for International Economics.

Department of Finance Canada. [1990]. *Canada and a Mexico-United States Trade Agreement.* Ottawa (July).

Dornbusch, Rudiger. [1990]. "U.S.-Mexican Trade Relations." Testimony before the Subcommittee on Trade, Committee on Ways and Means, U.S. House of Representatives. Mimeo, June 14.

Finger, J. M., and M. E. Kreinin. [1979]. "A Measure of Export Similarity and Its Possible Uses." *The Economic Journal* vol. 89 (Dec.).

Hart, Michael. [1990]. *North-American Free Trade Agreement: The Strategic Implications for Canada.* Halifax: Institute for Research on Public Policy.

Industry, Science and Technology Canada. [1990]. "North American Trade Liberalization: Sector Impact Analysis." Ottawa (Sept.).

Lipsey, Richard G. [1990]. "Canada at the U.S.-Mexico Free Trade Dance: Wallflower or Partner?" Toronto, C. D. Howe Institute, vol. 20 (Aug.).

Purcell, John F. H., and Dirk W. Damrau. [1990]. "Mexico: A World Class Economy in the 1990's." New York, Sovereign Assessment Group (Aug.).

Schott, Jeffrey, J., ed. [1989]. *Free Trade Area.* Washington, D.C.: Institute for International Economics.

Waverman, Leonard. [1993]. "The NAFTA Agreement: A Canadian Perspective," *Assessing NAFTA: A Trinational Analysis,* edited by Steven Globerman and Michael Walker, Vancouver, Fraser Institute.

Wonnacott, Ronald J. [1990a]. "The Canadian-U.S. Experience in Auto Trade Since 1965: Its Relevance for Free Trade Negotiations with Mexico." Toronto, C. D. Howe Institute, vol. 24 (Dec.).

————. [1990b]. "U.S. Hub-and-Spoke Bilaterals and the Multilateral Trading System." Toronto, C. D. Howe Institute, vol. 23 (Oct.).

————. [1990c]. "Canada and the U.S.-Mexico Free Trade Negotiations." Toronto, C. D. Howe Institute, vol. 21 (Sept.).

16

International Unions and NAFTA

Joseph Mangone

The UAW has taken a dim view of the negotiations that have been undertaken by the governments of the United States, Mexico, and Canada that are generally referred to as negotiations on a North American Free Trade Agreement (NAFTA). In fact, we opposed granting the administration an extension of its authority to bring back an agreement to Congress under rules known as "fast-track," which allow no amendments and require a vote after limited consideration.

We did not take that negative position because we wanted to ignore the increasing number and intensity of economic ties between the United States and Mexico or because we determined that there were no important issues that could be usefully discussed. We arrived at our position based on the administration's stated goals and objectives for the U.S.-Mexican talks. Those goals were limited to trade and investment, pure and simple. There was no room in the negotiations for directly addressing the economic and social conditions of workers (their pay, working conditions, workplace rights, and living standards), or the environmental impact of existing patterns of production and trade and the expected impact of patterns fostered by a new agreement.

There are many other issues that were not acceptable to the Bush administration as negotiating subjects, like sustainable development strategies, democratic political development, human rights, immigration, and a host of others, all of which are essential facets of America's future and the future of our relationship with Mexico and Canada. But these were not acceptable subjects of negotiation. We worked with a coalition of groups from around the country, some of them based in Washington, others based around the country in places like Minneapolis. And we worked with similar coalitions

in Canada and Mexico that shared our reservations about the narrow objectives and limited agendas of their own governments.

So we opposed the fast-track extension. Unfortunately, we lost in the
House of Representatives by a rather small margin. We announced at the
time that this was not the end of our interest in this issue, that we would
continue our commitment to develop a trinational dialogue that would address the intense needs of workers in all three countries for better working
and living conditions, and we have done just that. And we will continue in
this effort because our members have a strong interest in reaching a trinational, worker-oriented understanding of the problems facing the three countries.

One of those problems is dealing with differences among the United States,
Mexico, and Canada in the legislation and enforcement as they affect workers. Before jumping into this area, we need to look at the recent past as it
has affected the economic and social condition of workers.

In 1982 economic depression struck in Mexico when the U.S. economy
dived into the most severe recession since the 1930s and interest rates soared,
making interest obligations on Mexico's foreign debt unpayable. Since then,
living standards for the vast majority of working Mexicans have fallen substantially and unemployment has remained high. The poverty and hardship
experienced by most Mexicans during this period were intensified by the
Reagan and Bush administrations' response to the weighty burden of debt
on Mexico's government. The International Monetary Fund and the World
Bank, along with private banks in the United States, led by the U.S. Treasury
Department, pushed Mexico to repay its debt obligations in full by squeezing
living standards and draining capital from the Mexican economy.

The resulting economic debacle has had a direct effect on American workers. As the dollar value of real wages in Mexico fell below those in Korea,
Singapore, Brazil, and other developing countries, U.S. firms moved production to Mexico, or threatened to do so unless American workers lowered
their wages and benefits, weakened workplace protections, or made other
concessions. Sadly, some workers have been forced to accept these conditions to preserve their jobs.

The UAW and other unions have watched with anger and horror the rapid
expansion of maquiladora production in response to Mexico's debt crisis.
American jobs moved across the border to pay predominantly young women
far less than one dollar per hour. The living conditions in the rapidly growing
Mexican border towns are appalling and the stories of toxic waste dumping
are truly frightening.

The maquiladoras constitute a model of economic development tied to having wage rates among the lowest in the world to attract multinational corporate investment that produces for foreign, not domestic, markets. Poorly paid
workers cannot afford to buy "internationally competitive" products.

American workers did not fare well in the 1980s either. While we have not been subjected to the economic deprivation experienced by Mexican workers, we have suffered from declining average real wages, paltry productivity improvement, an escalating public and private debt burden, and a concentration of new employment in low-wage jobs. Employment in industry after industry in which international trade is a significant factor has declined in the past ten years despite the high and rising level of productivity in these industries. The Reagan and Bush administrations' economic and trade policies helped encourage this decline, while favoring the growth of service industries with no international competition. The relatively low wages and inadequate health and pension benefits that characterize jobs in these industries keep millions of American workers and their families struggling week to week to make ends meet. Thousands of UAW members displaced by international trade have suffered steep declines in their living standards and the well-being of their families and communities has suffered as well.

Our experience with maquiladora production tells us what to expect if a free trade agreement accelerate this process and precludes alternative approaches. Certainly, there will be more U.S. and other foreign companies shifting production to Mexico, as an alternative to U.S. production, to pay pitifully low wages that perpetuate poverty rather than relieve it. Workers in previously protected Mexican industries, such as its domestic auto industry, will face intense pressure to lower their wages to the maquiladora level, just as American workers have faced this pressure. In the process, many will be displaced from their jobs.

The Mexican low-wage economic development strategy has its corollary on the U.S. side of the border. By linking its economic fortunes with Mexico, the United States opens up a vast reserve of low-wage labor that allows the past decade's policy of creating millions of low-wage jobs to continue. Unfortunately, this policy discourages domestic investment in technology, machinery, and other capital equipment needed, along with investments in education and training for workers, to raise living standards for American workers.

To perpetuate the path of the past ten years, as the governments in both countries seem to endorse, would be disastrous for workers in both countries. We must make a break with the policies of deregulation and denationalization, and move toward rational development that puts the interests of workers ahead of corporations, that puts higher wages ahead of higher profits.

The efforts of unions are one of many forms of response to these conditions and it is important for unions in both countries to become stronger if the aims of our governments are to be thwarted.

There are mechanisms available to put additional pressure on the governments and companies that are fostering the competition between American and Mexican workers. One of these is the Coalition for Justice in the Maquiladoras. This coalition of labor, environmental, religious, and activist groups has developed a code of conduct for U.S. companies operating plants in Mexico. The code incorporates respect for U.S. and Mexican laws concerning labor rights and standards, environmental standards and practices, and social responsibility to workers and communities. The UAW has been a part of, and worked with, the coalition and the AFL-CIO has played an important role in the coalition's work. It is still at an early stage and there are no major victories to announce at this point, but they will come and Mexican and American workers' interests will be served by those victories.

The UAW has worked with unions in other countries throughout its history through the International Metalworkers Federation. The IMF has brought unionists in the auto, steel, electrical and electronic, and shipbuilding industries together to solve mutual problems for a hundred years. There are affiliates of the IMF in Mexico and we look forward to working with them and other Mexican unions to build relationships that promote our common interests and stifle the greed of the multinational corporations that seek to divide us.

The potential forms of cooperation are almost unlimited. The most common forms of multinational support and cooperation have consisted of information exchanges related to organizing or bargaining; industry-wide and company-wide meetings of unionists to discuss developments relevant to them all; regional meetings for workers in particular companies or industries to exchange information and discuss strategies; educational conferences to address the problems of women workers, white-collar workers, skilled workers, and others. All of this exchange and coordination is going on now internationally and the UAW participates in it, as does the Canadian Auto Workers Union (CAW). There is no need for new institutions or new organizations to take NAFTA negotiations into account. We must take advantage of the mechanisms that exist, like the IMF, and forge new relationships that reflect the increasing economic and social ties among the United States, Mexico, and Canada and the need to defend the interests of workers from the growing influence of multinational corporations with the three governments and in the economies of the region.

Now, there are people of good intention who tend to oversimplify the situation of workers in Mexico. Just as the labor scene in the United States includes advances for workers in certain industries or companies within an overall dismal picture, so the same is true for Mexico. And there are different labor voices in Mexico with different positions on free trade, on politics, on development. But they are all unions and, just as the UAW and the Teamsters may disagree, that does not mean some unions should not be recognized and others ignored or opposed.

The government and the labor movement in Mexico have had a long history together. The ruling party, the PRI, has been in office for decades. Until the most recent decade, workers in Mexico made important advances in wages and living standards, labor laws, and social standing. There have been different perspectives within the labor movement in Mexico and these differences exist today. This means that coordination with workers in Mexico will not be a simple, quickly accomplished task. The UAW and many American unions, however, have more than begun to establish formal and informal contacts and relationships that will become stronger in the days and years ahead.

We cannot fully discuss or understand the labor situation in Mexico today or its history or the relationship between workers and unions in the countries involved in NAFTA negotiations. What we can do today, and what we must do, is to dedicate our energies and our activities toward building a counterforce to the power of the multinational firms that use the slogan of "free trade" to promote their own agenda: to minimize labor costs at the expense of the incomes of their workers; to substitute their interests for the national interest in government policymaking; to undermine social standards that limit their operations. We can do it through the coordinated efforts of American, Mexican, and Canadian workers directed at NAFTA negotiations. And we will do it.

17

The North American Free Trade Agreement Negotiations and the Canada-U.S. Free Trade Agreement: Revisiting Unfinished Business

Keith Martin

THE CANADA-U.S. FREE TRADE AGREEMENT

The Canada-U.S. Free Trade Agreement (FTA), signed on January 1, 1989, represents a watershed in Canadian trade policy. By formally recognizing the central role of trade to Canada's continued prosperity, and particularly the importance of the United States in Canada's trade picture, the FTA reflects a new Canadian vision of how to manage its economy and ensure prosperity, a vision founded on a rejection of protectionist and inward-looking economic policies as tools to achieve economic development. The FTA should also be viewed in the context of a general worldwide movement toward more open markets internationally. In this more general context, the FTA can be seen as a formal recognition of the benefits of globalization and an important but not dramatic commitment to continue policies based on the premise that open international markets lead to a more efficient and productive allocation of resources than the mercantilist alternative.

While these general principles are important, the FTA negotiators recognized the complex intellectual and practical issues raised by trade liberalization, and consequently the agreement left many issues to be resolved or dealt with more comprehensively through other avenues or other negotiations. Two principal avenues were seen as particularly appropriate. First, the Uruguay Round negotiations of the General Agreement on Tariffs and Trade (GATT) offered the opportunity to deal with such issues as subsidies, intellectual property, agriculture, and trade in services. As well, the FTA negotiators set up explicit mechanisms for continued discussions and negotiations on a host of issues, including automotive trade, rules on technical standards, accelerated tariff reduction, and, most important, subsidy and dumping issues.

The Uruguay Round offers the most important short-term opportunity for Canada and the United States to obtain a resolution to some of the issues that were not dealt with in the FTA. A successful and comprehensive outcome to the Uruguay Round negotiations of the General Agreement on Tariffs and Trade could potentially result in greater adjustment for Canadian industry than the FTA, especially in some sectors such as agriculture, textiles, and footwear. By offering a multilateral forum for discussion on these issues, the political difficulty of Canadian concessions is less acute than in a bilateral, Canada-U.S. negotiation. This must be weighed against the less comprehensive outcome that a multilateral negotiation is likely to offer on many, although not all, issues.

In addition to the Uruguay Round, the FTA was seen as an avenue for addressing unsettled trade issues between Canada and the United States. Within the FTA, mechanisms were created for the continued discussion of matters outstanding from the negotiations. Foremost among these mechanisms is the bilateral working group mandated by Articles 1906 and 1907 of the FTA to negotiate new definitions on subsidies and dumping, and to negotiate new rules on constraining or reforming trade remedy laws, as they apply between Canada and the United States. While the working group has done some preliminary research, negotiations have been put off until the completion of the Uruguay Round.[1]

NAFTA

At the conclusion of the FTA negotiations, the Uruguay Round as well as the FTA mechanisms created to allow for continued negotiations were the only formal avenues available for resolving unsettled business from the FTA and for building on the agreement where its achievements were marginal. An unexpected third avenue for resolving outstanding issues from the Canada-U.S. FTA and for expanding on the agreement has presented itself in the form of the NAFTA negotiations. However, it is important to note that Canada's intention in participating in NAFTA is not to explore a new avenue for revisiting these outstanding issues. Canada's primary reason is to protect the law, spirit, and integrity of Canadian-U.S. FTA. NAFTA also permits the creation of a continental trade zone as opposed to the creation of two overlapping zones, one between Canada and the United States and one between Mexico and the United States. The latter arrangement would create a hub and spoke system that would give the United States an advantage over Canada and Mexico as a destination for investment. A longer-term reason for Canadian participation in the NAFTA talks, and one that is often neglected, is that the negotiations offer Canada an opportunity to gain preferred access to a potentially dynamic Mexican market. While revisiting the FTA's unfinished business may not have been the Canadian government's primary imperative in joining these negotiations, these talks do offer a new opportunity for progress on some of these issues.

Some have expressed concern that regardless of the reasons for Canadian participation in NAFTA, these negotiations produce a challenge to the multilateral system. The negotiations on a NAFTA offer an opportunity to rapidly liberalize sectors of the North American economy. Regional trade liberalization allows countries within a geographical boundary the opportunity to open up their markets more rapidly and more deeply than is possible in a large, multilateral forum like GATT. This provides targets for future GATT negotiations to aim for and allows for the exploration of what is possible at the frontier of trade liberalization. By establishing rules that are consistent with the principles and objectives of the multilateral system and by incorporating legal and technical language that borrows from GATT, NAFTA negotiators can reinforce the multilateral system as opposed to challenging it. Canada's decision to appoint Canada's ambassador to GATT as the chief negotiator in NAFTA is an encouraging and reassuring sign that the Canadian government recognizes the need to ensure compatibility between GATT and NAFTA.

The Canadian motivations in joining the NAFTA negotiations (protecting the FTA, preventing a hub and spoke system, gaining preferential access to Mexico, and revisiting issues left from the FTA) have been noted. The next question is how Canada can fulfill this mandate. Canada can largely protect the FTA, prevent the worst aspects of a hub and spoke system, and gain some preferential access to Mexico by meeting the minimalist Canadian demands on tariff elimination and rules of origin (a core agreement).[2] Canada can fully offset the hub and spoke system and gain the same access to Mexico as the United States by signing onto a full, comprehensive NAFTA as opposed to just a core agreement. This latter approach would in a comprehensive NAFTA also allow Canada the opportunity to meet the objectives that are examined in some detail in this chapter. Such an achievement would not only profit Canada and the United States, but also Mexico, which would benefit from a NAFTA that was more comprehensive than the FTA.

The minimalist Canadian objective in NAFTA is a common triparty agreement on rules of origin and on tariff elimination. If Canada signed onto only these aspects of NAFTA, the agreement would consist of a trilateral core agreement and a bilateral Mexican-U.S. extended agreement (with the possibility of a third Canadian-Mexican extended agreement). For reasons that are related to GATT consistency and the promotion of Canadian interests, one trilateral comprehensive NAFTA is most desirable. However, proceeding from minimalist demands to other demands is analytically useful and corresponds to one possible outcome of the negotiations.

Rules of origin should be common within a North American free trade zone to avoid the costly administrative system that would be created by two sets of rules of origin, one for U.S.-Mexican trade and one for Canadian-

U.S. trade. By agreeing on one set of rules, NAFTA can provide for continental trade that is not restricted by unclear and inconsistent regulations. The negotiators will also have to carefully consider the implications of highly restrictive rules of origin. While tight rules can ensure more sourcing within a market, investors have less incentive to locate within a market when they are restricted in their ability to source offshore without losing tariff-free access within the market. Restrictive rules are also contrary to the principles of open competition that underlie trade liberalization. They additionally decrease the competitiveness of products that would benefit from higher levels of sourcing from third markets, limiting the ability for those products to compete internationally.

Achieving tariff elimination rules that are common to Canada, the United States, and Mexico is also a minimal objective of Canada. Tariff elimination is a defining characteristic of free trade zones, and a principal objective of Canada in joining the NAFTA talks was to prevent a hub and spoke system whereby the United States had separate free trade agreements with Mexico and with Canada. In such a system, goods produced in the United States would gain tariff-free access to both Canada and the United States, while goods produced in either Canada or in Mexico would only be able to obtain tariff-free access to the United States. Such a system would make the United States more attractive as an investment destination than either Canada or Mexico, a situation that Canada seeks to avoid by achieving common tariff elimination rules.

Canada's objective beyond these minimalist demands is to seek where possible to build upon and refine the FTA. The FTA negotiators were unable in the time available to them to negotiate comprehensive rules on all of the issues related to Canadian-U.S. trade, and so NAFTA provides an opportunity to develop new or more comprehensive rules on a wide variety of trade issues of importance to Canada.

TRADE ISSUES IN CANADA

Technical and Legal Issues

The experience of two years of the FTA has provided the Canadian and U.S. administrations with information about where the agreement did not adequately deal with barriers to trade between the two countries. This experience will also be valuable with respect to a North American free trade zone, although a new learning curve will also have to be experienced in the postimplementation period of the NAFTA, especially as regards Mexico. Canada and the United States continue to face difficult administrative, technical, and legal problems in such areas as customs declarations, labeling requirements, nontariff barriers, paperwork, and other bureaucratic matters. The opportunity to simplify and facilitate trade between Canada and the

United States and within North America in general by drafting clearer rules should not be lost.

Government Procurement

NAFTA could build upon the FTA's marginal achievements in establishing rules on government procurement, by further limiting the ability of governments and their agencies to favor domestic firms over foreign competitors. NAFTA could also include refinements to the bid challenge mechanism created within Canada by the FTA for the investigation of complaints about procurements that fall within the scope of the FTA (the United States already had a bid challenge mechanism in place prior to the FTA). However, most interesting is the possibility that NAFTA could apply government procurement rules at the subfederal level. The ability to devise such rules presumes the ability of the federal government in each country to enforce treaty obligations at the subfederal level. The United States has suggested that it has the constitutional power to do this. Mexico has also suggested that it has the authority to force compliance to NAFTA's subfederal government procurement rules. Canada's ability to ensure its trade partners in NAFTA that government procurement provisions at the subfederal level could be judicially or administratively enforced by the federal government is much more doubtful, although the adaption of the current constitutional provisions on an economic union could provide the federal government with the institutional authority to enforce such rules.

Agriculture

Canada could gain from liberalized rules in agricultural trade within North America without much adjustment, since on the one hand it is not a large competitor with Mexico's agricultural products, while on the other hand it is a potentially large importer of these products, especially fresh fruits and vegetables. While interests in the southern United States are likely to seek a minimalist outcome to the agricultural discussions, Mexico may well demand heightened access to the North American market, an outcome that would generally benefit Canadian consumers without threatening Canadian producers. Where Canada is more vulnerable is in its support of supply management techniques to support farmers' income. This system has been challenged internationally within GATT, and Canada in the Uruguay Round has officially been in support of opening markets in agriculture at the same time as it has supported a strengthening of Article 11 of GATT, which allows supply management systems to be exempted from the general provisions of the agreement.

Energy

Canadian interests in oil and natural gas call for secure access to the United States. In this regard, the industry's interests would be satisfied by maintaining the status quo, since this would continue to provide Canada with more advantageous access to the U.S. market than Mexico has and would continue to make Canada a more desirable location than Mexico for international energy investors. Furthermore, Mexican success in excluding energy trade from NAFTA would limit the development of the inefficient Mexican industry, and this would in turn provide Canada with an additional advantage relative to Mexico. However, while the status quo is acceptable to Canada, Canadian negotiators should not block any Mexican offers to open their energy market within North America. Canadian expertise in exploration and pipeline development would make liberalization of the Mexican industry attractive to Canada, by offering Canadian firms new investment opportunities in Mexico.

Safeguards

The rules on safeguards in the FTA are stringent and provide for binding arbitration to settle safeguard disputes, probably with the intention of determining adequate compensation for the industry subjected to a safeguard action. NAFTA should adopt these rules, since they reduce the incentive to use safeguards casually. Binding arbitration to settle safeguard cases is an important element of the FTA, since it offsets the greater power of the United States relative to Canada in safeguard disputes and because it promotes an adjudicative, objective process for determining fair compensation to firms facing safeguard action. Canada should ensure that binding arbitration also applies in the NAFTA.

Subsidies and Countervailing Duties

Canada and the United States were unable in the free trade agreement negotiations to settle on a common definition of subsidies and the appropriate scope of countervailing duties. The United States considers many Canadian policies to require unacceptable levels of subsidization, even though these practices are considered by the Canadian government to be legitimate and to be sanctioned by the international trade system. Canada considers many U.S. trade remedy practices as de facto trade harassment, while the United States considers these laws to be necessary to force exporters to the United States to trade fairly and to offset unfair foreign subsidy practices. Because of the inability of the FTA negotiators to resolve these issues and settle on a common definition of subsidies, it was agreed that these questions would continue to be the subject of negotiations. Articles 1906 and 1907 of the

FTA commit both governments to continue to negotiate on these issues, and provides a five-year timetable, with the possibility of a two-year extension if necessary.

Until these issues are resolved, the FTA provides for appeals of the determinations of domestic trade authorities on subsidization and dumping to be made to a bilateral, Canadian-U.S. panel. Chapter 19 of the FTA sets out the rules for this panel, which is limited to interpreting the domestic trade remedy legislation on countervailing and antidumping duties. Nevertheless, this appeal process has proven to be important to Canada, which as a small country considers itself vulnerable to unilateral U.S. trade remedy actions.

The issue of what system should be in place if NAFTA is successfully negotiated has been the subject of much debate. The Mexican government has indicated that while its preference would be comprehensive new rules on subsidies and dumping, its minimum demand is incorporating Chapter 19 provisions into NAFTA. Despite the mandate of Articles 1906 and 1907, Canada and the United States have avoided tackling difficult subsidy issues bilaterally; their preferred approach has been to emphasize the multilateral route as the most appropriate avenue to deal with subsidy issues. In the event that GATT talks are successful, many of these difficult issues may be resolved, although multilateral progress on subsidies will not likely diminish Mexican demands for a panel system for appeals of domestic trade remedy determinations.

Many Canadians have expressed strong reservations about Mexican access to a Chapter 19 system. For example, the Committee on Canada-U.S. Relations in an official, joint resolution, states that "The dispute settlement provisions of Chapter 19 of the Canada-United States FTA dealing with trade remedies should not be incorporated into a NAFTA." One of the reasons for these reservations is that Canada and the United States set up the Chapter 19 provisions as a temporary measure, pending agreement on subsidies and dumping. To give Mexico access to these provisions would result in a weakening of the argument that the ultimate objective was new rules on subsidies and dumping. Furthermore, it has been suggested that the U.S. Congress would not consider restrictions on the U.S. right to apply its trade remedy law, and already considers the panel system to be an infringement of legitimate U.S. jurisdiction. This argument suggests that political imperatives may prevent the achievement within NAFTA of the same type of rules that the FTA achieved. Furthermore, some have argued against Mexican access to a Chapter 19-type system on the grounds that the Mexican trade remedy system is not transparent and is inadequately judicial.

The primary Canadian interest is to ensure that NAFTA in no way restricts the continued bilateral existence of the Chapter 19 provisions of the FTA. Canada should also consider promoting further discussion of subsidy and dumping issues to the extent that it is possible and politically feasible for progress to be made within the NAFTA negotiations. Mexico may in many cases be sympathetic to Canadian views, in which case Canada should not lose an opportunity to revisit some issues that it was not possible to resolve in the FTA.

Dumping and Antidumping Duties

Dumping occurs when a good is sold in an export market at a price that is lower than the price a good is sold at in its domestic market.[3] However, it is normal corporate behavior for a firm to differentiate between markets and to price below its costs of production for short periods of time (companies would be unlikely to sell below marginal costs for any period of time, but could be willing to temporarily sell below costs of production if this allowed them to offset some of their fixed costs). Furthermore, such behavior is sanctioned domestically so long as it is not predatory in nature. However, across borders such goods can be subjected to offsetting antidumping duties. Such treatment is particularly problematic in a free trade zone, where in theory differential pricing can be rendered ineffective by buying the good where it is being sold more cheaply, and reselling it in the market where it is being sold at a higher price.

The Committee on Canada-United States Relations of the Canadian Chamber of Commerce and the United States Chamber of Commerce have played a leading role on this question by commissioning a major study on the issues raised by the elimination of dumping laws as they apply between Canada and the United States. The study found no legal or technical reasons for which dumping laws could not be eliminated as they apply between Canada and the United States, and replaced by a substitute regime based on competition law. With the elimination of all tariffs between Canada and the United States by 1998, and the explicit commitment in Article 1907 of the Canada-U.S. FTA for both parties to "seek to develop a substitute system of rules" on subsidy and dumping issues, the imperative for moving toward the speedy achievement of such an objective is strong.

Some have suggested that NAFTA negotiations offer an opportunity for advancing the work on eliminating antidumping law as it applies between Canada and the United States. However, similar concerns arise on this issue to those raised regarding the inclusion of Mexico in Canadian negotiations on restraining the United States in its application of its countervailing duty law. One such concern is that Mexican participation in these negotiations would complicate an already technically and legally daunting challenge. It has also been suggested that the U.S. Congress would be unwilling to amend domestic trade remedy laws as they apply to Mexico, and that such provisions within NAFTA would reduce the likelihood of its passage into law. While these are important issues to which Canadian negotiators must be sensitive, they should not prevent a thorough discussion within NAFTA on the eventual elimination of dumping laws among all three countries. If a comprehensive NAFTA is negotiated, such a development will ultimately have to take place. The negotiators would be doing the cause of trade liberalization a service if they at minimum created a mechanism for the further discussion of such issues. They should also not lose sight of the balance of concessions and gains that a trade agreement represents. It is desirable for an agreement in its core form to address most of the important issues before implementation; after implementation, bargaining positions, political will, and negotiating strategies all shift markedly.

Services

Canada and the United States negotiated arrangements on trade in services in the FTA that mostly provided for standstills, as opposed to a liberalization of trade. It is hoped that GATT can achieve a significant liberalization of trade in services. Such an achievement should also be possible in NAFTA. Canada and the United States see Mexico as a market in which they have a comparative advantage in trade in services, and so both countries will push for liberalization to take place in this sector. In such a case, new opportunities may also become available for Canadians in the United States if these rules are applied trilaterally. Achieving more liberalization of trade in services in NAFTA than took place in the FTA should be a key goal of the negotiators.

While the principle of national treatment has been a cornerstone of trade liberalization internationally, in some sectors other principles may make more sense. In financial services, where regulatory regimes can limit market access when it is based on national treatment, several other principles have been advanced as preferable. The Canadian industry is currently supporting opening markets based on the principle of de facto national treatment with comparable market access, which in many respects is conceptually similar to reciprocity. The important issue is whether the provisions on financial services liberalize trade in a way that is fair to the industry in North America.

Transportation

NAFTA offers a new opportunity to negotiate rules on rail transportation and in trucking, since transportation was left out of the FTA. The establishment of fifth freedom rights[4] is important to the Canadian industry, which would need to use the United States as a base to penetrate the Mexican market. The trucking industry in all three countries has opposed granting cabotage rights[5] within NAFTA. Air transportation is not being examined in NAFTA, and this sector is the subject of separate Open Skies negotiations between Canada and the United States.

Telecommunications

Telecommunications is another key sector where NAFTA offers an opportunity for Canadian interests to be advanced in an industry in which Canada has an international presence and a comparative advantage. Trade in this sector requires good rules on government procurement, since many telecommunications purchases are made by governments and their agencies. As with all high-technology fields, trade in the telecommunications sector also requires transparent and enforceable rules assuring the protection of intellectual property in foreign markets.

Intellectual Property

Intellectual property rights were intensively discussed in the FTA negotiations. However, Canada was unwilling to go as far on intellectual property issues as the United States desired, and in the end the United States chose to exclude the provisions tentatively negotiated from the final agreement on the basis that no agreement on intellectual property was better than a suboptimal agreement. Intellectual property rights are key to exports in high technology, and NAFTA offers an opportunity to attempt to establish strong North American rules for the protection of intellectual property. Mexico has improved its legislation on intellectual property protection, which is now seen to be at world standards. Consistent and timely enforcement of intellectual property rules, and proper compensation for breaches of the law, will be objectives sought by negotiators in NAFTA.

General Dispute Settlement

Chapter 18 of the Canada-U.S. Free Trade Agreement provides for a two-step process for dealing with disputes. First, an ad hoc panel drawn from a roster and consisting of Canadian and U.S. citizens responds to the terms of reference of a dispute and issues a recommendatory report within strict time limits. The Canada-United States Trade Commission (CUSTC), a ministerial-level organization created by the FTA, then meets to discuss the panel report and negotiate its implementation. Because these are negotiations, Canada is susceptible to the U.S. application of its greater power. This is especially the case since the panels are ad hoc, the reports recommendatory, and their content open to interpretation. The addition of Mexico to the Chapter 18 provisions of the FTA in a new North American zone would be beneficial to the process and to Canadian interests. It would offset asymmetrical U.S. power in Chapter 18 negotiations, and would provide for disputes to be settled in a trilateral as opposed to bilateral context, which can improve the dynamics of resolving a disagreement. NAFTA offers other opportunities to improve the provisions of Chapter 18 of the FTA. This includes formalizing the process to limit the scope for negotiations, such as the establishment of a permanent tribunal as opposed to the current ad hoc panel process, agreement to have trilateral panels so as to get around the difficulty of having three nationals of one country and two nationals of another country on a five-person panel examining a bilateral dispute, and agreement to have the chair of a panel be from the nondisputant country. Canada should in general seek to increase the adjudicative nature of the Chapter 18 process.

NEW ISSUES IN THE NAFTA NEGOTIATIONS

Labor Standards

NAFTA negotiations will likely address some issues that were not the subject of serious discussions in the FTA. Labor standards is one. There is fear that standards in North America will be lowered in a North American free trade zone, as competitive pressures induce companies to move to the country with the lower standards. Several points need to be made here. First, Mexico has made efforts to raise its standards to international levels, and much of the attention of negotiators will be focused on the enforceability of these new Mexican commitments. Furthermore, it is not clear that markets with lower standards benefit from or attract investment due to these lower standards. High standards increase productivity, lead to a more motivated workforce, decrease labor turnover, and are strategically important to companies that emphasize quality. Most competitiveness experts stress innovation and quality over cost control as key to the success of companies. In this regard, it is helpful to note that within the United States, California with its high standards has had a better record economically than Louisiana, which has lower standards; within Canada, Ontario has had a better record economically than provinces with inferior standards.

Some industries are labor-intensive and low-technology, and in these sectors more attention has to be paid to the issue of labor standards. Furthermore, it is appropriate to seek avenues to improve standards and promote worker safety. It is important to note, however, that most if not all countries see labor regulation as a sovereignty issue and balk at attempts to mandate how they regulate on such issues. Negotiators may prefer to set minimum standards that must be met by all parties, for example, with the possibility of snapbacks of previously agreed tariff reductions in the event that these standards are not met. The more complex issue is how to measure whether a country has achieved and properly enforced such provisions.

Environmental Issues

Many of the points made above apply with equal force to environmental issues. While environmental issues are not being discussed as part of the NAFTA negotiation process itself, parallel discussions are taking place on environmental issues. Some environmentalists fear that in a zone free of tariffs, Mexico would have a competitive advantage due to its alleged low environmental standards. According to this argument, industries in the free trade zone would have higher costs in Canada and the United States than in Mexico, where the expense of meeting environmental standards would presumably be lower due to less stringent rules and weaker enforcement of rules. It bears mentioning that Mexico has unilaterally improved its environmental standards, and has committed itself to strict enforcement of these standards in the future. The question is whether these improvements are adequate, whether enforcement is likely to be effective and consistent, and whether competitive pressures will either draw investment to Mexico due to lower environmental standards there, or result in a lowering of standards in Canada and the United States.

These new issues are being raised because of the unique nature of NAFTA, which involves the negotiation of a free trade agreement between two highly developed, industrial states and a developing country. However, experience to date suggests that those countries with low environmental standards do not benefit from these policies, and that the lower standards in these countries is largely a result of their fiscal constraints. Trade liberalization, by generating wealth, will provide Mexico with the tools to improve its environmental record. There is a positive correlation, not a negative correlation, between high environmental standards and general prosperity. Finally, it is also worth noting that the vast majority of trade and investment is between countries with high environmental standards and high incomes, putting into question the suggestion that open trading regimes will lead to disinvestment from countries with strong environmental standards to those with lower standards.

The importance of maintaining and raising environmental standards and enforcement within all three countries in NAFTA requires that careful attention be paid to these important matters. Many recommendations have come forth. One intriguing suggestion is that the United States, Canada, and Mexico use a portion of the wealth to be generated by trade liberalization to fund a pool that would finance new projects to increase environmental standards and promote sustainable development. It is worthwhile for officials to explore these and other ways in which governments can cooperate to improve environmental standards. Such projects should not confuse issues, however. Trade liberalization increases wealth, and this in turn increases the ability of a country to fund expensive environmental projects. The primary focus of negotiators should be to liberalize trade, recognizing that this is fully compatible with the objective of sustainable development.

NAFTA and GATT Article 24

It is essential that NAFTA, like the Canada-U.S. Free Trade Agreement, be fully consistent with the General Agreement on Tariffs and Trade. GATT is the key instrument internationally for trade liberalization, and it is in the interest of Canada to seek a comprehensive outcome to the Uruguay Round negotiations. NAFTA must be consistent with Article 24 of GATT, which allows for an exception to the most favored nation rule[6] for comprehensive free trade zones that meet a number of GATT tests. Furthermore, as noted earlier, NAFTA must be compatible with not just the legal and technical wording of GATT but also with its spirit. For example, the rules of origin should not be so high as to unreasonably restrict the ability of investors within North America to source from third countries without losing tariff-free access to the North American market. These objectives are central to the achievement of an outcome in NAFTA that is consistent with and promotes general international trade liberalization.

Canadian participation in NAFTA is part of a more general recognition within Canada of the importance of trade liberalization to a small, trade-dependent country. By participating in this process, Canada is able to protect its interests within the FTA while exploring the possibility of gaining preferred access to the potentially dynamic Mexican market. Furthermore, this process allows Canada to revisit issues that were not fully negotiated in the FTA.

Canadian interests demand that priority attention be placed on the multilateral system. A comprehensive, successful outcome to both GATT and NAFTA would allow Canada to diversify its trade relations throughout the world by promoting internationally the competitive advantages it achieves regionally through North American trade liberalization. By rationalizing its industries and increasing competitive pressures on the domestic economy, Canada will be better placed to succeed in penetrating new international markets. Such global competitiveness is key to Canada's continued prosperity and wealth.

NOTES

1. The government's decision not to pursue subsidy negotiations bilaterally until the completion of the Uruguay Round has been generally accepted. However, there is less support for the decision to wait until the completion of the Uruguay Round to discuss antidumping issues. While antidumping will be discussed in the Uruguay Round, the round is not likely to go far on these issues and the parameters of the multilateral negotiations will be far more constrained than in the FTA negotiations. This is because different conceptual issues are raised by antidumping law in a trade zone free of tariffs.

2. If Canada does decide to only sign a core agreement, and leaves Mexico and the United States to sign a separate agreement that is more comprehensive, a partial hub and spoke system would be created, in that only the United States would have comprehensive agreements with the other two parties in the zone. Some of the features of the Canada-U.S. and the Mexican-U.S. agreements would be common. Companies interested in those features would then find provisions related to their

concerns incorporated into two treaties that the United States has signed, one with Mexico and one with Canada. This would make the United States a more attractive destination for investments for companies in those sectors. A core agreement and a separate, more comprehensive agreement would also present challenges to the GATT system that one comprehensive agreement would not, and would complicate the North American trade system instead of simplifying it.

3. In Article 6 of GATT and in the Antidumping Code negotiated in the Tokyo Round, dumping is defined as selling a product "into the commerce of another country at less than its normal value . . . for the like product when destined for consumption in the exporting country."

4. Fifth freedom rights allow a party to load in market a, unload in market b, reload in market b, and unload in market c. Clearly, for Canada this would be important, since it would allow a Canadian trucker to go into the United States with one load, and reload to go into Mexico with a new shipment. In the absence of fifth freedom rights in NAFTA, Canadian truckers would have much more limited access to the Mexican market.

5. Cabotage rights allow a party to load in market a, unload in market b, reload in market b, and then unload in market b. Such a right allows for foreign parties to provide competition to the domestic industry within its own boundaries.

6. The two pillars of the multilateral system are the National Treatment rule and the most favored nation rule. Under national treatment, imported goods are treated no differently than are domestic goods. The most favored nation (MFN) rule provides for a concession offered to one member of GATT to be offered to all of its members. Clearly, this rule is violated in a free trade zone, where the members of the zone offer each other concessions not available to others. This exception to the most favored nation rule is only allowed in the case of a comprehensive free trade zone that provides for significant trade liberalization. However, the GATT record on denying Article 24 exceptions from the MFN rule has been unimpressive.

18

Unions and Transnational Boundaries

M. E. Nichols

We have seen Mexican labor leaders struggle to improve the maquiladora system despite pressure from U.S.-based corporations and the Mexican government. We have seen the federales move to check the books of all the labor leaders who have been in leadership for a good while and who have taken a strong stand against the maquiladora officials who will do what the operators want, and to keep out strong unions in other areas. We expect that the negotiation of a free trade agreement that does not effectively address these issues will see even more erosion of labor rights for Mexican workers.

We see Mexican union leaders who oppose the operators being pushed aside by the government, which favors newer union leaders more willing to go along. CWA local 6229 President Richard Tarver, who has had a long experience with maquiladoras, reports that government is seeking to split the Mexican labor movement by supporting union officials who will do what the operators want, and to keep out strong unions in other areas. We expect that the negotiation of a free trade agreement that does not effectively address these issues will see even more erosion of labor rights for Mexican workers.

A U.S.-Mexican FTA poses a double threat: the loss of jobs for U.S. workers and an even worse exploitation of Mexican workers. Our strategy at this time is to continue to demand strong labor, human, and environmental rights as part of any trade agreement with Mexico. We fought this issue in Congress when we opposed the extension of the fast-track authority. Although we lost, we opened up many eyes in Congress to the abject conditions that most Mexican workers live and work in, particularly in the maquiladoras. We will be fighting just as hard in the Senate when the final agreement comes up for approval. The AFL-CIO and CWA support expanded world trade and open borders. But we are also pragmatists and realists.

Mercantilism, not unrestricted free trade as practiced by our nation, is still the most powerful force in the world economic system trade today. For evidence, we look no farther than the failed round of GATT talks, which broke down over Europe's insistence on maintaining high levels of agricultural subsidies.

The vision of an open world system equally benefiting all peoples remains just that—a vision. In November 10, 1991 *Washington Post* editor Jodie T. Allen points out that "as careful readers of Adam Smith will note, a faster growing world economy does not guarantee any one country will have a larger share in that growth, or even maintain its current share."

Winners and losers have already emerged in the new world economic order and if the current trade system remains unchanged the gap between the have and have-not nations will only continue to widen in the future. Many third world nations, for instance, are insistent on protecting and sustaining their competitive advantage, which they view as an abundant, low-wage workforce, employed in primitive conditions designed to attract foreign transnational corporations.

While average U.S. real earnings increased by a meager 3.7 percent since 1983, a time during which our nation experienced the longest peacetime expansion in its history, manufacturing wages since 1980 jumped by 18 percent in Germany.

The current recession also reveals the extent of structural unemployment that has developed in our economy over the past decade. We will hear more about this as we examine the failures of the recovery to gather any steam or momentum.

We need to examine the proposed negotiations with Mexico within the broader context of a new global economy that is no longer dominated by the United States. Even now, the Department of Labor tells us that only about 37 percent of jobless workers qualify for unemployment benefits—a dramatic reversal over past recessions when upwards of 80 percent of unemployed workers received jobless benefits. The difference? In the name of greater international competitiveness, we have seen the rise of the so-called flexible workforce comprised of part-time, temporary, seasonal, and contract workers who do not qualify for unemployment benefits, who have exhausted benefits, who do not work for covered employers, or who have not been employed long enough to be eligible for benefits.

And, yet, our national leaders continue to ignore the social cost of our trade policies as they cling to the mistaken belief that the free market and private capital are enough to deal with these problems. Our trade negotiators dismiss the concerns of organized labor by making exaggerated promises of economic prosperity based on unrealistic numbers spewed forth by computer models. In 1979, for instance, the U.S. special trade representative's office estimated that the last round of GATT talks would yield benefits to U.S. consumers that later analysis revealed were fifteen times higher than what we eventually received.

This is a consistent pattern followed by our trade negotiators. Similar overblown promises of future economic benefits are being heard in justification of a free trade agreement with Mexico. We need look no farther than to our Canadian neighbors to see the potential for disaster a free trade agreement with Mexico would mean for both American and Mexican workers.

When we negotiate with Mexico, we are bargaining with a nation that is deep in debt and still suffering from a severe economic depression, a country with a weak record of enforcing labor, environmental, safety and health, minimum wage and child labor laws, a nation with lower living standards, a less educated and less healthy population, a nation plagued by structural unemployment.

Ironically, during our negotiation of the free trade agreement with Canada, we found ourselves in a reversal of roles. The Canadians enjoy a higher standard of living compared to us, they have healthier and better educated workers living in a society with strong social, labor, and environmental laws. To Canadians, the United States is the low-wage competitor, with weaker unions and social programs and ineffective economic regulation.

Now, nearly three years later, even the staunchest promoters of the FTA with the United States are having a difficult time defending their position in Canada. Plants are shutting down and fleeing to the United States where wages are lower and unions are weaker. The government is under increased pressure to reduce Canada's social programs in response to competition from U.S.-based companies. The Canadian Labour Congress estimates that more than 226,000 Canadian jobs have been lost as a result of the U.S.-Canadian FTA.

In response to these trends, CWA is joining with our foreign counterparts to engage in joint actions to effectively counter the multinational corporations who travel the globe seeking the lowest wage rate. We joined with the Canadian auto workers, the communications electrical workers of Canada, and two international labor secretariats, the postal, telegraph, and telephone, and the International Metalworkers Federation in a conference about Northern Telecom in October 1990.

This company is engaged in a variety of antiunion activities here, including the illegal electronic wiretapping of union supporters. They also fired key union leaders in Turkey after they led a successful strike, and continue to work with government authorities in Malaysia to prevent the unionization of the workers at their two plants there. Our goal is to build an alliance to deal with Northern Telecom's antiunion behavior and to protect the living standards of Northern Telecom workers around the world. The October conference was an outgrowth of our successful strike against Northern Telecom in 1989. We were engaged in a bitter six-week strike against the company where we represent 600 of the 15,000 workers employed by Northern Telecom in the United States.

The company decided to take us on in collective bargaining. When we were forced to strike, the company replaced every one of our members, which they can do under U.S. law. We reached out to our brothers and sisters in the Canadian labor movement for help. The Communications Workers of Canada and the Canadian auto workers enthusiastically responded to our appeals. CWC President Fred Pomeroy was personally involved in our efforts to reach a settlement. At one point, he even sat with us at the table when bargaining resumed. We conducted joint activities, mobilization drives, and education efforts. We eventually reached a fair contract with Northern Telecom and all of our members were rehired. We would never have had a successful resolution of this strike without the involvement of the Canadians.

In 1990 at our convention in Toronto, we signed a cooperation agreement with the communications workers of Canada that pledges us to continue these joint activities. In fact, a Northern Telecom executive was quoted as saying this agreement will have a significant impact on their operations "because of the globalization of the industry." This pact is not a prelude to merger between our unions. We both recognize and support our mutual independence. But we also recognize our mutual interdependence in the new international economy. We are already engaged in similar cooperative activities with the leaders of Mexico's telephone workers union as they face the challenge of foreign ownership of their nation's telecom system.

Greater international solidarity between unions must become the pattern of our relationships in the future. CWA is among the U.S. unions who are in the vanguard of this movement. We see a simple and straightforward goal for the future as the world continues to shrink. Whenever and wherever one of our employers moves off-shore to a foreign land, there they will find a strong, free trade union waiting for them.

At the same time, CWA President Bahr has called for a less confrontational approach on the part of international companies. Just as many companies today see no boundaries to their business opportunities, they should see no boundaries to their labor-management relations. Many experts in this country, for example, believe that labor-management cooperation is essential to the competitiveness of a company in the global economy.

Why should we not look to that advice in the way a company conducts its business on the international level? In the telecommunications and other industries, unions from around the world already are beginning to target specific employers for joint action. But this need not be confrontational.

On three occasions, President Bahr and the president of the Japanese Telephone Workers met with the CEO of Nippon Telephone and Telegraph to talk about procurement policies—specifically pushing ATT's union and American-made products.

We know we have made a difference. Last year, the CEO of Nynex, at the suggestion of agency for international development, asked President Bahr to go to Thailand where the Telco unions are an obstacle to Nynex winning a large contract. In fact, we even see the day when a worldwide group of workers from all of the unions representing a transnational will gather for an international conference to discuss common problems, concerns, and suggestions for improving conditions for workers. CWA has already offered to take the lead in calling for a joint international meeting of labor and management with any of the U.S.-based transnational corporations in the telecommunications industry.

In conclusion, we see many opportunities for international labor to respond to these developments if we begin now to coordinate our strategies and our activities. If there is a new day dawning over an international marketplace, we should also wake up to the possibilities and the necessity of new and different international labor-management relations.

19

The Impact of NAFTA on Collective Agreements in Canada: Issues and Trends

Claude Rioux

During the past decade one of the most divisive political debates in Canada focused on the Canadian-U.S. Free Trade Agreement (FTA). We experienced a highly polarized debate that was widely discussed in forums, conferences, and the media. Many people and organizations were wary of the consequences of the FTA on the social fabric of Canada, among which was the labor movement. Even though the agreement is now in its fourth year, feelings are still very much alive on this issue.

In fact, just a year after the agreement was passed and signed by the two governments, Canada was plunged into a severe recession and its manufacturing sector was badly hurt. By way of illustration, between the first quarter of 1989 and the second quarter of 1991, about 273,000 jobs were lost in the Canadian manufacturing sector, according to data compiled by the Economic Council of Canada. There are a number of contributing factors. One is the value of the Canadian dollar, which is at its highest level in the past ten years. Others relate to productivity questions such as unit labor costs, industrial structure, and lagging technological innovation.

But FTA has also had an important effect. This is particularly true in the furniture industry. It was anticipated that this labor-intensive industry was bound to suffer from the implementation of the FTA (Rioux, 1988).

In the same period of time, 21,000 jobs were lost in Quebec alone. This industry is still characterized by a great number of small and medium-size firms, often undercapitalized or family-owned. Thus it was vulnerable to the increased competition coming from U.S.-based firms. Much of this story also applies to the garment and textile industries as well as the domestic appliances and "white" goods industries. Many of these firms are now trying to improve their competitiveness by importing from the United States or abroad components such as wood panels, hardware, glass and mirrors, electrical components, paint and varnishes—all goods that are generally more expensive in Canada and cheaper in the United States. This is the result of lower prices, the relative value of the Canadian dollar as regards the U.S. dollar, and the reduction in tariffs. Moreover, over the past three years, imports of furniture and appliances from the United States have increased dramatically. This very short introduction illustrates the extent to which the FTA is a significant source of change in the economic environment of important segments of the Canadian manufacturing sector.

It is difficult to make any final assessment of the overall effects of the FTA on the entire Canadian economy. The agreement is still relatively recent and attempts to make an assessment are complicated by the severe recession that we have experienced during the second and third years of the FTA. We will need more time to study its impact very carefully, but there are definite signs that some industries will have great difficulties surviving in a continental market.

SIMILARITIES AND DISTINCTIVE CHARACTERISTICS

If you were to look at a Canadian collective labor agreement, you would find many features in common with an American one, and vice versa. Many subjects are similar. Even the language is similar, the major difference being in Quebec where the use of French is mandatory. The wording is also the same, as is the syntax and even the idioms. All of our agreements have such provisions or articles as grievance and arbitration procedures, union recognition, seniority rules, disciplinary codes, and so on.

This is by and large the result of a historical process. The most important unions and corporations that were engaged in the development of the Canadian collective bargaining system were from the United States. They brought with them their culture, procedures, patterns, and behavior pertaining to their vision and practice of industrial relations and personnel management. In particular, many practices were "imported" from the United States: pattern bargaining, union management sponsored fringe benefits programs, job evaluation systems, and craft definitions of jurisdictions. Thus, there are many similarities in both the formal and the substantive aspects of collective agreements in both countries.

Over the past three decades, however, we can also observe significant changes in Canada. First, public sector employees have become increasingly unionized and have developed distinctive collective bargaining agenda and processes. For instance, the public sector collective bargaining process is generally highly centralized at municipal, provincial, and federal levels. Their contracts are usually very detailed and their negotiations are conducted within specific framework of laws and regulations. This formal setting will not be hampered by the FTA. If some changes are to occur, it will likely be on the more substantive aspects of their contracts. In particular, governments will attempt to keep their contracts within the ambit of their overall economic policies and criteria, the latter being under the influence of the philosophy and the general objectives pursued by the implementation of the FTA.

A second significant change in the Canadian industrial relations scene is what is known as the "Canadianization" of the labor movement. The best known examples are those of the paperworkers, the energy and chemical workers, and the auto workers unions. It is not an exaggeration to suggest that this trend, where major unions separated from their international "parent" unions, was to varying degrees related to serious dissatisfaction and even disapproval, of the policies, priorities, and agenda set by these international unions. In splitting, these Canadian unions obtained greater autonomy, were able to develop their own philosophies, and had more scope to set their own objectives and determine the ways and means needed to pursue them.

Finally, there is a distinctive aspect of the Quebec legal environment that is both formal and substantive. In that province, labor agreements like all other contracts are subject to a civil code originally derived from French statutory law. This situation is unique to Quebec. There are of course, labor code provisions governing labor agreements, but their interpretation and enforcement are subject to the rules established under the civil code. Thus, we have had to make a number of adjustments in labor agreements, especially as regards language, in order to take account of this particular situation.

THE LEGAL ENVIRONMENT

Generally speaking, it can be argued that Canadian labor law is more supportive of unionization and collective bargaining (Weiler, 1990). The Canadian labor movement also has a tradition of commitment to the enlargement of social programs and, over the years, it has developed a comprehensive agenda on social issues (Robinson, 1991).

Thus, in Canada, it is easier to get a certification. It is also easier to collect union dues under the "Rand formula," which is widely diffused in labor agreements. Moreover, in some provinces, there are regulations controlling or, even in the case of Quebec, forbidding the use of strikebreakers. On the other hand, the social safety net, especially the medical and hospitalization assistance programs, is very helpful since we do not have to negotiate it. In what is a highly contentious area for U.S. collective bargaining, that means that in Canada we only have to bargain over issues such as prescriptions and related matters, short- and long-term disability insurance, and dental care.

Indeed, trade unionists have expressed concerns over the impact of the FTA on social programs as they fear that such programs could be threatened by the strong economic pressures arising out of the implementation of the

FTA. They anticipated, and it still appears to be the case, that these pressures would emerge not only because of increased competition, but also because the conservative political and corporate elites in Canada would share the individualistic values that appear so well entrenched among their American counterparts.

Caution of the longer term is thus required because changes in these values and programs could effect significant alterations in the overall collective bargaining process in Canada.

COLLECTIVE AGREEMENT ARTICLES PROMPTED BY THE FTA

We should expect increasing competition from U.S. firms, as the FTA gradually takes effect. But the FTA is just a part of a much more complex situation. It must be kept in mind that the FTA was implemented in the context of the increasing globalization of markets, and it is difficult to disentangle the relative effects of each. The FTA will act as a facilitating mechanism in this process of globalization. In the short run, therefore, it will have an effect similar to that of an "accelerator." Let us look at the impact of this new force on collective bargaining in two particular industries, for example, automobile assembly and forest products, and then consider its implications for some specific collective agreement articles, notably work rules, fringe benefits, pay structure, and terms of agreements.

In the fall of 1990 the Canadian Auto Workers (CAW) renegotiated their agreements with the Big Three automobile producers, GM, Ford, and Chrysler. In Canada, the union was able to negotiate base pay increases for each year of a three-year agreement. In the United States, the UAW negotiated a base pay increase for the first year of its contracts and a lump sum for the second and third years. In so doing, the CAW successfully continued the wage-bargaining policies that it set in the early 1980s. Moreover, the CAW not only avoided lump sum payments but also the profit sharing that featured prominently in the UAW agreements. This was a serious test case for the Canadians, since negotiations began after the FTA was adopted. The auto workers negotiations in Canada tend to be critical for the manufacturing sector at least, and their outcome is widely scrutinized by both unions and employers.

While the CAW was negotiating in the auto industry, it was also pursuing similar objectives in the airline industry. Indeed, it obtained provisions protecting the purchasing power of its members, which was regarded as a "good deal" because the CPI was expected to rise significantly following the introduction of the new federal goods and services tax. Both of these cases were important. Their results suggest that the bargaining power of the Canadian Auto Workers Union appears greater than that of the UAW during this same period (Katz and Meltz, 1991). The other interesting point is that this very dynamic union was able to negotiate its own agenda not only on wage issues but on other questions such as training, job security, and other benefits.

The forest products industry is strategic in the overall Canadian economic structure. Just the pulp and paper sector alone represented 10.8 percent of total Canadian exports in 1990, mainly to the United States, and ranked first in terms of value added: $8.851 billion in 1987 as opposed to $4.751 billion for the automobile industry (CPPA, 1990).

Most of the Canadian output (newsprint is the main commodity) is traded freely between our two countries. However, there are also important segments such as fine paper, specialty and packaging grades, and lumber, which have been protected by tariffs. Overall, it is an industry that is very much exposed to any changes in international markets. Before the FTA, the negotiation of Canadian contracts tended to follow a path quite distant from that of the United States.

In 1990 Canadian unions had to renegotiate contracts for all the mills in eastern Canada (some 108 mills and 50,000 employees). They obtained a 17.0 percent base pay increase over the life of a three-year agreement and some improvements in vacation pay. However, for the first time in twenty years they had to make major changes as regards flexibility. This brings us to some of the changes occurring, in the context of the FTA, in certain specific articles of Canadian collective agreements.

Work Rules

During the 1990 pulp and paper negotiation, all of the companies requested that we negotiate more flexible work rules for maintenance workers. In particular, we introduced a new concept based on mutual aid between different trades as well as on some elements pertaining to the teamwork concept. Employers were also permitted to maintain operations during two statutory holidays. This was settled after very tough discussions and, in some cases, after strikes.

This is a good illustration of changes that can originate from the United States. For many years, pulp and paper mills located in the southern states had incorporated such work rule provisions. Their collective agreements referred extensively to flexibility in assignments, "general mechanic" classifications, the team concept, and "run through" operations. It is not coincidental that we were obliged to introduce such changes into our collective agreements in the Canadian forest industry. Indeed, it was the result of this tough new economic context ushered in by the FTA.

We were, on the other hand, quite successful in negotiating clauses protecting job security, training, and safe working practices. Again, however, these clauses, as they are linked to work rules, will come under further pressure for change.

Fringe Benefits

As long as our national medical and hospitalization assistance programs are kept intact (there are pressures to introduce deductible or extra-billing charges in some provinces), there is unlikely to be major changes in our agreements. Many employers recognize that this public system is cheaper than in the United States and it gives room to both parties when they are negotiating compensation packages since we do not have to make the kinds of tradeoffs that are so common in the United States, namely, between wage increases and the cost of privately insured medical benefits. As regards pension benefits, suffice it to say that the laws and regulations pertaining to private schemes were improved markedly a couple years ago and that the federal and provincial pension programs remain a good base.

Pay Structure and Terms of Agreement

The 1990 auto workers negotiations were critical; fortunately the CAW was successful in keeping its pay structure intact. Otherwise, there would have been a significant increase in the pressures for change in pay structures in other negotiations. For example, lump sum payments are to be found in the U.S. pulp and paper industry and on some occasions Canadian employers referred to such practices. Another difference is that U.S. pulp and paper agreements often feature what are called "starting rates," a practice that contrasts markedly with our contracts since we do not have such rates.

Terms of Agreement

While the standard term of agreement in Canada is between one and three years, with a legislated minimum of one year throughout Canada and a legislated maximum of three years in the province of Quebec, several U.S. contracts are characterized by much longer terms. For example, there are contracts whose terms are of four, five, or six years in duration in the southern pulp and paper industry.

However, this does not mean that we cannot extend the term of contracts in Canada. We recently experienced a new way to address this issue. An important specialty steel company, international in origin, asked its Quebec-based union to extend the collective agreement beyond the usual three-year term. This company was committed to making a major investment at its site located in Tracy (Quebec). In order to ensure that industrial peace prevailed during the construction and start-up period, both parties agreed to set up a special mechanism to replace the conventional termination procedures of their contract. Provided that the investment materialized it was agreed that, at the end of the third year, both parties would have ultimate recourse to a final offer interest arbitration procedure to settle their agreement. If negotiation failed, an arbitrator would then be empowered to mediate and eventually decide which offer should be upheld. Both parties set aside their right to strike or lockout. In return, the company agreed to include in the memorandum of agreement articles related to job security guarantees for existing employees over the next six years, joint training program, and a joint total quality control system. In this new competitive age, this agreement was seen as an innovation.

Even without modifications in labor laws, we are likely to see more such agreements in the future as they can be linked or included in strategic business decisions.

Information Sharing

In the context of increased competition, unions are also likely to ask for first-class information about financial results, business planning, and investment. We are seeing more such demands from unions and, in some firms, there have been experiments where unions and management are sharing this strategic information. There is much scope to expand this important aspect of collective bargaining and we can extend the purpose of the collective agreement to cover such strategic issues.

CONCLUSION

During the coming years, the most sensitive parts of the collective bargaining agreement will be those related to work rules. It is there that most of the changes will occur. As there are increased links between the two countries, it will affect work organization in the workplace. Canadian unions will have to meet this challenge and they are able and ready to address this issue in a responsible way.

What is perhaps more ominous is the conservative agenda of the Canadian government. There are, to some extent at least, strong signals that medicare, unemployment insurance benefits, and programs financing public education are all under considerable scrutiny as the government seeks to cut back on public spending. It is this threat that could introduce the most critical changes in Canadian collective bargaining.

NOTE

I would like to thank, for his assistance and comments on an earlier version of this chapter, Gregor Murray, Department of Industrial Relations, Universite Laval.

REFERENCES

Rioux, Claude (1987). "Libre-échange et pratiques du syndicalisme au Canada et aux États-Unis: Rétrospective et perspective." In *Un marché, deux sociétés?*

Libre-échange, aspects économiques, ed. Pierre J. Hamel ACFAS, Cahiers Scientifiques 51, pp. 158–73.

———— (1989). "Free Trade, Change, Flexibility and Adjustment." In *Flexibility and Labour Markets in Canada and United States*, ed. Gilles Laflamme, Gregor Murray, Jacques Bélanger, and Gilles Ferland. Geneva: International Institute for Labour Studies, pp. 297–314.

Weiler, Paul (1990). *Governing the Workplace-The Future of Labor and Employment Law*. Cambridge: Harvard University Press.

Robinson, Ian C. (1991). *Organizing Labour: Explaining Canada U.S.-Union Density Divergence in the Post War Period*. Unpublished Ph.D. Diss., Yale University.

Canadian Pulp and Paper Association (1990). *Reference Tables*, Montréal.

Katz, Harry C., and Noah M. Meltz. (1991). "Profit Sharing and Auto Workers Earnings—The United States vs. Canada." *Relations industrielles* vol. 46, no. 3, pp. 515–30.

20

Provisions of Collective Agreements: A Comparison of Selected Portions of Labor Agreements Negotiated in Canada and the United States

Marcus Hart Sandver

The purpose of this chapter is to identify and discuss differences in the contents of labor agreements negotiated in the United States and Canada. The reason that this topic is important can be traced back to the U.S.-Canada Free Trade Agreement (FTA), which became effective on January 1, 1989. If the promises for the FTA are correct, then we can expect to see more movement back and forth across the border of U.S. and Canadian firms. The results of this chapter will perhaps give union leaders and management negotiators from both sides of the border a better sense of what to expect and a greater insight into the expectations of their counterparts.

The data upon which this chapter is based have been gathered from a variety of sources. The data on collective agreements negotiated in Canada come from the library of a large midwestern law firm with which the author has a long-term and continuing consulting relationship. Specific hypotheses and hunches are largely the product of conversations with several partners of the firm who have had extensive collective bargaining experience in both the United States and Canada. The sample of Canadian contracts is small (n = 9), but represents a good cross-section of major manufacturing corporations. The sample contracts are all from Ontario. The companies and the unions that have negotiated the agreements are as follows:

1. Hercules Canada, Inc. and United Steelworkers of America
2. Dow Chemical, Inc. and Energy and Chemical Workers Union
3. Canadian Home Products and United Food and Commercial Workers
4. DuPont Canada and International Brotherhood of Teamsters
5. General Electric Canada and United Electrical Radio and Machine Workers of Canada

6. Amoco Fabrics and Fibers, Ltd. and IWA-Canada Local 1–600

7. Westinghouse Canada and United Electrical Radio and Machine Workers of Canada

8. Accuride Canada, Inc. and National Automobile, Aerospace and Agricultural Implement Workers of Canada

9. Columbian Chemicals Canada, Ltd. and the International Brotherhood of Teamsters

The comparison group of contracts will be that found in the Bureau of National Affairs' *Basic Patterns in Union Contracts* and the source materials included in the *Collective Bargaining Negotiations and Contracts*. Due to time and space limitations it will not be possible to make comparisons between every item in every contract. As a result six subjects of negotiations are compared: management rights, union security, grievance and arbitration procedure, representation issues, subcontracting, and duration.

MANAGEMENT RIGHTS

A statement of management rights is an important component of all labor agreements. An inspection of the nine Canadian agreements reveals that all of them contained a statement of management rights. A closer inspection of the nine agreements reveals that in seven of these the management rights clause was so broadly written that there were no expressed limitations on management to make rules or to direct, control, and supervise the workplace. An example of a relatively limited management rights clause can be found in the Hercules agreement:

Management of the Plant

The right of the Company to manage its enterprise and to direct employees is hereby reserved in each and every detail except as such right shall be specifically abrogated by this Agreement. The Company agrees that these functions shall be exercised in a manner consistent with the terms of this Agreement, and all promotions, demotions and transfers of employees shall be in conformity with the seniority provisions of Article 7 of this Agreement.

A more detailed and more representative statement of management rights is found in the Westinghouse agreement:

Management Rights

It is recognized that management of the Plant and direction of the working forces are fixed exclusively in the Company, which maintains all rights and responsibilities of management not specifically modified by this Agreement.
The exercise of such rights shall include but not be limited to:

(a) The right to hire, assign, increase and/or decrease the work forces, promote, demote, transfer and make temporary lay-offs for lack of business and materials.

(b) The determination of: the number and location of plants, the products to be manufactured, the methods of manufacturing, schedules of production, kinds and locations of machines and tools to be used, processes of manufacturing and assembling, the engineering and design of its products, and the control of materials and parts to be incorporated in the products produced.

(c) The making and enforcement of rules and regulations, not inconsistent with this Agreement, relating to discipline, safety and general conduct of the employees, and to suspend or discharge or otherwise discipline employees for just cause.

To enable the Company to keep its products abreast of scientific advancements the Company may from time to time, without reference to seniority hereinafter set forth, hire, teach, transfer, or assign duties to technically trained persons and technical students and deal with them as it deems advisable. This practice, however, shall not adversely affect the employees in the bargaining unit.

The Company agrees that these functions will be exercised in a manner not inconsistent with the terms of this Agreement.

Claims of discriminatory up-grading, demotion or transfer, or a claim that an employee has been suspended or discharged without just cause may be made the subject of a grievance and dealt with as provided in the Agreement.

A study of over four hundred labor agreements negotiated in the United States by the BNA reveals that management rights were more likely to be expressly limited by the contract than for those negotiated in Canada. In particular, the BNA study found that in 86 percent of the contracts they studied there were some limitation on rights.[1]

In particular, the unrestricted right of management to make rules was only found in 36 percent of the agreements studied.[2] The group of Canadian contracts studied for this chapter seems to give management the unrestricted right to promulgate rules in the majority of cases.

UNION SECURITY

In all the Canadian contracts studied there was an express provision for the union shop and the check-off of union dues. Representative language can be found in the Canadian Home Products agreement:

Article 4—Union Membership

1. All employees covered by this Agreement shall become members of the Union on attaining seniority as provided by this Agreement.

Article 5—Check-off

1. The Company agrees and is hereby authorized to deduct from the wages of each employee who is a member of the Union the amount of the monthly dues as estab-

lished by the Local Union. Union dues collected will be forwarded to the Financial Secretary of the Local by the 15th of the month where the dues were collected.

The prevalence of the union shop in the Canadian agreements may well be due to the concentration of the companies in Ontario. In a national study of U.S. agreements the BNA research showed that only 62 percent of the U.S. agreements included union shop type of provisions. Even in the north-central and midwestern regions of the United States the percentage of agreements with union shop provisions was only 67 percent. The percentage with a check-off of union dues was about 90 percent nationwide.[3]

Interestingly, two of the Canadian contracts contained "hold harmless" provisions, an item that is becoming increasingly common in U.S. labor agreements in wake of the *Hudson* decision by the U.S. Supreme Court.

GRIEVANCE PROCEDURES AND ARBITRATION

All of the Canadian contracts contained some provision of grievance procedures and arbitration. A typical procedure would be found in the DuPont agreement.

Article X—Grievance Procedure

(a) Any dispute, grievance or misunderstanding (hereinafter called "grievance") involving occupational classification, wages, seniority, hours of work or other working conditions which any employee or group of employees may desire to discuss and adjust with the Company, shall be handled in accordance with the provisions of this Article.

(b) While an employee may discuss a grievance with his foreman at any time, a request for retroactive adjustment need not be entertained by the Company unless the grievance is presented in writing within thirty (30) days of the date of the incident which gave rise to the grievance. Any grievance shall be deemed to have been withdrawn if, after an answer has been given at any step, more than thirty (30) days have elapsed before the grievance is carried to the next step.

(c) The employee shall first take up his grievance directly with the foreman of his department. If the matter is not resolved by the foreman, it shall be handled as follows:

Step 1. The employee may report the matter to the steward elected to represent his group, who, together with the employee may take up the matter with the foreman and shall at the same time present to the foreman a written summary of the grievance. If the written decision of the foreman does not settle the matter to the satisfaction of the employee or four (4) regularly scheduled working days have elapsed since the grievance was submitted under the provisions of this step, the employee and the steward may:

Step 2. Take up the matter with the appropriate member of supervision above the foreman as designated by the Company from time to time. If the written decision of the appropriate member of supervision does not settle the matter to the satisfaction of the employee or twenty-one (21) days have elapsed since the grievance was submitted under the provisions of this step, the steward may:

Step 3. Submit the grievance in writing to the Union Bargaining and Grievance Committee which may bring the matter to the attention of the Site Manager by presenting to him or his appointee the written statement of the grievance. The Union Bargaining and Grievance Committee may then discuss it with the Site Manager or his appointee at a time to be agreed upon. If the Site Manager or his appointee does not settle the matter to the satisfaction of the Union Bargaining and Grievance Committee within six (6) weeks after the grievance has been submitted under this step, the provisions of Article XI may be invoked.

(d) All decisions arrived at by agreement with the Site Manager, or his appointee, and the Union Bargaining and Grievance Committee with respect to any grievance shall be made in writing and shall be final and binding upon the Company and the Union.

(e) Nothing in this agreement shall be deemed to take away the right of an individual employee to present any personal grievance to the Company.

Procedure for Arbitration Proceedings

1. The party desiring to submit a matter to arbitration shall deliver to the other party a notice of intention to arbitrate. This notice shall state the matter at issue and state in what respect the agreement has been violated or misinterpreted by reference to the specific clause or clauses relied upon. The notice shall also stipulate the nature of the relief or remedy sought.

2. Within ten (10) days after the date of delivery of the foregoing notice, the party initiating arbitration shall notify the other party of the name of its representative on the arbitration board and the other party shall appoint its representative within ten (10) days of receipt of this notification.

3. In the event either party shall fail to appoint a representative to the arbitration board within the delay provided, the other party may request the Minister of Labour of the Province of Ontario to appoint a representative on behalf of the defaulting party.

4. When the representatives have been appointed they shall meet forthwith to choose a chairman, who, with the two (2) representatives, shall constitute the arbitration board.

5. Should the representatives fail within five (5) days to agree on a chairman, the Minister of Labour of the Province of Ontario may be requested by the representatives or either of them to appoint a person who shall be chairman of the arbitration board.

Of the group of nine Canadian labor agreements, two had a two-step grievance procedure, six had a three-step procedure, and one had a four-step procedure. In the provisions for arbitration in the Canadian contracts, eight of the nine provided for a three-person panel of arbitrators and one provided for a single arbitrator.

In the BNA study of U.S. agreements the results revealed that about 50 percent of the contracts had three-step grievance procedures and something over 20 percent had a two-step procedure, and about the same number (over 20 percent) had a four-step procedure. In the U.S. agreements, about 80 percent call for the services of a single arbitrator, while 15 percent call for a tripartite board of arbitration.

UNION REPRESENTATION

The language on union representation has to do with the rights of union representatives to conduct union business or to handle grievances on company time. A review of the Canadian contracts revealed that six of these allowed union stewards to investigate grievances "on the clock" within certain limits, two contracts allowed "on the clock" investigations with no specified limits, and one contract prohibited the conduct of any union business on company time. In reference to the handling of union business other than grievance investigation, two contracts allowed time off paid by the company for the union officer to conduct union business, six contracts allowed unpaid time off to handle union business, and one contract made no mention of this topic.

An example of a very liberal union representation provision is found in the Accuride contract:

Article IV—Union Representation

Section 1—The Company shall recognize four (4) zone committeepersons plus a Plant Chairperson from the Plant. Such Plant Committee shall constitute the in-plant committee and negotiating committee. Each committee member shall be appointed by the Union for each zone. The Plant Committee to be on steady days within their zone.

Section 2—Each committeeperson shall be an employee of the Company. The Union shall notify the Company in writing from time to time of the names of the committeepersons, the effective dates of their appointment and the names of any of the former committeepersons whom they are replacing or discontinuing and of the name of the Chairperson of the Committee.

Section 3—The Union shall have the right to appoint up to one off-shift committeeperson on each of the shifts within each of the four (4) committee zones. The objective of this structure is to result in as many grievances and complaints being resolved at Step 1 of the Grievance Procedure as is possible. Such appointed committeepersons shall be accountable to the elected zone committeeperson regarding required representation duties carried out on behalf of the committeeperson. The appointed committeeperson may not process a grievance to Step 2 unless agreed to by the elected committeeperson. The Union shall have the right to appoint an alternative committeeperson in the absence of the regular committeeperson.

Section 4—During periods when there are 350 or more employees in the Bargaining Unit, the Plant Chairperson shall be permitted to have up to eight (8) hours paid time per regular shift while on the premises for the sole purpose of:

a) Attending 2nd and 3rd shift step grievance meetings.

b) C.A.W. Local 27, Unit 17, paperwork and recordkeeping.

c) Preparing Union notices.

d) Maintenance of Union notice board postings.

e) Discussions with the Employee Relations Manager or his designate.

f) Meetings with employees not at work regarding Union business in a conference room or other suitable facilities.

The Plant Chairperson shall account for the paid time as per the above to the Employee Relations Manager or his designate. It is understood that the above duties will continue for a period of one (1) month following the reduction to below 350 employees. This provision does not inhibit a co-operative approach which results in the inclusion of other duties providing such co-operative arrangements have the ongoing agreement of both the Employee Relations Manager and the Plant Chairperson.

Section 5—The Plant Chairperson shall be supplied with office space which includes:

a) Telephone with a separate line and number. The full cost to be paid by the Union.

b) Desk and chair.

c) Filing cabinet.

Section 6—In the event the Plant Chairperson is replaced, and he has sufficient seniority, he shall be given the choice of returning to his former classification, or electing to be declared surplus.

Section 7—The Plant Chairperson shall receive top straight time base hourly rate plus cost of living allowance excluding off-shift and overtime premiums.

Section 8—When the Plant Chairperson is absent on a full day in terms of Leave of Absence provisions on Union business, the alternate Chairperson shall be relieved of his normal job duties to fulfill the designated duties of the Plant Chairperson. In cases of absence for other reasons, the alternate Chairperson shall be relieved of his normal job duties to fulfill the designated duties of the Plant Chairperson from the second full day on. This provision not to apply during the summer vacation shutdown or the Christmas to New Year Holiday periods.

The BNA review in 1989 found that in about 36 percent of the U.S. agreements surveyed union activity was expressly prohibited on company time. Most of these prohibitions have to do with solicitation of new members and with dues collection. Unfortunately, the BNA data are not reported with enough specificity on this point to make definitive statements about how time to handle grievances by union representatives is dealt with in most U.S. labor agreements.

SUBCONTRACTING

The review of the Canadian contracts show that two of the agreements allow management an unrestricted right to subcontract bargaining unit work, two prohibit management from subcontracting, and the remainder (5) are silent on the issue. An example of an agreement that allows broad rights to subcontract would be the Accuride agreement:

Article XXIII—Subcontracting

The following procedure will be followed regarding subcontracting: The Company will advise the Union of cases where outside contractors are to be engaged to do installation work within the plant. Regular continuing maintenance work will be performed by maintenance employees consistent with the needs of the Company. The needs of the Company shall be determined on the basis of avoiding production delays, time requirements, and ability of the Company to perform the work with respect to available skills and equipment.
The Union will be advised of the work to be performed and how long the outside contractor is expected to be in the plant.

A much more restrictive provision on management rights to subcontract is found in the Dow Chemical agreement:

Contracting Out—The Company agrees that outside contractors will not perform maintenance work in the plant. This Article will not prevent the Company from contracting out work involved in new construction, nor work of a magnitude or type not within the capability of the Maintenance department. It is the intention of the Company to continue the normal growth of the Maintenance department.

The BNA survey of contracts shows that subcontracting as mentioned in 54 percent of all U.S. labor agreements and that this percentage has been steadily increasing since 1979. In the United States, subcontracting is almost never strictly prohibited (perhaps reflecting the N.L.R.B.'s *Milwaukee Springs* thinking) but it often requires advance discussion with the union (in about 50 percent of the agreements surveyed). In the current legal environment of the United States, if subcontracting is not specifically limited then the decision to subcontract would be regarded as a management right.

DURATION

A review of the Canadian contracts show that two of the nine contracts were for a period of less than two years, four were for two to three years, and three were for three years or longer. Of this last group of three contracts, only one was for three years exactly, the other two were for four years.

In the BNA survey, 80 percent of the contracts were for three years, 13 percent were for two years, and 5 percent were for four years. The Canadian contracts were predominately of shorter duration than the "typical" U.S. agreement, although two of the agreements were for four years, which would be regarded as a rarity in the United States.

CONCLUSION

Based on a reading of a small number of Canadian manufacturing contracts in Ontario the following generalizations seem justified. Generally speaking, Canadian contracts seem to contain very detailed and broad statements of management rights, more detailed and more broad than in the United States, especially regarding management's rights to promulgate rules. In general, union security provisions are stronger in Canada than in the United States, with the union shop being almost universal. The grievance procedure in Canadian contracts is usually a three-step process (as it is in the United States) but in Canada the arbitration procedure is much more likely to be a tripartite panel than in the United States. In most contracts in Canada union representatives are allowed time "on the clock" (within limits) to handle and investigate grievances. Specific provisions are made to allow time off to handle negotiations in most Canadian contracts although this is usually unpaid. Strict prohibitions on union activity during work hours are somewhat unusual in Canada and are more common in the United States. Subcontracting is mentioned in less than half of the Canadian agreements and where it is mentioned, about half prohibit subcontracting and about half specifically allow it. In the United States subcontracting is mentioned in the majority of agreements, and it is virtually never prohibited. Finally, in the United States the vast majority of contracts are for three years. In Canada, most contracts are for less than three years although a significant minority are for longer than this.

The lesson to be learned from this brief chapter is that the explicit or stated rights of both labor and management seem to be stronger in Canadian agreements than those in the United States. Negotiators from the United States can expect more lengthy negotiations about rights and principles than they might experience in the United States. Canadian negotiators, especially management negotiations, may find U.S. unions more concerned with limiting management rights than in Canada, but at the same time more willing to negotiate longer-term contracts. In the end, however, both parties to the negotiations from either side of the border will find more similarities than differences in their transnational bargaining experiences.

NOTES

1. Bureau of National Affairs, *Basic Pattern: Management and Union Rights*, p. 65–1. 1989.
2. Op.cit. p. 65–3.
3. BNA op.cit. p. 87–3.

21

The Impact of NAFTA on Labor

Stephen I. Schlossberg

Back in the old days when there was a Soviet Union, our TV news broadcasts brought us annual images of May Day Parades when missiles and tanks and all sorts of weapons of destruction were paraded through the streets of Moscow. On one such occasion when Khrushchev was the prime minister and general secretary of the Communist party, a flange of people in business suits marched by—a whole city block full of them. Khrushchev responded to an inquisitive colleague, "Those are economists. You would be surprised at the damage they can do."

It is hard to get economists to agree on things. If two economists are in a room, you are going to have at least two opinions. That is why Truman always wanted a one-armed lawyer, because most lawyers say "on one hand, and on the other hand." He did not want to deal with all those hands. For our purposes, we do not want a one-armed economist or a single viewpoint. We need a good healthy discussion of strategies for confronting the situation.

There is some disagreement as to the wisdom of certain actions and when to carry them out. First, we seem to agree on worker protection in certain industries. Despite some disagreement over the extent of protection, there is agreement that policies need to be adjusted to take care of workers. There also seemed to be agreement that America could make it in the world only as a high-tech, highly skilled competitor to Germany, Japan, and other industrialized exporting nations, not as a third world nation, existing on making only bicycles and bicycle-makers' wages.

Skills will bring productivity. A statement that came out of the Committee of Rome projected that increases in productivity mean that people can live a little better tomorrow than they do today. That was a western, not a

Japanese, definition. Productivity will eventually lead to higher standards of living. That is a given.

Many agree that market economies are the most efficient in the world and that they can produce great results in terms of value, quality, and productivity. Many of the countries in Eastern Europe really were "basket cases." Making them more efficient, and at the same time more democratic, seems to be an undisputed goal. Democracy and the value of freedom has come home as never before to people all over the world. The market, however efficient it is, cannot take care of the protection of human beings and the environment.

Postcolonial Africa is also beginning to show signs of moving toward democracy and the achievement of market economies. Building a democracy is not a simple matter of learning technical skills and entrepreneurial tactics. It is not only knowing how to set up a vocational education system and how to run a labor market; not only knowing how to keep labor statistics and calculate national productivity rates, or knowing what the cost of living and the price of goods really are. It is much more. There are intricate labor-market systems that are institutions in their own right. Increasingly, the process involves independent, strong trade unions. Remember, it was such forces that made the first real cracks in the Eastern and Central European countries. That union was Solidarity.

In the ILO, we call for a social dimension in all the work we do. This call has been heard by the great lending institutions, the World Bank, the International Monetary Fund, and individual countries wanting to do work in Central and Eastern Europe. If you set up a market economy so that it works too fast and too hard, and the suffering is too great, and people have too big a price to pay, then you risk pushing the people back to authoritarianism, whether of the right or the left. So the ILO has insisted on the necessity of looking at the social dimension in every economic and political decision worldwide. We are insisting that this social dimension, more than safety nets, be a vital component of any successful system.

In the European Economic Community, the EEC, twelve nations have come together and decided that a single market makes economic sense, that knocking down artificial barriers will bring great benefits to the entire region. The EEC has taken on the task of removing politically sensitive border controls and national restrictions that once kept goods, services, labor, and capital from moving freely within the community. However, many of the people in those twelve countries, not just the trade unions, but certainly led by them, are worried about certain implications of this liberalization. They were concerned that the social policy achievements of some of Europe's great nation-states, forged in long, hard work over the years, might be lost. For instance, in Germany co-determination has made businesses more efficient. Cooperation as a way of life in Germany has made their skilled factories the best in the world. They have outdistanced the United States and Japan, the United States being second and Japan third in the percentage of skilled goods exported. One reason for their preeminence is that they are willing to spend the necessary money to invest in human capital. They also care about the institutions that protect human beings. There is no doubt about the necessity of labor unions, trade unions, and free trade unions in European industrialized society. If Canada has higher taxes than the United States, so does every postindustrial industrialized country in the world. All of Europe has higher taxes than the United States and we are reading lips and looking for ways to avoid taxes when 35 million U.S. citizens are not covered by any kind of health insurance and the homeless sleep on grates not three blocks from the White House.

The social dimension is so important. Canada had a lot to worry about when it made a free trade agreement with the United States because, as some people say, the bad often forces out the good and they had a lot to protect peoplewise. They were, for instance, worried that the United States would say that the Canadians should stop subsidizing employees and employers by providing national health insurance. Instead, we in the United States are going to decide that we cannot exist without some form of national health insurance and some controls on medical and health care costs. Maybe it will hit home when we realize that Canada, a country right here on this continent, is able to do it. Maybe we can learn from each other.

Your decision on the North American Free Trade Agreement (NAFTA) has already been made for you. The Congress has voted a fast track for the president and there is no way that will be changed. There is not one chance in ten thousand that any bill introduced by Tom Harkins is ever going to get anywhere to undo that. NAFTA is on the way. The choice is yours. Will you cry and pound the wall or will you fight to add a social dimension and begin to work on it now? Will you begin to build allies among the many decent people in business? Will you establish links with Mexican unions, not only the federation, the government-involved, and connected unions, but the independent unions as well? Will you call on the International Confederation of Free Trade Unions and other multilateral organizations like the Organization of American States? Ask them to help you because you are trying to add the ingredient of social justice that makes our society different from a jungle.

You must devise adequate protection for people and communities and firms that are joined by an agreement that benefits the whole. NAFTA benefits the whole because there seems to be no chance of anyone stopping it. It can benefit everyone if enough people can influence it in the right way. That is what you should be working on right now. Do not spend your time saying that there will be no tide tomorrow, but in planning a strategy to harness the tide for the common good.

Tell the people of this country that they should plan to have worker assistance in heavy training, as recommended in the Brock, Magaziner, and Marshall Report. Secure a commitment that we will spend money on education and training and on keeping human beings healthy and alive, even if we have to invest in them. We invest in other things. We invested in defunct savings and loans and in wars in Kuwait. We need to invest in human beings.

Make your cry to the North American Free Trade Agreement a call for social justice and work to get allies on the environmental side, on the religious side, on every other side. Do not say, "Stop the train!" but put a car on the train for *people* so they can live comfortably. Go out and talk to your reference groups, talk to your unions and companies and say, What kind of a world do we want? Do we want a world in which we can really boost the living conditions of workers? Do we really want to stamp out child labor? Do we want to enable Mexicans to enjoy life a little more? That is the goal of the labor movement—to make workers better off.

Do not spend your time talking about whether there will be a free trade agreement. Talk about what kind of agreement it is going to be and if it has the right social dimension.

In the final analysis, it is how a society treats its young, its old, and those who lose out on the good things in life for one reason or another. NAFTA gives this nation, Canada, and Mexico the opportunity to demonstrate that they are worthwhile societies that recognize people as social as well as economic beings. Shall we have a fair and compassionate society—in essence, a decent society—or shall we opt for greed and the law of the jungle?

22

Mutual Labor-Management Concerns to Be Addressed in a North American Free Trade Agenda

Gary Sorensen

Many predictions have been made as to the job losses NAFTA will bring to Minnesota. We have no way of knowing how many employers are awaiting the signing of a free trade agreement that will send them scurrying south of the border. Certainly there are some financial incentives that could convince companies to give Mexico a try. And if major competitors from other states or countries are already taking advantage of such incentives and threatening to outstrip them in the marketplace, some Minnesota companies could decide their survival depends upon them doing likewise. Current economic hard times for some will undoubtedly contribute to that happening.

And there will likely be other impacts. The overriding philosophy of free trade is to let countries do what they do best. As the economies shift into those areas, even a successful Minnesota transition into better jobs and new industries will mean some unemployment and retraining along the way. Mexico's enhanced ability to compete for export markets, agricultural competition that could end protection on commodities and force lower prices, continuing technology transfer, and industrialization are other factors that will likely contribute some problems.

But we are already in the process of losing jobs to other states and countries, and some of it is our own doing. We still tend to cling to Tayloristic management and old-fashioned ideas. We are still trying to solve the problem by throwing more workers at it, having to squeeze wages and reduce training and cut benefits in order to achieve the productivity our competitors are able to accomplish.

A 1991 study revealed that eight out of nine new jobs being created by Minnesota businesses were being created elsewhere. Too many of these lost opportunities and jobs that we have already lost are being replaced by low-paying, part-time jobs with few benefits and no future. Minnesotans have been left behind with no marketable skills and little means to access better opportunities. These things will continue to happen if we try to continue in isolation. The North American Free Trade Agreement is only a small part of the overall global situation confronting us. Minnesota's workers must compete with the rest of the world.

ECONOMIC DEVELOPMENT/BUSINESS RETENTION

As Jack Kemp recently said, "You can't create employees until you've created employers." It will do little good for us to pour dollars into retraining affected workers if they have no place to go with their new skills. We are already working on initiatives with the Department of Trade and Economic Development to coordinate and improve efforts in this area. As a minimum, we must do the following.

We must court responsible employers who will provide jobs with a future. We must realize that we cannot survive with companies that come here to find the cheapest workers. That will doom us to a low-wage, low-skills economy. The socialized costs that go with that are already becoming difficult for some areas to bear.

We must promote the concepts of total quality management and high-performance work organizations. The workers need to be involved. Greater efficiency and dedication to a well-trained staff will mean greater productivity and better wages—and a better future for the employer and workers. Employers should be prepared to dedicate resources to employee development and cooperative mechanisms between labor and management.

We must work to keep existing employers. We need to develop cooperative efforts between state departments to identify the early signs of trouble for employers. We must devote expertise and resources to providing consulting and technical services so that our businesses become more competitive. We already have some companies helping each other in that regard, and we have others approaching regional centers for such help. In order to be successful in any of these efforts, we must also maintain a good business climate for Minnesota employers by providing tax structures and business incentives that will be an invitation to stay.

We must promote entrepreneurship and do everything possible to foster new businesses. Smaller companies are still the key to growth and we must find ways to help them get started. We may be able to do some of that by changing unemployment insurance laws and using benefits for business start-up projects. Other incentives will have to be initiated.

We must market our labor force—something that we have not done a great job of in the past. Not only do we need to sell well-trained people with a great work ethic to attract new employers, but we also need to market the special skills of the currently unemployed to existing employers. Our

job service offices and other agencies and groups working with the unemployed must coordinate efforts to move these people into the right jobs.

In the years ahead our department will seek out and establish relationships
with those employers who subscribe to these philosophies. They will be the
ones to whom we will try to refer qualified workers, to develop training
contracts, to provide with performance incentives. They will be vital to our
success and our future. They will insure that we do not keep recycling people
through the unemployment insurance and dislocated worker systems.

IMPROVING EDUCATION AND TRAINING

We also feel that it is vital to get involved in improving education. We
have asked our own employees to do so not only on behalf of the department,
but on a personal basis as well. Business, labor, and society as a whole must
do the same thing.

Too many of our young people come out of school who do not have any
idea what it is really like to work on a regular basis for an employer, to feel
a sense of obligation to that workplace, to punch a clock every day and make
sure that they take care of that job. They do not come out of school with
the necessary skills. The biggest fear expressed by many employers is not
only that youth coming out of school will not have the skills they need, but
that they will not even have the ability to learn the skills.

Latest estimates are that two-thirds of Minnesota youth will fall into the
"Forgotten Half" category in years ahead. If we do not do something, they
are going to be the ones with the low wages, the low skills, and no future.
We have to make the adjustments that will give them the kinds of jobs they
will need and prepare them for those jobs.

We stand to be the first generation who does not leave things in a better
situation for our youth than we had it left for us. We must turn out a labor
force that is better prepared for the jobs of the future and better prepared
to meet the everyday needs of employers.

To accomplish that we must seek improvements in the elementary and
secondary education systems. Getting a good education and learning proper
work skills and ethics must be more important than earning some part-time
dollars and having a good time. All of us, as workers and citizens, must
demand that our schools do a better job in this area. And we must get
involved in helping to plan for it. Such concepts as those contained in
"Minnesota 2000" and "America's Choice: High Skills or Low Wages" must
be endorsed and adopted.

Vocational and higher education must be improved. We simply cannot be
training people for jobs that are going to be low-wage, low-skill, or obsolete
in a few years. Curriculums must be revamped to be sure that we are
retraining people for jobs with a future. More public money must be devoted
to these areas instead of to the college-oriented. The necessary skills to

compete in the workforce of the future must be an element of every training program.

Training in the workplace must be accelerated. While this may be a difficult time to start it, we should expect and encourage employers to devote time and resources to employee development, to begin the training that will realize maximum potential and productivity and allow employers to improve their own situation. Cross-training and retraining should be a way of doing business. Again we will look favorably toward employers who provide such training.

We must encourage workers to begin preparing for their own futures— to give up having a good time in their off-work hours and look toward helping themselves and others to better prepare for the workplace they will have to fit into in the coming years. That may include coming up with some public dollars to help pay for such efforts.

HELPING DISLOCATED WORKERS

Trends are already underway that will undoubtedly leave us with some unemployed and dislocated workers in the coming years. There will be continued downsizing, cutbacks in government and defense-related jobs, additional megamergers, and other phenomena that will add to the already swollen ranks.

The already mentioned training by employers could help, making it easier to move them into related jobs or new areas that they have had a chance to prepare for. In terms of helping dislocated workers, we already have a fairly good system in place in Minnesota. There are a number of things that we can do to improve on the delivery of services to those affected.

The federal government is going to have to kick dollars into the pot. The amounts currently given to states for dislocated workers are pitifully small and fail to meet existing needs. Besides pressuring for increases in EDWAA dollars, we might also look at expanding trade adjustment assistance. TAA provides a more comprehensive package of benefits and assistance than EDWAA, and helps to overcome more of the barriers to reemployment.

It was because of the minimal federal dollars coming in for dislocated workers that Minnesota enacted its own dislocated workers tax. We may find that even with the current collection of $18 to $20 million each year, we will not have the money to address all of the training needs and associated costs when those affected by this agreement are added in. Ways to maximize existing resources will be critical.

We currently have a lot of service deliverers. Job service offices do trade adjustment assistance. Service delivery areas, private industry councils, job service, and a host of other vendors compete with each other to deliver the dislocated worker programs. There are strengths and weaknesses in that situation. There must be coordination of efforts and elimination of duplicate administrative costs. The maximum dollars must go to the clients.

We have to quit competing with each other and share resources and information. For instance, the natural place for people to go for placement should be job service. We have the greatest access to employers. We are the natural starting point because workers come to us first to file for unemployment benefits. And we have the experience. Yet we still have new vendors starting up, offering placement as part of their service, getting a grant to do so, and then hiring someone off the street to do placement for them. We simply should not have contracts that award dollars to vendors to perform services already available for free or through established agencies, such as placement, testing, and counseling.

And we have vendors isolated from the total picture, neglecting to coordinate efforts and share opportunities. One of the things that is happening in job development is we have everybody with their own little base of employers and openings. If their own people do not fit into an opening, they just close the book on it instead of feeding it to another group who might be able to put one of their workers into it. We need to improve things not only to avoid wasting opportunities, but also to spare employers from a myriad of program representatives and sales pitches.

One of the other things that we need to do is improve ways of moving dislocated workers into new employment. Many of those people can be returned to work immediately or moved into related work with a minimum of training. We have to find ways to get people into new work at minimum cost, instead of assuming that everybody has to be retrained.

In some cases, we have spent too much time and money putting people through a total retraining process only to have them go into the new work and make far less money than they were making before or that they could have made by just making a quick transition into another job or related occupation.

We need to encourage more on-the-job training contracts. As the quality of our workforce improves and employers implement their own training systems, transferrable skills will encourage easier transition into new jobs. In the meantime we should encourage employers to use on-the-job training options and look for ways to subsidize such arrangements. It represents the quickest and least expensive way of making the transition to new work. The trend in recent years has been away from such arrangements. We should encourage the federal government to restore such programs and push for more use of available retraining funds for these purposes.

We need to improve on our early intervention in the whole process, to minimize the disruption that these people are going through in their lives. We may have to look at some changes in or stricter enforcement of the laws regarding early notice, as there is currently some manipulation that impedes early intervention. Current procedures have not always been successful at identifying companies in time for rapid response units to intervene and prevent plant closures. We have to get there before the doors close so that we are not just taking unemployment claims and trying to pick up the pieces.

UNEMPLOYMENT INSURANCE BENEFITS

Minnesota's unemployment insurance fund is facing a potential crisis. Whatever pieces we have to pick up from this agreement will add to the burden. Employers who leave or close the doors will not be around to pay the tab for their workers, so the socialized cost to all Minnesota employers will be increased.

One of the things we may have to consider is increased taxes or freezes on benefits. We are into a trend of paying out more than we are taking in. The minimum employer tax decreased to .1 percent for 1991. With automatic increases to the maximum weekly benefit amount triggering in and some extensive payouts expected as we recover from the recession, projections are that the fund could even go into debt and we would have to do some federal borrowing. We will likely kick in solvency assessments for employers—perhaps 10 percent, or even 15 percent of the tab they are paying now. We may have to look at higher tax rates for employers and/or freezes on benefits.

In a worst cast scenario, a more serious recession could lead to heavy borrowing, which also brings the possibilities of interest payments, federal penalties, even lost tax credits. The cost of all of this could be quite high for Minnesota employers.

Another thing we can look at that might help workers is to enhance the approved training provisions for unemployment insurance. Current law prohibits us from approving training for anyone with "marketable" skills. What that means is that for the person with basic entry-level skills, there is always a job out there. So if they approach us about using their benefits to gain some retraining, we have to say "No" because they can likely find a job. There is always another low-paying, low-skill job out there. Such an approach makes it more difficult for such individuals to escape the cycle and usually means that we will continue providing unemployment benefits or social subsidies to them in the years ahead. We may need to reassess this approach and encourage any claimant with only basic skills to engage in retraining at every opportunity.

We should allow individuals to try new work without endangering their unemployment benefits. Under current law an individual who tries a new job runs the risk of losing benefits if he or she later decides the job is not suitable and voluntarily quits—even if the job was not suitable in the first place. That person can only escape that situation in the event of a layoff or serious medical problems. We are looking at adding a provision that will allow claimants to try new work under certain conditions, without risking the loss of benefits.

Some states are currently experimenting with programs that allow lump-sum payments of benefits to finance self-employment ventures or convert into on-the-job training subsidies for employers. Minnesota should at least look at such possibilities and other ways to convert existing funds into jobs.

23

Implications for Labor-Management Relations of the Proposed North American Free Trade Agreement

Jeremy Wright

In the 1930s national economies were essentially closed economies. The pace of international technological change was slow. Agricultural and other primary products had traditionally traded duty-free. International trade in services was not significant. In manufacturing and value-added goods, tariffs had escalated to 40 percent. International trade and commerce ground to a virtual standstill.

It was not until after the Second World War that a process to reduce these high tariffs were found. GATT came into being in 1948. This provided an international rule book and a forum where a schedule of reciprocal reduction in tariffs could be hammered out between the industrial nations. This focused essentially on trade in manufactured goods. Since then, the number of industrial and industrializing countries has grown. "Closed" economies have become "open" economies.

The anatomy and importance of trade have also changed. As evidenced by the current discussions of the Uruguay Round, there are now attempts to rectify the original omissions of trade in agriculture and services. However, environmental, labor, and social matters are still in GATT limbo, mainly because the third world sees the issue of cheap labor as their major international competitive advantage; they too should have the right to develop and sort out their chronic balance-of-payments and growing debt problems.

The postwar period has seen an increase in the pace of technological change unprecedented in human history. Germany, Japan, and some other Far Eastern countries have systematically set about securing world leadership in a variety of sectors. Capital markets have gone global. Multinational corporations can now do their research and development and establish production facilities anywhere on the globe.

Against these open global dynamics, trading blocs are being formed. Australia and New Zealand, and Canada and the United States have signed free trade agreements. The European Common Market, a broader arrangement than a free trade area incorporating free labor mobility, a common currency, and common social, labor, and environmental standards, came into being in 1992.

THE DYNAMICS OF NAFTA

Set against this background of rapidly changing patterns of international investment and trade, the proposed North American Free Trade Agreement is perhaps one of the most complex trade agreements ever attempted. There are vast structural differences between the Canadian, Mexican, and U.S. economies.

Canada is a resource-based economy "at the crossroads," with a "greying" population of some 27 million.

The United States is the world's largest industrial country, but has recently also become a debtor nation. Over the past decades, considerable corporate attention has been given to takeovers, share buybacks, and junk bonds. Net U.S. corporate investment, expressed as a percentage of GNP, has been falling. The U.S. domestic economy, still essentially predicated on the Henry Ford production line and cheap hydrocarbons, now faces challenges in the global marketplace from both high-technology and low-wage economies.

Mexico is a developing nation under GATT, with all the special rights and privileges that this entails. It has a young, burgeoning population (average age of fifteen), which is estimated to grow from the current 85 million to some 140 million early in the next century, perhaps even surpassing the U.S. population later in the century. There are currently some 10 million unemployed, and a million new labor market entrants each year.

From the Mexican perspective, the advantages of freer access to the U.S. market, more international investment, and more employment for their burgeoning labor force are clear. Industrial growth is imperative not only to deal with their unemployment, but to create a larger industrial base to finance the increasing demands on social and community infrastructure, including education, sewage, and water.

From the U.S. perspective, the reactions are less straightforward. For some the prospect of access to Mexican labor with wages of some US$4.00 a day is the answer to offshore competition. For others freer access to this growing market appears to offer significant commercial opportunities. For others these siren songs offer nothing more than the rocks and shoals of growing imports, lower U.S. and Canadian wages, and rising domestic unemployment.

How can a North American company compete with wages of $4.00 a day? Rep. Rahall (W. Va.) noted, for example, that FINSA Grupo Arguilles is promising U.S. companies fully fringed labor costs of $1.25 per hour, and referred to another company that holds seminars on how to save $25,000 per assembler per year.

From the Canadian perspective, matters are equally complex. There are a number of U.S. branch plants north of the border; the Canadian exchange rate has risen steadily since the signing of the bilateral trade agreement. Unemployment is at the 10 percent mark. The same reactions also apply. How can one possibly compete, outside of the resource sectors, with essentially the same technologies and maintain Canadian social programs, Canadian wage levels, and Canadian jobs? A trilateral trade deal appears totally different in kind to bilateral trade. In many ways the Canadian and U.S. economies are similar. The Mexican economy is vastly different.

Mexico publicly counters this with arguments that a trading bloc of 360 million will benefit all three countries; most Mexican exports are largely duty-free; and Mexico has already reduced its tariffs from 100 percent to a current weighted average of 8.5 percent.

Trade theory has it that eventually some new equilibrium will establish itself. But in this case:

- Mexican population and labor supply statistics suggest that it will take some time for any wage pressures to occur.
- It may therefore be some time before the Mexican purchasing power rises to a level where they can afford imported goods.
- There are distinct possibilities that social and environmental dumping will occur without adequate social and environmental safeguards. There will be significant long-term costs which, on top of the current demographic pressures on Mexican infrastructure, may outweigh some of the short-term employment benefits to Mexico.
- If competition is based on wages, U.S. and Canadian wages would trend inexorably downward toward the Mexican levels.

How, then, can NAFTA be crafted to take account of the emerging concerns of the next century, and still benefit all three countries?

The worst case scenario is that parts of "corporate America" with "trailing-edge" products or technologies will myopically see Mexican low-wage labor as their corporate salvation and the North American answer to offshore competition. They would then move south, trying to survive. Companies that cannot cut the international mustard lose international market share, suffer through a period of declining profits and cost-cutting measures, shed labor, and are eventually forced to close their doors. This will merely postpone the inevitable. The real corporate answer is not to produce trailing-edge products with cheap labor, but to design and develop new leading-edge technologies and products, preferably green products and processes.

Mexico will lose under this trailing-edge product scenario, as their sole benefits will be some short-term low-paying jobs. Closures will follow. This will do little for the overall Mexican well-being.

From the U.S. and Canadian perspectives, this dynamic would probably also be accompanied with a "ripple-back" effect in the wages area. Some corporations will say to their North American labor force, "If you don't take a cut in wages, we will move to Mexico." This will massively exacerbate labor-management relations, which will become increasingly adversarial. The same type of arguments apply to the Canadian jobs and wages and to the Canadian social security system.

NAFTA is ultimately about raising standards of living in the three countries. The crafting of such an agreement, which will allow the three countries to live together for the next century, will not be easy. But if nothing is done in all of these areas, matters will trend down to the lowest common denominator. In the ultimate analysis, this is in nobody's interest.

THE WIN/WIN/WIN SCENARIO

Corporations that develop leading-edge products and processes have the world as their market (subject to national and cultural differences in tastes and patterns of consumption).

There are areas where a win/win/win scenario can be contemplated. Europeans have recognized that labor and environmental costs are all part of the costs of production. They have gone to extreme lengths, albeit in a Common Market framework, to ensure that there is a level playing field. But the playing field is anything but level. Of interest is the extent to which the United States lags behind its two trading partners on women's issues and maternity leave, the issues of right to work states, and issues of enforcement of standards on the Mexican side, and the extent to which the three countries lag behind European social practice.

For all of the reasons outlined above, it is now clear that a win/win/win agreement must ensure that Mexico gains more than some short-term, low-wage jobs, and that there are some dynamics set in place that ensure the raising of Mexican standards of living, and not the decline of U.S. and Canadian standards of living to those now pertaining in Mexico.

Given the need for a level playing field, it can therefore be argued that NAFTA must establish *ex ante* enforceable provisions for the highest possible international environmental, health and safety, and labor standards. These would have to be enforceable if the goods or services were traded, and failure to comply with these standards should be made subject to some form of trade remedy.

If there is a will to do this, then different provisions can be crafted. These could take the form of "snap-back" (tariff reductions snapping back if the labor and environmental rules are not implemented). Firm-specific or product-specific duties could also be imposed in the same way as "countervail" now operates. Failure to meet the highest environmental and social and labor standards would be deemed to be a "trade-distorting" subsidy.

Recognition of the importance of environmental and labor concerns have been given preliminary recognition in Memoranda of Understanding. These are a start, but they do not provide any teeth, are not as yet part of any formal agreement, and there is as yet no mechanism contemplated such as the European Commission that would set or enforce such NAFTA standards.

Rather, the conventional GATT view still argues that social issues are purely domestic concerns, affecting the intrinsic national sovereignty, and have no place in a trade agreement.

Mature and sober thought for the twenty-first century would suggest otherwise. The ultimate purpose of any free trade agreement is that all members benefit. The environment is a common good. Some corporations might well object from their narrower perspective. But there is the over-riding issue of a balanced agreement and the "greater good."

Another major issue is that of the relationship among trade surpluses, corporate profits, the return to labor, and the retirement of national debt. These four issues are not usually looked at in the same breath. Yet, in the longer term, they all have to do with the distribution of benefits from any agreement.

The longevity of NAFTA and the social stability of the three countries ultimately depends on the creation of surpluses, the distribution of those surpluses, and the rate of retirement of outstanding debts. Corporate longevity depends on the amount of productive reinvestment and the technological capability to remain at the leading edge of progress. If any one of the countries goes socially or financially bankrupt, the longer-term political and economic ramifications will be horrendous.

There is therefore a need to begin to examine the theoretical alternatives for the distribution of benefits of NAFTA not just among the three countries in terms of the traditional short-term quantitative trade flows, but among the three key partners in the three countries—government, business, and labor.

This is an extension of the question of swapping debt for environmental preservation. The exercise of *ex ante* linking the proper distribution or application of the benefits from NAFTA leads to new and interesting stabilizers.

Matters are sufficiently complicated when a free trade agreement is contemplated between two developed and a developing nation that new and imaginative options to balance trade, investment, employment, standards of living, and the matter of debt need to be developed.

THE CHANGING NATURE OF LABOR-MANAGEMENT RELATIONS

Much recent work has been undertaken in the OECD, in the World Economic Forum, and in the United States (Harvard and MIT Sloan School of Management), for example, which suggests that the achievement of new leading-edge processes and products is largely dependent not on "white-coated top-down R&D" or on the size and number of layers of traditional managerial hierarchical systems, but on the knowledge base, skills, and contributions of people and cooperative forms of corporate organization. The new system is a "customer first" system. It is "people first" system—not a "people last" or "customer last" system. This is an ongoing global trend.

Part of the new dynamic for the twenty-first century can be summed up in Figure 23.1. New technologies lead to new skills, which lead to new technologies, and thence to new skills . . . all within a new imperative of "going green."

Concurrently, the traditional managerial pyramid is flattening and inverting, giving rise to new responsibilities and roles in what Robert Kelly calls the "gold-collar worker." In the ultimate analysis, well-paid jobs and wages do not depend on yesterday's production processes, yesterday's products, and yesterday's skills whether managerial or labor. They ultimately depend on the knowledge base and skills of people and the extent to which they can serve customer needs.

Corporations, sectors, states, and nations that adopt this dynamic will find themselves pulling ahead of the pack. Those that do not will fall behind.

The real issue at stake in NAFTA is whether the traditional "top-down" feudal or ancient Egyptian pharaoh view of labor will condition the NAFTA agreement. If it does, then it can be expected that this will lead to one type of outcome. Many lower-paid jobs will filter down to Mexico; there will be social and environmental dumping, leaving behind intractable unemployment problems and growing city and ghetto unrest. The adversarial nature of North American social and industrial relations will grow. A trailing-edge industrial structure will then result.

If it does not, then attention can be given to twenty-first century issues and the conditions that will strengthen the respective economies, sectors, industries, and firms.

Therefore, decisions will have to be taken as to whether international competitiveness and survival ultimately depend on the development of leading-edge products and processes, on teamwork, participation, and rising standards of living; or on trailing-edge products produced with cheap wages and falling standards of living.

SUMMARY

If precautions are taken at the outset to ensure level social and environmental playing fields with rising standards, all countries will generally level up rather than the United States and Canada leveling down. All three countries, with proper allocation of the benefits among all the social partners

Figure 23.1
Go Green

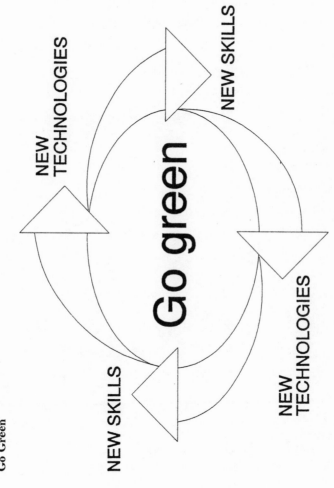

from trade and a proper longer-term handling of the debt issue, will stand to gain. But if insufficient attention is given at the outset to the issues of dynamic national development within a NAFTA level playing field, the costs may prove to outweigh the benefits.

Bibliography

AFL-CIO. "The Pocketbook Issues AFL-CIO Policy Recommendations for 1992," p. 23. Pamphlet reprinted from the National Economy section of the *Report of the Executive Council of the AFL-CIO to the Nineteenth Convention*, Detroit, Nov. 1991.

AFL-CIO News. "Jobs Exported to Mexico," Apr. 29, 1991.

Arregui, Edur Velasco. "El Desafio Sindical al TLC: productividad, empleo y slarios." *El Cotidiano*, no. 41, mayo–junio de 1991, Universidad Autonoma Metropolitana Unidad Azacapotzalco, Mexico, p. 12 prepublication draft.

Bernstein, Aaron, and Susan Garland. "There's More Than One Way to Say 'Job Training.' " *Business Week*, Sept. 7, 1992, p. 30.

Blomstrom, Magnus, and Edward N. Wolff. *Multinational Corporations and Productivity Convergence in Mexico*, NBER Working Paper No. 3141. Cambridge, Mass.: National Bureau of Economic Research, 1989.

Bureau of National Affairs. "Operating Standards for Maquiladoras Sought in U.S.-Mexico FTA Legislation." *International Trade Reporter*, Feb. 20, 1991, vol. 8, no. 8, p. 279.

Campbell, Bruce. "Goin' South—Two Years Under Free Trade," *Canadian Dimension*, Jan.–Feb. 1991.

Cohen, Robert B., and Kenneth Donow. *Telecommunications Policy, High Definition Television, and U.S. Competitiveness.* Washington, D.C.: Economic Policy Institute, 1989.

Cohen, Robert, and Alan Tonelson. *Doing It Right: A Winning Strategy for U.S.-Mexico Trade.* Washington, D.C.: Economic Strategy Institute, 1991.

Collins, Doreen. *The Operation of the European Social Fund.* London: Croom Helm, 1983.

Commission on the Skills of the American Workforce. *America's Choice: High Skills or Low Wages.* Rochester, N.Y.: National Center on Education and the Economy, 1990.

Cypher, James. *State and Capital in Mexico*. Boulder, Colo.: Westview Press, 1990.

Davis, Bob. "U.S., Canada, Mexico Find Differences on How to Give Teeth to Free Trade Pact," *Wall Street Journal*, Mar. 19, 1993, p. A2.

Diebel, Linda. "Will U.S. Dominate Hemispheric Trade by the Year 2000?" *Toronto Star*, Apr. 25, 1992.

Dillon, John. "Trade Talks Are the Key to the 'New World Order.' " *Pro-Canada Dossier* (Mar.–Apr. 1991), pp. 17–18.

Dornbusch, Rudiger. "It's Time to Open Up Trade with Mexico." *Challenge*, vol. 33, no. 6, Nov.–Dec. 1990, pp. 52–55.

Dornbusch, Rudiger. "U.S.–Mexico Free Trade: Good Jobs at Good Wages," Testimony before the Subcommittee on Labor-Management Relations and Employment Opportunities, Committee on Education and Labor, U.S. House of Representatives, Apr. 30, 1991.

Economic Justice Report. vol. 2, no. 3, Oct. 1991, p. 4.

Erfani, Julie A. "NAFTA's Ties to Political Authoritarianism in Mexico." *Industrial Relations Research Association*, Proceedings of the 1992 Spring Meeting, May 6–9, 1992, Denver, Colo., pp. 530–34.

Farrell, Christopher, and Michael J. Mandel. "Industrial Policy Call It What You Will, the Nation Needs a Plan to Nurture Growth." *Business Week*, Apr. 6, 1992, pp. 70–75.

Faux, Jeff, and Richard Rothstein. *Fast Track-Fast Shuffle: The Economic Consequences of the Administration's Proposed Trade Agreement with Mexico*. Washington, D.C.: Economic Policy Institute, 1991.

Faux, Jeff, and Todd Schafer, "Increasing Public Investment: New Budget Priorities for Economic Growth in the Post–Cold War World." Washington, D.C.: Economic Policy Institute, 1991.

Faux, Jeff, and William Spriggs. *U.S. Jobs and the Mexico Trade Proposal*. Washington, D.C.: Economic Policy Institute, 1991.

Friedman, Sheldon. "Trade Adjustment Assistance: Time for Action, Not False Promises." *AFL-CIO Reviews the Issues*, Report No. 53, Sept. 1991.

Greene, Walter E. "The Maquiladora—Japan's New Competitive Weapon." *Business*, vol. 39, no. 4, Oct.–Dec. 1989, pp. 52–56.

Grinspun, Ricardo. "North American Free Trade Area: A Critical Perspective." Paper presented at Facing North/Facing South, conference at the University of Calgary, Canada, May 1991.

Grinspun, Ricardo. "Are Economic Models Reliable Policy Tools? Forecasting Canadian Gains from Free Trade." Forthcoming.

Gutfeld, Rose. "Free Trade Accord May Hurt Workers in U.S., Study Says." *Wall Street Journal*, Oct. 1, 1992, p. A3.

Heilbroner, Robert. "Lifting the Silent Depression." *New York Review of Books*, Oct. 24, 1991.

Hufbauer, Gary Clyde, and Jeffrey J. Schott. *North American Free Trade: Issues and Recommendations*. Washington, D.C.: Institute for International Economics, 1992.

Fernandez Kelly, M. Patricia. "Technology and Employment along the U.S.-Mexican Border." In *The U.S. and Mexico: Face to Face with New Technology, U.S.-Third World Policy Perspectives*, no. 8, Overseas Development Council 151 (C. Thorup ed., 1987).

Kirkland, Lane. "U.S.-Mexico Trade Pact: A Disaster Worthy of Stalin's Worst." *Wall Street Journal*, Apr. 18, 1991, p. A15.

Koechlin, Timothy, and Mehrene Larudee. "The High Cost of NAFTA." *Challenge*, Sept.–Oct. 1992.

Kootnikoff, Lawrence. "Coming Together." *Business Mexico*, vol. 1, no. 1, Mar. 1991, pp. 4–38.

La Jornada. Mexico City, Oct. 8, 1990, p. 44.

Learner, Edward E. *Wage Effects of a U.S.–Mexican Free Trade Agreement*. NBER Working Paper No. 3991. Cambridge, Mass.: National Bureau of Economic Research, Feb. 1992.

Magnusson, Paul. "The High-Tech Brawl over Free Trade." *Business Week*, Apr. 6, 1992, p. 22.

Magnusson, Paul, Stephen Baker, David Beach, Gail DeGeorge, and William C. Symonds. "The Mexico Pact: Worth the Price?" *Business Week*, May 27, 1991, pp. 32–35.

Mead, Walter Russell. *The Low-Wage Challenge to Global Growth: The Labor Cost-Productivity Imbalance in Newly Industrialized Countries*. Washington, D.C.: Economic Policy Institute, 1991.

Middlebrook, Kevin J. "The Sounds of Silence: Organized Labour's Response to Economic Crisis in Mexico." *Journal of Latin American Studies* 21 (May 1989), pp. 195–220.

Moffett, Matt. "Stock Prices Drop Sharply in Mexico and U.S.: Mexican Market Sees Foreigners Streaming Out." *Wall Street Journal*, June 18, 1992, p C1.

Moffett, Matt. "Working Children Underage Laborers Fill Mexican Factories, Stir U.S. Trade Debate." *Wall Street Journal*, Apr. 8, 1991, pp. A12, A14.

Moody, Kim, and Mary McGinn. "From the Yukon to the Yucatan." *Dollars & Sense*, Nov. 1991.

Murray, Alan. "The Outlook and Now Good News on the Economy," *Wall Street Journal*, Apr. 12, 1993, A1.

Oravec, John R. "AFL-CIO Lists Problems with Mexican Trade Pact," *AFL-CIO News*, Vol. 38, No. 5, March 1, 1993, p. 5.

———. "Workers Ask Congress to Save U.S. Jobs." *AFL-CIO News*, vol. 37, no. 8, Apr. 13, 1992, pp. 1, 3.

Overseas Development Council, 1991, p. 4.

Papageorgiou, Demetris, Michael Michaely, and Armeane M. Choksi, eds. *Liberalizing Foreign Trade: Lessons of Experience in the Developing World*, 7 vols. Washington, D.C.: World Bank, 1991.

Peat Marwick Policy Economic Group. "The Effects of a Free Trade Agreement Between the U.S. and Mexico," Feb. 1991.

Peters, Susanna. "Labor Law for the Maquiladoras: Choosing Between Workers' Rights and Foreign Investment." *Comparative Labor Law Journal*, vol. 11, no. 2, Winter 1990, pp. 226–48.

Podgursky, Michael. "Estimated Losses Due to Job Displacement: Evidence from the Displaced Worker Surveys." Paper prepared for the Economic Policy Institute, Washington, D.C., Apr. 1991.

Rothstein, Richard. *Keeping Jobs in Fashion: Alternatives to the Euthanasia of the U.S. Apparel Industry*. Washington, D.C., Economic Policy Institute, 1989.

Sanderson, Susan Walsh. *The Consumer Electronics Industry and the Future of*

American Manufacturing. Washington, D.C.: Economic Policy Institute, 1989.

Schoepfle, Gregory K. "U.S.–Mexico Free Trade Agreement: The Maquilazation of Mexico?" Bureau of International Labor Affairs mimeo, U.S. Department of Labor, Apr. 18, 1990.

Schott, Jeffrey, and Gary Hufbauer. *The Realities of a North American Economic Alliance.* Washington, D.C.: Institute for International Economics, 1990.

Seib, Gerald. "Clinton Backs the North American Trade Pact, but Candidates' Stances on Issue Aren't Clear." *Wall Street Journal,* Oct. 5, 1991, p. A14.

Stanford, James O. "C.G.E. Models of North American Free Trade: A Critique of Methods and Assumptions." Testimony to the USITC Public Hearing on Economy-Wide Modeling of the Economic Implications of Free Trade Investigation No. 332–317, Apr. 1992.

Symonds, William. "The U.S. Can't Afford to Nickel-and-Dime Canada." *Business Week,* Mar. 23, 1992, p. 30.

Symonds, William C., and Paul Magnusson. "In Canada, The Free-Trade Deal Is Hardly Home Free." *Business Week,* Sept. 7, 1992, p. 53.

U.S. Congress, Office of Technology Assessment. *U.S.-Mexico Trade: Pulling Together or Pulling Apart?* ITC–545 (Washington, D.C.: U.S. Government Printing Office, Oct. 1992).

U.S. Department of Commerce. *Investing in Mexico,* Overseas Business Reports 5 (Dec. 1985).

———. *United States Trade Performance in 1988* (Sept. 1989), Appendix A. Ann H. Hughes, "U.S.-Canada Free Trade Agreement," pp. 57–60.

U.S. Department of Commerce, International Trade Administration. *U.S. Exports to Mexico: A State-by-State Overview, 1987–90.* Washington, D.C.: U.S. Government Printing Office, 1991.

U.S. Department of Labor, Bureau of Labor Statistics. *Displaced Workers, 1981– 85.* Bulletin no. 2289, Washington, D.C.: U.S. Government Printing Office, 1987.

U.S. International Trade Commission. *Review of Trade and Investment Liberalization Measures by Mexico and Prospects for Future U.S.-Mexican Relations.* Investigation No. 332–282, Phase II: Summary of Views on Prospects for Future U.S.-Mexican Relations, Oct. 1990, Washington, D.C.

———. Publication No. 2053, *The Use and Economic Impact of TSUS Items 806.30 and 807.00,* Aug. 16, 1988, Report to the Subcommittee on Trade, Committee on Ways and Means, U.S. House of Representatives.

———. *The Likely Impact on the United States of a Free Trade Agreement with Mexico.* USITC Publication 2353, Washington, D.C.: U.S. Government Printing Office, 1991.

———. *Economy-Wide Modeling of the Economic Implications of a FTA with Mexico and a NAFTA with Canada and Mexico.* USITC Publication 2516, Washington, D.C.: U.S. Government Printing Office, May 1992a.

———. *Economy-Wide Modeling of the Economic Implications of a FTA with Mexico and a NAFTA with Canada and Mexico: Addendum.* USITC Publication 2508, Washington, D.C.: U.S. Government Printing Office, May 1992b.

Velasco Arregui, Edur. "El Desafio Sindical al TLC: productividad, empleo y salarios," *El Cotidiano*, no. 41, mayo–junion de 1991, Universidad Autonoma Metropolitana Unidad Azacapotzalco, Mexico, pp. 23–24.

Weintraub, Sidney. *A Marriage of Convenience: Relations Between Mexico and the U.S.* Twentieth Century Fund Report. New York: Oxford University Press, 1990.

———. "Jobs on the Line." *Business Mexico*, vol. 1, no. 1, Mar. 1991, pp. 10–11.

———. "The Canadian Stake in U.S.-Mexico Free Trade Negotiations." *Business in the Contemporary World*, vol. 3, no. 1, Autumn 1990, pp. 127–30.

Whalen, Christopher. "Mexico's Government Creates Another Debt Crisis." *Wall Street Journal*, Mar. 12, 1992, p. A13.

Yeats, Alexander, and Refik Erzan. "Free Trade Agreements with the U.S.: What's in It for Latin America?" In Sylvia Saborio, *U.S.-Latin American Trade Relations in the 1990s*. Washington, D.C.: Overseas Development Council, forthcoming.

Index

About the Contributors

MARK ANDERSON (Office of International Trade, AFL-CIO, Washington, D.C.) has worked for the AFL-CIO since 1976, and has coordinated Federation activities on issues relating to international trade and investment since 1983. He currently directs the AFL-CIO Task Force on Trade.

MARIO F. BOGNANNO (Professor & Director, Industrial Relations Center, Carlson School of Management, University of Minnesota, Minneapolis) joined the faculty of the Industrial Relations Center in 1970. His teaching and research emphasis is in labor economics, collective bargaining and arbitration. He has published extensively in all of these areas. His most recent books are *Labor Market Institutions and the Future Role of Unions* (with Morris Kleiner, 1992) and *Labor Arbitration in America: The Profession and Practice* (with Charles Coleman, 1992).

BRUCE CAMPBELL (Research Fellow, Canadian Center for Policy Alternatives, Ottawa) is Research Fellow at the Centre for Policy Alternatives in Ottawa. He is currently advising the Government of Ontario on trade policy alternatives available to the province. Mr. Campbell has recently completed a study for the British Columbia government entitled, *The Enterprise for the Americas Initiative—Implications for Canada and British Columbia: Trade and Investment Alternatives.*

WILLIAM H. CAVITT (Director, Office of Canada, United States Department of Commerce, Washington, D.C.) is an International Economist and Director at the Office of Canada. He has primary responsibility as staff advisor for the development of departmental positions on international economic, trade, investment and commercial policy issues affecting U.S. relations with Canada. He was a member of the U.S. Delegation which negotiated the

U.S. Canada Free Trade Agreement (CFTA) and also was involved in negotiation of the North American Free Trade Agreement (NAFTA).

CALMAN J. COHEN (Vice President, Emergency Committee for American Trade, Washington, D.C.) joined the Emergency Committee for American Trade as Vice President in March 1981. He was formerly the Director of Congressional Affairs for the Office of the United States Trade Representative. Mr. Cohen also has served on the professional staff of the U.S. Senate's Democratic Policy Committee, where he advised on trade and international economic policy. In addition, he represented the Smithsonian Institution in Latin America. Mr. Cohen's Ph.D. is from Harvard University where he has been a Teaching Fellow. He has been a Visiting Scholar at El Colegio de Mexico in Mexico City.

JAMES M. CYPHER (Professor, Department of Economics, California State University, Fresno) has published numerous scholarly journal articles on the U.S. economy, U.S. military spending, U.S. foreign economic policy, the global economy and economic development. His most recent book *State and Capital in Mexico* (1990) was recently published in Spanish.

JEFF FAUX (President, Economic Policy Institute, Washington, D.C.) is the co author of *Rebuilding America*, the author of *New Hope of the Inner City*, and the co-author of *The Star Spangled Hustle*. He has researched, written, and published studies on a wide variety of economic subjects.

MANFRED FIEDLER (Vice President, Human Resource—International Honeywell Corporation, Minneapolis) has a broad understanding of cross-cultural issues, and he is an expert on the subject of globalization. Mr. Fiedler's primary objective is to expedite and foster Honeywell's approach toward global leadership from a human resources perspective. He serves on Honeywell's Mexico Operations Advisory Board.

WILLIAM C. GRUBEN (Senior Economist & Policy Advisor, Research Department, Federal Reserve Bank of Dallas) is the author of numerous articles and book chapters on U.S.-Latin American relations in trade and finance. He holds a Ph.D. in economics from the University of Texas at Austin, and also served as a research associate at the University's Institute for Latin American Studies.

MORLEY GUNDERSON (Director, Centre for Industrial Relations and Professor, Department of Economics, University of Toronto) has written extensively on the impact of free trade, with particular attention to its effect on labor market adjustments, workplace practices, collective bargaining, industrial relations and human resource management.

PHARIS HARVEY (Executive Director, International Labor Rights Education and Research Fund, Washington, D.C.) is a graduate of Oklahoma City and Yale Universities, and has spent much of his working life in Asia working for ecumenical organizations among worker, urban slum and peasant community organizers. He serves in his present post under assignment from the United Methodist General Board of Global Ministries. The International Labor Rights Education and Research Fund, a Washington-based non-profit organization working to broaden awareness of the importance of an international trading system in which the interests, safety and well-being of working people are positively considered and where competition based on degradation of labor standards is minimized.

ROBERT T. KUDRLE (Director, Freeman Center for International Economic Policy, Professor and Associate Dean, Hubert H. Humphrey Institute of Public Affairs, University of Minnesota, Minneapolis) is Associate Dean for Research at the Hubert Humphrey Institute of Public Affairs and Director of the Orville and Jane Freeman Center in International Economic Policy. He is interested in industrial organization, public policy toward business, international economic policy, and the political economy of social services. Much of his recent research has examined economic relations among the industrial countries. A Rhodes Scholar, Kudrle holds a master of philosophy degree in economics from Oxford University and a Ph.D. in economics from Harvard University.

ROBERT Z. LAWRENCE (Professor of International Trade & Investment, John F. Kennedy School of Government, Harvard University, Cambridge) is an expert in the field of international economics. Mr. Lawrence's books on domestic and international economic problems include *The North American Free Trade Area: An Assessment of the Research* (co-editor), *Can America Compete?*, *Saving Free Trade: A Pragmatic Approach*, and *Primary Commodity Markets and the New Inflation*.

THEA LEE (Research Fellow, Economic Policy Institute, Washington, D.C.) specializes in international trade issues. She received a B.A. in economics from Smith College and a master's degree in economics from the University of Michigan, where she is completing a doctoral program. She has worked as an editor at *Dollars & Sense* magazine in Boston and has taught economics at the University of the District of Columbia.

SUNDER MAGUN (Project Director, Competitiveness and Trade Study Group, Economic Council of Canada, Ottawa) is a specialist in international trade and labor economics. He has produced several papers on the impact of the Canada United States Free Trade Agreement on various sectors of the Canadian economy. He is Executive Director of the economics research organization, Applied Economics International.

JOSEPH MANGONE (Program Director, UAW National Community Action, Detroit) has been director of the UAW's National Community Action Program (CAP) Department, since 1985. The CAP staff and CAP councils across the country initiate and promote political activities, striving to secure economic and social justice for UAW members, their families, their communities and the nation. CAP conducts state and national legislative action, registration and get-out-the vote campaigns, UAW V-CAP dollar drives, leadership training institutes, CAP conferences and a variety of community projects.

KEITH MARTIN (Director of International Policy, Canadian Chamber of Commerce, Ottawa) is a trade specialist who has written on the General Agreement, on Tariffs and Trade, the Canada-United States Free Trade Agreement, and the North American Free Trade Agreement. He has worked at the Centre for Trade Policy and Law in Ottawa, and was Director, International Policy at the Canadian Chamber of Commerce from 1990 to 1993.

M. E. NICHOLS (Executive Vice President, International Communication Workers of America, Washington, D.C.) has served continuously as Executive Vice President of the Communications Workers of America since his election in 1980. Some of his union duties include responsibility for the union's education programs, community services, occupational safety and health, and minority concerns. He serves on a large number of boards and committees of various civic and charitable organizations.

KATHRYN J. READY (Department of Business Administration, University of Wisconsin—Eau Claire) teaches industrial relations, human resource management, and organizational behavior. She received her Ph.D. in Industrial Relations from the University of Iowa and her MBA from the University of Wisconsin—La Crosse. She has worked in industrial relations and human resources in industry. Her research centers on pattern bargaining, managing global organizations, and the changing markets and earnings for managers.

CLAUDE RIOUX (Director, Federation of Paper & Forest Workers (CNTU) Quebec City) has published extensively on labor relations in the paper industry, the impact of FTA on industrial relations in Canada, and on job flexibility and new pay-systems. He is a graduate of the Harvard University Trade Union Program.

MARCUS HART SANDVER (Professor, Management and Human Resources, Ohio State University, Columbus) has been at The Ohio State

University since 1976. Prior to coming to Ohio State, Mr. Sandver was at the University of Wisconsin where he received his Ph.D. in Industrial Relations (1976). He has published numerous articles and his most recent book is *Labor Relations: Process and Outcomes* (1987). He is working on a new book, *Labor Management Relations and the Workplace,* that will be published in 1993. In 1988 Mr. Sandver was a Fulbright Scholar in Turkey teaching and conducting research in international labor law and dispute resolution.

STEPHEN I. SCHLOSSBERG (Director of Washington Branch International Labor Organization, Washington, D.C.) has been the Washington office director of the International Labor Organization since 1987. With nearly a half-century in labor management relations, he has been a union organizer, a labor lawyer, a law professor, a lecturer, a civil rights activist and a federal official fostering labor-management cooperation. For nearly 20 years, he was general counsel and director of government affairs for the United Automobile Workers of America.

GARY SORENSEN (Assistant Commissioner, Job Service & Unemployment Insurance, Minnesota Department of Jobs & Training, St. Paul) has worked within the Job Service and Unemployment Insurance system since 1969. He has served on Private Industry Councils, Community Task Forces, and other advisory committees and continues to work with these groups and other agencies on work force and economic development issues.

ANIL VERMA (Associate Professor, Centre for Industrial Relations and Faculty of Management, University of Toronto) holds a joint appointment on the Faculty of Management and the Centre for Industrial Relations. His primary research interests are in the areas of management responses to unionization, participative forms of work organization and the contribution of human resource management policies such as employment stabilization practices, profit; shgain sharing and other innovations in industrial relations to Canadian competitiveness in international trade. Mr. Verma has published numerous articles in research journals and books. His most recent book is *Industrial Relations in Canadian Industry,* co-authored with Richard P. Chaykowski. He has taught previously at the University of Saskatchewan, the University of California, Los Angeles, the University of British Columbia and worked in the steel industry as an engineer for five years.

JEREMY WRIGHT (Global Economist, Itchenhouse, Ottawa) was a Senior Economic Advisor for the Canadian Federation of Labour in Ottawa until 1991, and is now a consultant on global economic affairs.